Cruising the Inland Waterways of Europe

Photographs by Stanley Rosenfeld

Cruising
the Inland Waterways
of Europe

Jarrett and Stanley Kroll

Harper & Row, Publishers
New York, Hagerstown, San Francisco, London

Dedication

To Julius Caesar, Trajan, Da Vinci, Thomas Jefferson, Napoleon, Robert Louis Stevenson and Irving and Electra Johnson, who discovered the waterways of Europe before we did, and to all those who are about to discover them, we affectionately dedicate this book.

All prices given for waterway tours are for general reference only. They are subject to change.

FIRST EDITION

Designed by Lydia Link

Maps by Clifton Line

Library of Congress Cataloging in Publication Data

Kroll, Jarrett.
    Cruising the inland waterways of Europe.

    Bibliography: p.
    Includes index.
    1. Europe—Description and travel—1971–
2. Waterways—Europe. 3. Kroll, Jarrett. 4. Kroll,
Stanley. I. Kroll, Stanley, joint author. II. Rosen-
feld, Stanley Z. III. Title.
D923.K7 1979   914'.04'55   78-2151
ISBN 0–06–012456–3

79 80 81 82 83 10 9 8 7 6 5 4 3 2 1

Contents

Captions for part and chapter title illustrations will be found on page 289.

Foreword

After crossing Europe in our own Ketch Yankee twenty-eight times in seventeen years my wife and I have enjoyed the Krolls' book of their waterways experiences to the utmost. Jarrett takes us right back to waterside cafés where we tied up, to locks through which we cranked our own way, to French chateaux that we explored too, and best of all to feeling alternately excited and peaceful while floating through the life of a foreign country.

Today, all of us who extoll cruising Europe's waterways can look to a great American father to back us up, for Thomas Jefferson wrote from the Canal du Midi in 1787. "I dismounted my carriage from its wheels, placed it on the deck of a light bark, and was thus towed on the canal instead of the post road. . . . I hired a bark to myself by the day and have made from 20 to 35 miles a day. . . . Of all the methods of travelling I have ever tried this is the pleasantest. I walk part of the way along the banks of the canal, level, and lined with a double row of trees which furnish shade. When fatigued I take seat in my carriage where, as much at ease as if in my study, I read, write or observe; my carriage being of glass all round admits full view of all the varying scenes thro' which I am shifted: olives, figs, mulberries, vines, corn and pasture, village and farms. I have had some days of superb weather, enjoying two parts of the Indian's wish: cloudless skies and limpid waters. I have had another luxury which he could not wish since we have driven him from the country of mockingbirds: a double row of nightingales along the banks of the canal in full song." Fortunately, this form of travel hasn't changed much since Jefferson's time and he joins me, the Krolls, and many others when he adds, "You should not think of returning to America without taking the tour which I have taken."

In the nineteenth century we have another good authority in Robert Louis Stevenson. He was writing about the barges that are our constant companions on the waterways. We gradually learn their unwritten code of boat behavior, we bow to their long experience and skill, and we are fascinated by their homes afloat. In "An Inland Voyage" he says, "Of all the creatures of commercial enterprise a canal barge is by far the most delightful to consider. . . . The man dreaming at the tiller sees the same spire on the horizon all day long. . . . and to see the barges waiting their turn at a lock affords a fine lesson of how easily the world may be taken. There should be many contented spirits on board, for such a life is both to travel and to stay at home. . . . There are few callings, I should say, where a man gives up less of his liberty in return for regular meals."

My wife and I did our inland voyaging all in one way—in our own boat—but the Krolls have investigated every way an inland voyage can be done, for every age, every ability, every taste, and every pocketbook. How kind of them to do all this research for the rest of us, and what a good time they obviously had doing it. And for someone who doesn't want to leave home, Stan Rosenfeld's pictures are a wonderful cruise in themselves.

We first knew the Krolls when this inland cruising idea was just germinating. Now they are experts. They started with a fair experience of boats, but even more important with enthusiasm and an intelligent determination to learn everything there was to find out on the subject of floating in Europe.

Of course there's lots more to the whole experience than getting the boat from here to there. The Krolls lead you to delights in food and wine, to history in forts and castles, and especially to the development of Europe's network of waterways going back to Roman times. Every now and then you are with Caesar's legions or Napoleon's armies, or in the ferocious Dutch battles at sea with the Spaniards. As we learned from the same experiences and "sights," it seemed like getting a whole second education. Europe and its past, which is also our past, came alive and meaningful. But the reader is not in a classroom. He is sometimes coping with the flat tire of a rusty rented bike, or hauling the boat out of the mud by main force, or meeting a Charollais bull in *his* pasture, or propping a 12-year-old with a bad cold by a window while the ship moves on.

So step aboard, let go the lines, turn the wheel, and see what is round the bend.

Irving M. Johnson

Introduction

Taking to the water—the inland waterways of Europe—may be the most enjoyable and fulfilling way for the traveler to explore and experience that continent. It is safe, exciting, exotic, and—above all—within the budget of most people. You can charter, for example, a comfortable diesel-powered do-it-yourself five-passenger houseboat on many of the French and British canals for under $300 per week. At $9 per person per day, this certainly qualifies as one of the most economical vacation possibilities.

Many of the historic European waterways were used as navigable passages as far back as Roman times. They criss-cross the continent, twisting and turning through the most interesting and scenic parts of Europe—reaching even into the Swiss Alps—far from the traditional tourist routes. Whether you're an experienced boating person, a confirmed landlubber, a parent with a desire to introduce your children to a unique and educational vacation; whether you're a person seeking the real, uncommercialized Europe or an inveterate traveler bored with the fast-paced hustle through the "standard" capitals, floating through Europe can become a new vacation answer.

If you have never been on a boat or are looking for complete relaxation free from responsibility, you'll find a multitude of passenger and excursion boat possibilities. You can hire any size boat you wish—small motor and sailing yachts, converted hundred-foot steel barges, even a Rhine steamer with plush facilities that rival passenger liners. Little boating experience is necessary for many waterway trips, as your boat may never exceed five miles per hour, nor stray more than twenty feet from the river or canal bank.

If you can afford the time and expense to transport your own boat to Europe to cruise the waterways, you'll want to know what kinds of boats are best suited for waterway cruising, the details of the arrangements you must make to get your boat to and from the best cruising areas, how to equip and outfit your boat, documents and insurance details, the costs involved—even how to receive mail and telephone calls enroute. Though this sounds awfully complex, more and more people are cruising Europe's waterways on their own boats every year.

This book, as do many others, owes its origins to an unsuccessful search for a comprehensive book that we'd hoped someone else had already written. As "boatniks" of long standing, experienced in craft ranging from outboard-powered inflatables to a fifty-five-foot ocean-racing yawl, we'd long been seeking a good source of information on the European waterways. What we found was scattered, frequently out-of-date, and invariably frustratingly incomplete. Our course was clear—why not write our own? The research promised to be fascinating, to say the least, and the prospect of enticing others into a world that we've so keenly enjoyed for so many years was more than a little attractive. Here then are the results of several years' intensive research and travel. We loved every minute and every mile of it.

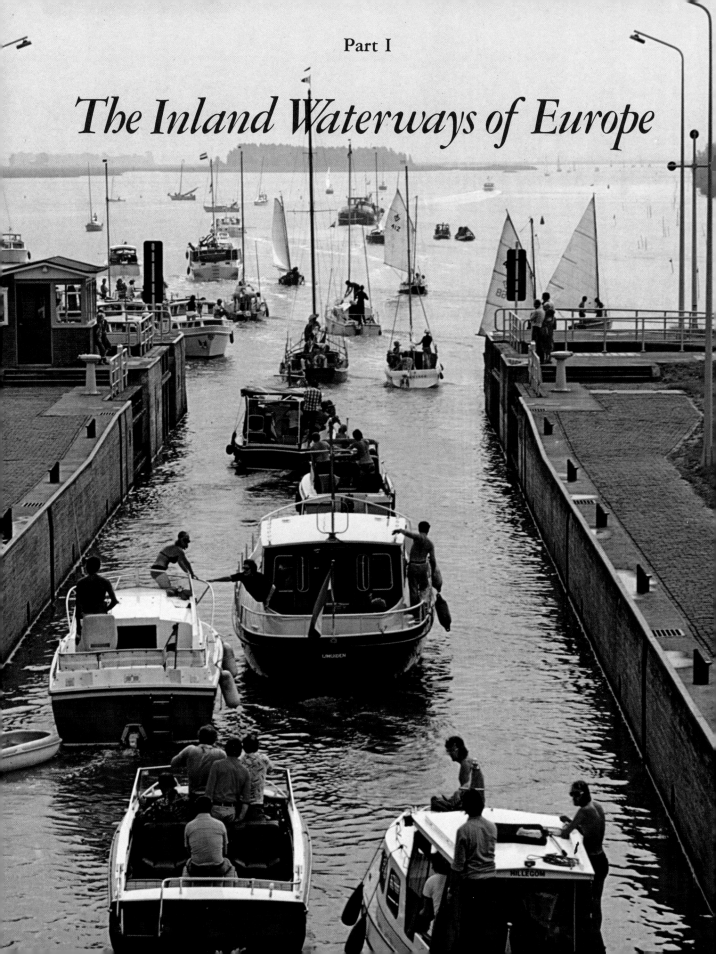

Part I
The Inland Waterways of Europe

1

Discovering Southern France

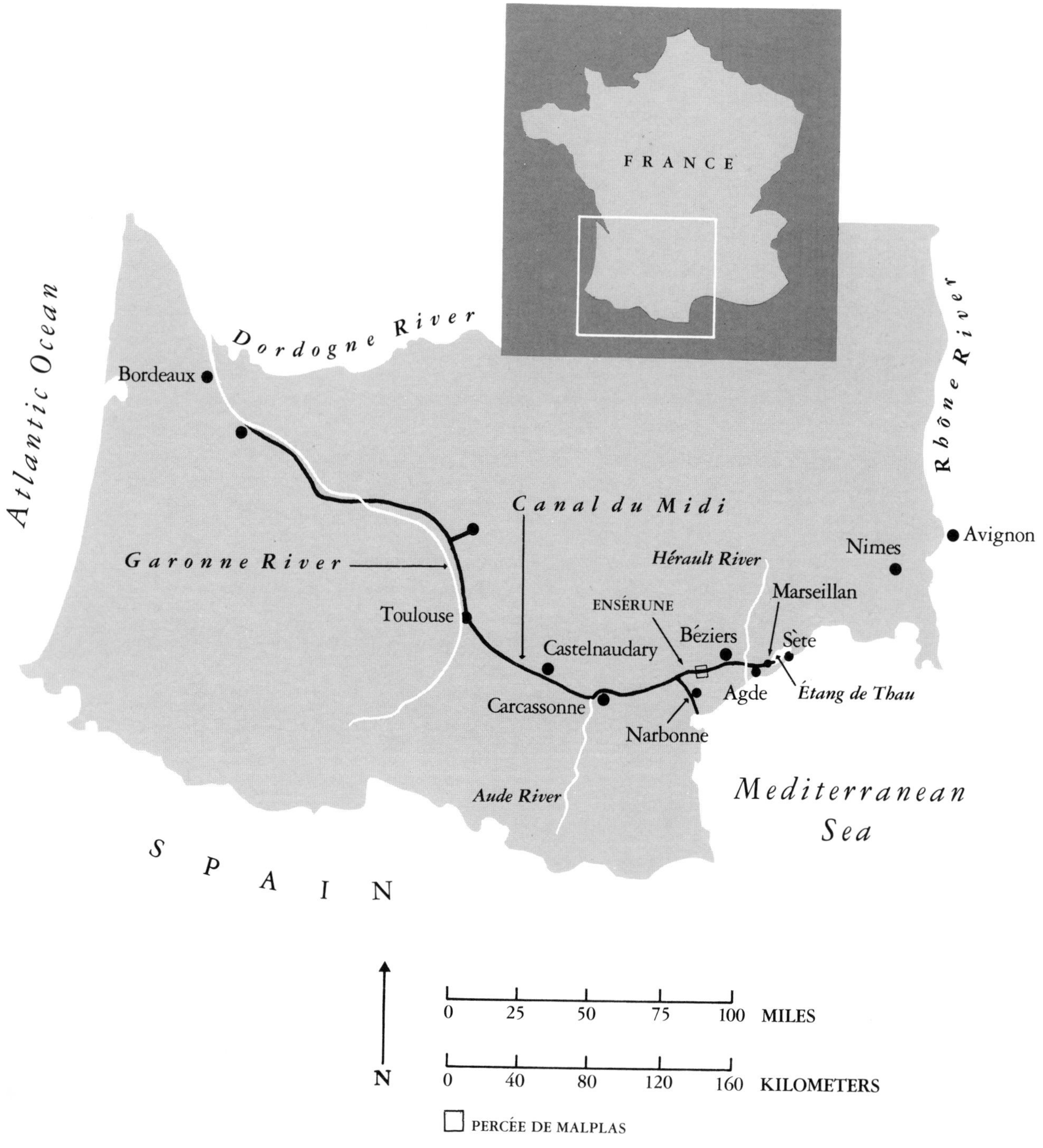

Atlantic Ocean

Dordogne River

FRANCE

Rhône River

Bordeaux

Canal du Midi

Garonne River

Hérault River

Nimes

Avignon

ENSÉRUNE

Marseillan

Toulouse

Béziers

Sète

Castelnaudary

Agde

Étang de Thau

Carcassonne

Narbonne

Mediterranean Sea

Aude River

S P A I N

| 0 | 25 | 50 | 75 | 100 | MILES |

| 0 | 40 | 80 | 120 | 160 | KILOMETERS |

N

☐ PERCÉE DE MALPLAS

A Cruise on the Canal du Midi

"Écoutez-moi! Écoutez-moi!"—listen to me!—insisted the seven-year-old street urchin Michel in the central square of Ventenac, province of Languedoc, the sunny southern countryside of rural France.

"We are *écoutez*ing, but——" and he was off again, tearing through the French language at an indecipherable frenzy. The problem was, of course, that we just couldn't assimilate French at anything over 10 w.p.m.

Michel was a member of the "police force," he said, and he brandished an old Wild West cap pistol to prove it. That much we could understand. He had also put himself in charge of keeping the stray cats out of Ventenac's square; he threw sticks at them. And he lived above the Restaurant Pigalle, Ventenac's quiet, lovely café. He'd show us a real French restaurant, he said.

He did, and our family of five enjoyed a marvelous French country dinner of quiche, lamb chops, fresh *haricots verts,* a selection of local cheeses, fresh fruits, oven-fresh bread, and delicious local table wine (they don't let you drink less than a liter here), for just over $13.

After this feast we ambled back to our Blue Line cruiser, the six-berth, picture-windowed, wildflower-filled vacation home we had chartered for our week's tour of the Canal du Midi. The boat was tied to a tree at the foot of the village bridge, on the motionless waters of the canal. Reflecting on the day's good fortune, we hoped our boat would continue to drift into such pleasurable ports.

But perhaps we are getting a little ahead of ourselves; we should explain how we happened to be floating down the waterways of France. As boating and blue-water sailing enthusiasts of long standing, we habitually paid our monthly homage to nearly every boating magazine. In one of those magazines, sometime in 1972, we read of a slow trip through southern France on a self-drive boat. This sparked our interest and, our eyes newly opened, we found a copy of Irving and Electa Johnson's book, *Yankee Sails Through Europe.* The more we read, the more appealing the idea of traveling the canals of Europe became until, unable to stand armchair traveling any longer, we finally booked a cruise for our girls' April vacation in 1974.

Looking back on that first trip on one of Europe's glass-smooth ribbons of water, we smile to think how little we realized what we were undertaking. That seven-day trip covered little more than 100 miles westward along the seventeenth-century Canal du Midi, from the Mediterranean to Castelnaudary. But it was also the beginning of a four-year odyssey that would take us through thirteen countries, from the Land of the Midnight Sun to the Pyrénées, from the British Midlands to the Black Sea. It was to be an odyssey filled with passion: the quiet passion of discovering a magnificently extravagant mode of travel that allowed many quiet hours of contemplation, the luxury of relaxation and indolence, and the spontaneity of interacting with nature and with people.

For Jarrett our trips were the culmination of a little saying her parents had taught her when she was growing up: "Don't hurry, don't worry, and don't forget to smell the flowers."

Cruising the canals of Europe allowed us to smell the flowers and to meet the people who had planted them, the children who picked them, and the lovers who wished on them. We seldom traveled at a speed of more than four miles an hour—just fast enough to heed the cries of the mockingbird and whippoorwill, to exchange smiles and greetings with the people along the way, and, of course, to breathe that wonderful, flower-fragrant air.

Birth of the Canal du Midi

The Canal du Midi, built in the grand style of the Renaissance, has been described as "the greatest feat of civil engineering between Roman times and the nineteenth century." Running from the Mediterranean west to Toulouse, it forms a navigable waterway some 160 miles long, containing 65 locks.

It fulfilled a centuries-long commercial need: Until the middle of the seventeenth century, vessels from the Atlantic Ocean could reach inland on the River Garonne only as far as Toulouse. Despite the fact that this river route was tricky—prone to floods in winter and drought in summer—many smaller vessels preferred it to risking the Spanish peninsula, the Straits of Gibraltar, and the attacks of pirates from the North African coast. The combination of river and overland routes was infinitely safer, if not easier.

Since Roman times there had been many schemes to link Toulouse to the Mediterranean by canal, but the technical problems involved—primarily the limited supply of water for the high and waterless region east of Toulouse—defeated them all.

Leonardo da Vinci, who is credited with inventing the modern mitre-gate "pound lock" still in use on canals today, suggested linking the Atlantic with the Mediterranean by joining the rivers Garonne and Aude. But he, too, was stymied by the problem of collecting enough water to fill a canal through the highlands, one of the driest areas in all of France. So this much-needed corridor had to await construction for another hundred or more years.

The problem was solved in the mid-seventeenth century by Pierre-Paul Riquet, salt-tax collector, amateur engineer, and Baron of Bonrepos, in the course of his tax-gathering journeys on horseback through the region. He realized that there was ample rainfall in the Black Mountain about 40 miles to the north and observed that, when it rained, "half the water goes toward Toulouse and half toward the Narbonne." Concluding simply enough that if water were collected into reservoirs it would do likewise, he is reputed to have exclaimed the French equivalent of Eureka! and to have hurried off in the direction of the Black Mountain. The whole problem of a waterway across southern France had been solved in a single flash of inspiration. However, it would take Baron Riquet the rest of his long life to finish the Canal du Midi, and he would die nearly penniless and battle-scarred by politics in the process.

Riquet financed most of the original planning and surveying from his own personal funds because of official skepticism about his plan. Finally he obtained a royal edict for the new canal from Louis XIV, the "Sun King," in 1666. Having been given the go-ahead at the age of sixty-two, Riquet wasted no time. By January 1667, 2,000 laborers were at work on the vast dam to supply the feeder systems in the mountains; by March 15 the work force had doubled. In November two foundation stones were ceremonially laid in the walls of the lock leading from the Garonne at Toulouse, and work had begun on the canal proper. At the peak of construction the labor force numbered more than 12,000, including 600 women who carried soil in baskets on their heads for the equivalent of a penny a load.

After fifteen years of work, having introduced many remarkable engineering innovations—feeder streams, floodlocks, staircase locks, a round lock, siphons, the world's first canal tunnel, and probably the first use of gunpowder for engineering purposes—having grown white-haired and white-bearded working on his life's project, and having finally accomplished the near-impossible, Riquet died as his canal moved within "one league of the Étang de Thau." The canal was opened just seven months later, with a celebration that included gaily decorated boats filled with musicians and proud high officials floating through the locks as cheering citizens crowded its banks. The canal has not changed much since that time, so well was it conceived and built.

Sunshine, the Sea, and the Vine

The Midi is the region of France south of the Loire River, stretching from the Atlantic to the Mediterranean. *Midi* literally means midday, where theoretically the sun always shines. Within the Midi is the province of Languedoc, where the people still speak an ancient variant of the French language known as the *langue d'oc,* or Occitan, which is quite distinct from the official French of the north. Here the way to say yes is *oc,* not the expected *oui.* And, in French as in other languages, the way in which one says yes is more than a little important.

The people of the Languedoc are a mercurial Ligurian and Iberian mixture, shorter, darker, and chunkier than their Celtic and Teutonic northern cousins. Full of verbal extravagance and gusto, dedicated to the sea and the vine, they conduct most of their business in the streets. It is said of this hot-blooded region of rough people and rough wine that "even the grannies love a good brawl."

The wines of Languedoc are little known outside France, for they are primarily modest table wines, but in fact they represent the bulk of French wine production. Here, on the relatively wide and flat coastal plain, from the Spanish border on the Mediterranean to the mouth of the Rhône River, and far inland, lush vineyards stretch as far as the eye can see. The Languedoc offers some red, white, and rosé wines of better quality, such as the Clairettes found around Montpellier and Gaillac. The reds of Carcassonne, the sparkling white of Limoux, the fine reds of Narbonne, and the reds from Corbières (which were appreciated by the Romans) are all accorded by the French government the coveted Appellation of Controlled Origin (A.O.C.).

Innocents Abroad

April, we had been told, was not too early in the year to enjoy this sunny region. We hoped that the advice was accurate; however, the beginning of our first trip was not auspicious. Our lack of travel experience showed in our somewhat naïve planning. While we had done our library work well before leaving, we had planned to fly directly from New York to Paris and from Paris to Toulouse, then to take the train from Toulouse to Marseillan, a small town near the Mediterranean, at the eastern end of the canal. There our 34-foot Blue Line cruiser awaited us. We expected to start right off on our 105-mile trip along the Canal du Midi to Castelnaudary, just east of Toulouse. The only thing we had forgotten to plan for was sleeping time! After having traveled, two adults and three children, for more than fourteen hours, we found we were in no condition to set off on a boat when we arrived. From that time on, whenever a transatlantic flight preceded a waterway trip, we always planned at least a day's respite before launching ourselves onto a canal.

The three children were Stan's daughters: Laura, then fourteen years old, Beverly, twelve, and Janet, ten. Their diaries, recording impressions and first-time canal travels through young eyes, have brought us many warm moments in the years since the trip. And they have been of great value in jogging somewhat older, more sluggish minds in writing a full account of the trip.

As we arrived that afternoon in early April 1974, sleep-drugged and bleary-eyed, our first view of the little port of Marseillan, through torrents of cold, wind-swept rain, was of a bleak and sodden landscape. The port on the Étang de Thau was full of little deserted-looking boats, and the surrounding terrain was uniformly flat and unbroken in every direction.

We ran through the open doorway into the Château du Port, lugging our duffel bags out of the driving rain. The lobby was deserted, its cold marble and stone decor adding echoes to the chill in the air. Had we not been so tired, and had our taxi still been standing by, we might well have willingly picked up our duffels and trundled right on back to New York.

Fortunately, Mr. Van Heek, amiable host of both the Château and the Blue Line cruisers base, soon appeared, greeted us heartily in perfect Dutchman's English, and

Along the Rampe Paul Valéry in the old port of Sète, net mending and conversation fill the quay with colorful sight, sound and smell of the sea. Sète, between the Mediterranean and the Bassin de Thau, is at the junction of the Canal du Midi, which leads west to the Atlantic Ocean, and the Canal du Rhône, entrance to the heartland of Europe.

showed us to our waiting boat. There we promptly collapsed, awakening only when our stomachs told us it was dinnertime. The rain had stopped and the wind was diminishing as we donned sweaters and walked to the hotel for dinner. In the intimate and casual candlelit dining room, on the open fire before us, Mrs. Van Heek prepared steak and *pommes frites* for the girls, then, in the kitchen, the most delicious, delicate monkfish in garlic cream sauce for us. Wine arrived automatically in big pitchers; water had to be ordered. If we were not yet convinced, this was proof enough that we had arrived in the Midi of France, which Lawrence Durrell, in *Monsieur,* called "a separate Mediterranean nation . . . unashamedly pagan in attitude . . . leaner and thirstier than the north." Thirstier, anyway.

Prelude to the Cruise

After a good night's sleep we were ready to begin our first day of cruising at about 10 A.M. But before casting off, there was the town to be explored and groceries to be bought, activities which the entire family enjoyed immensely.

As with much of the coastal region from Marseille in the east to Narbonne in the west, Marseillan was founded in the sixth century B.C. by Greek sailors, who introduced the vine to the region and exploited its fertile fishing grounds. Fishermen and vinegrowers still, the Marseillannais now produce a huge quantity of wine for vermouth, and Noilly Prat, the largest French vermouth firm, has its open-air maturing parks here.

Making the vermouth is a complex and time-consuming process. They begin by filling large wooden casks with Clairette, Picpoul, and Bourret grapes, plus some Muscat whose fermentation has been stopped by the addition of brandy. The casks are then set out in the large open-air maturing parks for up to two years—in which time as much as 10 percent of the contents will evaporate—before they are blended with special herbs and spices.

Beyond its industry Marseillan is notable for the warm and vivacious people who live there, people who smiled, offered us old-fashioned courtesies, and appeared unhurried and unaffected by clock time.

After checking out most of the local merchants we returned with our grocery bags bulging and felt we were now fully prepared to begin our cruise. Mr. Van Heek soon arrived to orient us concerning the boat's operations and maintenance. Having persuaded the motor to perform after a few secret rituals, he took us for a trial run into the Étang de Thau, showed us the general direction of the opening to the Canal du Midi, and gave us the go-ahead. We dropped him off at his dock and, by one o'clock, were on our own, heading out into the Étang de Thau.

The Cruise Begins

The Étang de Thau is a shallow, tideless saltwater lake separated from the Mediterranean Sea by a low, narrow land spit. Covering just under 20,000 acres, the largest of several such lakes on the Languedoc coast, it is famous for its oyster and mussel farms.

Its little ports glinted and winked in the afternoon sun. The most notable of them is Sète, built on the narrow isthmus separating the Étang from the sea. Situated between both bodies of water, Sète welcomes the seagoing cargo vessels carrying— to the fury of the southern *vignerons*—Algerian and Italian wine and exporting much of the Hérault's enormous 600 million liters of wine per year.

From our boat we could see in the foreground the old port, with its pleasure boats and fishing trawlers draped with the acres of nets used for catching tuna, sardines, and anchovies. Behind the port the town climbs in terraces up the side of Mont St. Clair. Sète's native son, the poet Paul Valéry (1875–1945), lived here ("I was born in one of these places where I would have loved to have been born," he said) and is buried in the Cimetière Marin, which he made famous in a poem of the same name.

We headed southwest from Sète toward two lonely stone jetties, one of which held the lighthouse marking the opening to the canal. From here to the first lock, four miles away, the canal was swampy, almost junglelike, with dragonflies droning past and an occasional snake sunning itself on the surface.

Eel fishermen tended nets that stretched across the waterway. Sometimes they needed waking with a polite hoot so that they might drop their nets for us to pass. One man appeared to give weighty consideration to not responding at all to our needs. Finally he shrugged in resignation and heaved his considerable body up from the damp ground to lower his net. As we passed he warmed up and gave us a smile and a little wave.

After skirting the southern shore of the little Étang de Bagnas, the canal swung north toward Bagnas Lock, presumably the last lock built on the canal. For us it was our *first* approach to our *first* lock on our *first* canal. We were hesitant, a little nervous. As we passed under the little low bridge before the lock gates, Stan's normally steady hand at the wheel wavered and the boat wiggled suddenly, narrowly missing the sides of the bridge. Then our bow entered the lock, and Stan nosed it slowly to the left side to let Laura, who had been chosen to do the honors, climb the black iron ladder to ground level. This she did with surprising aplomb, then hurried, as instructed, to the front of the lock to tie our bow line, then back to secure our stern line to a hefty bollard.

Out of the tiny lockside cottage walked our first *éclusier* (lockkeeper), who gave us a nod and a smile in greeting and went directly to work to close one of the back gates with a black iron crank. Laura knew that part of her job would be to operate her side of the lock, so she began cranking her gate closed, working in mirror-image of the *éclusier*. He nodded approval and, when she had finished, led her to the front gates, which were already closed. In unison they began opening the paddles to let water from the higher level ahead to fill the lock. We began to rise slowly, the water in the lock chamber bubbling and frothing beneath our little boat, which was doing a disciplined version of the rhumba as we rose. The entire process took just about ten minutes; then Laura and the lockkeeper laboriously cranked the heavy front gates open, and we emerged into a landscape entirely new to our eyes.

Two miles further on we crossed the River Hérault and, after another 200 yards, entered the famous Round Lock of Agde, an outstanding example of the boundless ingenuity of Pierre-Paul Riquet and his engineers. Its design allows barges to rotate and to have a choice of leaving through one of two gates—one continuing the Canal du Midi toward Toulouse, the other offering a short branch canal south to the ancient fishing port of Agde.

Known to the Greeks who settled there in 500 B.C. as Agathé (the good place), Agde thrived as a seaport until the twelfth century, when it was gradually supplanted by Montpellier, Aigues-Mortes, and later Sète. Now it's a town of peasants, vinegrowers, and fishermen, famed for its fortified Cathedral of St. Étienne, a church built of black lava from Mont St. Loup and once used for defense against Saracen pirates.

Just past the round lock the canal hugs the coastline of the Mediterranean,

A hire-cruiser underway in the old harbor of Marseillan, eastern service base for Blue Line Cruisers. To the left is Château du Port, a hotel with Languedocian charm in an area noted for its oysters, snails, vermouth, beaches and poets.

skirting the ancient fortified market and pilgrimage town of Vias. Then, after a long straightaway, we saw ahead of us a forbidding assemblage of steel girders, chains, pulleys, and menacing guillotinelike sluice gates spanning the canal. These gates represent a unique and clever solution to the problem of crossing the Libron River, one of the canal's most persistent trouble spots. Under normal conditions the Libron is an insignificant stream, but as often as twenty times a year it is subject to violent flashfloods. With its ingenious system of sluice gates—basically locks with retractable tunnel-shaped gates through which a vast torrent can be diverted—the canal can peacefully intersect the capricious river even when it is in violent flood.

At this point we were as close to the Mediterranean as we were going to get this trip—a mere 500 yards from La Redoute, home of Club Méditerranée, with its excellent beach, horseback riding, and all the amusements associated with the world-renowned resort. Later in the season, we imagined, this would be a popular watering spot for canal travelers; now it was just an unassuming place, quiet as the rest of the countryside, bursting silently with April's sweetness and pregnant with spring.

Just beyond the tiny village of Cers we stopped for the night. Beverly's diary records, "It's really neat! We stopped for the night by just jumping ashore and tying up to trees alongside the canal." The girls decorated our table with wildflowers picked from the banks, and we roasted a chicken on board and enjoyed a memorable evening of quiet conversation amid the sounds of frogs, crickets, and the water gently rippling past our boat.

The morning of our second day found us still lazy, and it was toward ten o'clock before we got under way. Within half an hour we had passed through the Villeneuve Lock, graced with pretty flower gardens and a smiling lockkeeper in classic French-blue working overalls. Beverly and Janet shared responsibility for ascending the lock ladders and working the paddles with the lockkeepers. Though neither of them knew more than a few words of French, Beverly found herself, at the double lock of Béziers, in a full-fledged conversation with the lockkeeper, who began by teasingly pointing out how strong she was as she wound the lock gates open and shut. This twelve-year-old was discovering firsthand that language differences didn't have to be a barrier to communication.

Béziers—the Grim Past

The locks led into the handsome Port Neuf, a wide canal port on the edge of the agricultural and viticultural town of Béziers, already a thriving town when the Romans arrived in the province they called Aquitania. They recognized the beauty and strategic importance of its superb location high on a plateau above the River Orb and made it their colony of Baeterrae Septimania. In 35 B.C. the Seventh Legion was headquartered there.

The most tumultuous chapter of its history occurred in the thirteenth century, when Béziers was the center of the heretic Christian sect known as the Albigensians. The whole of the Languedoc is haunted by the memory of their tragedy.

A gentle and reverent people, the Albigensians devoted themselves to preaching, teaching, caring for the sick, and consoling the dying; they were pacifists and vegetarians who were absolutely opposed to the Roman Catholic Church, holding that its symbols and rituals were earthly and evil. They were considered a threat to the Church because they were converting to their way of thinking ever-increasing numbers of Languedoc people—who were by no means submissive children of the Church to begin with.

In 1208 Pope Innocent III called for the elimination of the heretics ("worse than the pagans") in a new Crusade, and he promised the lands of the heretics to those who joined the Crusade. Bishops, prelates, and papal legates were among those who took part, under an army commanded by Crusader Simon IV de Montfort, who pursued the campaign with every cruelty and horror.

In 1209 Béziers was defended by Viscount Raymond-Roger de Trencavel, but on July 22 the Crusaders forced their way into the city and put every one of its 15,000 inhabitants to the sword. Legend has it that the abbot Arnaud-Almeric, commanding the invasion, was approached by one of his officers, who informed him that the town was about to fall. "Within the walls," the officer said, "there are many adherents to the true faith. How are we to tell them apart from the heretics?"

"Kill them all," Almeric replied. "The Lord will know his own."

The old and the sick, with women and their children, had taken refuge in the churches, 7,000 of them in the Madeleine alone. The Crusaders did indeed kill them all, including the priests, and then they set Béziers on fire. Boasting, Almeric himself reported to the pope that "nearly 20,000 of the citizens were put to the sword, regardless of age and sex."

The Crusaders went on to Carcassonne and subdued it despite its elaborate fortifications. Simon de Montfort assumed the title of count of Béziers and Carcassonne; an entire civilization, the legacy of the Greeks and the Romans, was crushed, and the whole of Languedoc fell to the king and the barons of the north.

Despite this grim history, Béziers is once again a prosperous town of about 90,000, the country around it largely devoted to producing wine of excellent quality. In the A.O.C. category there is Clairette du Languedoc, a heavy, dry white wine from the region between the rivers Orb and Hérault. The vineyards growing Clairette du Languedoc comprise about 2,800 acres; average production is less than 1.5 million liters, most of it sold in Béziers in the Friday afternoon wine market.

Home of Riquet

Béziers' most illustrious son was Pierre-Paul Riquet, to whom we owe the construction of the Canal du Midi. Born here on June 29, 1604, to Florentine immigrants originally named Arrighetti, Pierre-Paul identified himself so completely with his adopted country that, to the dismay of his teachers, he refused to learn Greek, Latin, or even French, preferring to speak in the local tongue, Occitan. His father, Guillaume, practiced as a lawyer in Béziers and was appointed one of the thirty managers of the city, wielding considerable local influence.

In January 1618 one of the many schemes for a canal between the two seas came up for consideration by the council, and Guillaume was one of the majority who voted against it, perhaps because its proposed route led through Narbonne and not Béziers. But this—and doubtless other schemes for a canal to link the two seas—was widely discussed in the Riquet household, and the idea fired the imagination of the young man.

Displaying a natural flair for the sciences and mathematics at the Jesuit College of Béziers, Pierre-Paul was destined to become—or so his father thought—a financier and man of business. Then, at the age of twenty-six, he was appointed collector of the lucrative salt tax, which in time provided him with the intimate knowledge of the countryside that later enabled him to solve the tricky water supply problems.

Béziers remembers Riquet with a broad, shady, tree-lined promenade that marks the line of the old town walls, and a statue of him by David d'Angers stands in the central square.

Béziers Today

It was lunchtime when we reached the Port Neuf, and we soon found a cozy bistro neatly tucked into a line of buildings near the waterfront. Here, in search of a "quick lunch," we discovered the full magnitude of our language deficiencies. Having been given a menu offering the typical big French midday meal—really dinner, not lunch—we deployed Beverly to pose the question, *avez-vous des sandwiches?* Her courage outweighed her linguistic prowess, however, and we soon saw her being bodily escorted (owner at one elbow, his wife at the other), her feet literally off the floor, her eyes wide and amazed, past our table, out the back door, and into a courtyard.

Oh dear, Janet thought, they're kicking her out. What did she *say?* Beverly thought they were taking her to see their lineup of sandwiches. In fact she ended up being gently deposited by the well-intended restaurateurs in the bathroom. She returned to the table laughing so hard that tears streamed down her cheeks. The quest for sandwiches clearly needed some new champions. Laura, who had had two years of French training, tried with greater success, and we ended up with hero-like sandwiches on crusty French bread.

After lunch we strolled the Boulevard Paul Riquet, admiring the beautiful fortified church of St. Nazaire, rebuilt in the thirteenth and fourteenth centuries following its destruction in 1209. We stood on the terrace belvedere nearby, gazing out over the lovely Béziers region that stretches from the River Orb to the Canal du

Midi and up to the plateau that holds the remains of the ancient Oppidum(town) d'Ensérune. In the distance emerges Mont Caroux; to the southwest, the summits of the Nore and the Canigou. We marveled at the old church of the Madeleine, whose exterior stubbornly survived the burning of the town by the Crusaders. Then we stood on the New Bridge over the Orb and looked up to the towered line of the town above the steep rise of the riverbank. Then we returned to our boat three hours after we had left it.

For us it was here at Béziers that the canal became really exciting, both visually and from the engineering and historic points of view. Beyond the Port Neuf we ascended to the level of the Orb, and from the head of the locks the canal passed onto the sensational "new" (1857) aqueduct over that river. A magnificent stone structure of seven spans, it possesses the same air of monumental permanence and grandeur that typifies works from the reign of Louis XIV, yet it was built under a decree issued in June 1854 by the emperor Napoleon III.

As we moved slowly across the pont-canal in the warm spring sunshine, Jarrett and the girls climbed to the roof of the cruiser, dangled their legs through the open sunroof, and were rewarded with a magnificent view of Béziers. Its old gray houses climbed higgledy-piggledy up the steep slopes of the hill from Notre Dame Bridge to the former cathedral of St. Nazaire and the fortified bishop's palace that crowned its summit.

Riquet's Two "Supreme Follies"

Beyond the aqueduct the canal made a sweeping curve through a magnificent avenue of tall cypresses near the foot of the celebrated lock staircase of Fonserannes. The banks were full of Sunday picnickers, lovers, and children collecting wildflowers and boat-watching as they walked along the canal.

The Fonserannes staircase would carry us up 80 feet in a distance of about 350 yards, from the level of the Orb to the longest pound, or level stretch, of the canal. Its seven chambers face the battlements of Béziers from across the valley of the Orb. Because boats cannot pass within the staircase, there are sometimes delays here, but we managed to time our arrival properly and were taken right into the first chamber along with a number of waiting boats. The ascent was eased by electrified equipment tended by the lockkeepers, which left our young crew free to tend lines and admire the view while chatting with passersby. The climb was spectacular and awe-inspiring, the water rushing into each chamber in a veritable millrace.

As we reached the summit and looked back over the Orb Valley far below and the city of Béziers across the river, we found it easy to understand why Riquet's critics thought him mad when he drove his canal to this point. To those without the advantage of seeing before them the completed canal, making this sharp drop navigable must have appeared impossible. With the lock staircase of Fonserannes—a magnificently theatrical last gesture—Riquet carried his canal down the steep slope to the banks of the Orb and silenced those critics. The Canal du Midi was then within sight of completion.

From the summit of Fonserannes the canal follows a pleasant, winding, tree-shaded route along the southern flank of the hill ridge of Ensérune. It carried us past the little village of Colombiers, whose charming Rue du Lavoir runs along the canal banks. This was the beginning of the longest level stretch of the canal—some 32 miles without a rise or fall. Then, just five miles beyond the summit, we reached the site of Riquet's second supreme folly, the famous Percée de Malpas.

This "bad passage" *(Mal pas)* was where the canal trouble really started. Riquet was attempting something without precedent; no one had ever tried to construct a tunnel for a navigable canal before, especially a 180-yard tunnel that had to be driven through crumbling, sandy stone. Riquet's opponents accused him of squandering their money for his own glory. Matters came to a head early in 1677 as the workers approached the point along the southern slopes of the Ensérune ridge, through which Riquet proposed to tunnel. The Crown yielded to the opposition and wrote Riquet to say that a commission would soon inspect the site and that if they felt dissatisfied they would order a suspension of work.

Riquet's fighting spirit was roused. He quickly withdrew all his workers from the other sections of the canal and mustered a huge labor force at the Ensérune tunnel site. As fast as the miners advanced, carpenters erected massive beams to support the roof and masons lined the walls with stone. In this way, they say, the first canal tunnel in the world was completed *in only six days.* When the commission arrived to inspect the "impossible work," they were utterly confounded to be led through the completed excavation by a triumphant Riquet.

Hercules, Hannibal, and Humanity

The site of the Malpas Tunnel is interesting and dramatic for other reasons. On top of the ridge separating the Aude and Orb valleys stand the remains of the only reasonably well-preserved pre-Roman settlement in France. The Oppidum d'Ensérune first came to light in 1915 when botanists noticed plants growing there that were native to Greece and unknown elsewhere in France. When the plants were dug up, shards of Greek pottery were unearthed—and an archaeological hunt of the greatest importance was under way. Scientists dug through three successive periods of habitation, going back to the sixth century B.C. and perhaps earlier.

Beneath the cisterns, drainage systems, paved roadways, and remains of walls left from the days when the Romans had their premiere colony at nearby Narbonne lay the granaries, silos, and terraced fields of the agricultural Gauls who had arrived in the third century B.C. (The oppidum then had a population of about 10,000.) And beneath that layer archaeologists discovered the remains of an ancient Greek trading colony, established as far back as 600 B.C. as the eastern end of an overland route from the Atlantic seaboard.

It was approaching dusk as we emerged from the Malpas Tunnel, so we moored near the grassy bank to spend our quiet third night. The next morning we were up early, walking to the summit of the Ensérune ridge. There we visited the museum, whose collection covers the evolution of Mediterranean art and civilization from the sixth to the first centuries B.C.

We emerged from the museum, returning from the past to the present as we stood on the north ridge and marveled at the scene below: the remarkable Étang de Montady, once a shallow lake and now a great expanse of fertile land divided into triangular fields shaped like great pie slices, all draining into a central collector. The drainage system, an astonishing feat of medieval engineering, authorized by the archbishop of Narbonne in 1247 and executed by monks, is still in use today. The waters are carried beneath the Ensérune ridge by an underground culvert 1487 yards long to the nearby Poilhes and Capestang étangs.

Though we were standing on a ledge only 400 feet above sea level, we could see north all the way to the Cevennes range, east to the Mediterranean, and, from a lookout point on the other side of the museum, south to the Canigou in the Pyrénées. Hercules had passed within sight of this hill on his quest for the golden apples of the Hesperides, and Hannibal, starting from New Carthage on the Mediterranean coast of Spain, had marched in the opposite direction toward Italy with 100,000 men and fifty elephants on his way to defeat the Romans on the River Po.

Tripping down the hill much faster than we had climbed it, we set off for new adventures along the canal.

Snaking a Sinuous Canal

From our mooring at the cavernous mouth of the Malpas Tunnel, the canal followed the southern slopes of the Ensérune ridge in a classic example of contour canal cutting. Winding this way and that, the sinuous line of the canal was signaled from afar by the continuous avenue of tall plane trees that marched alongside it in an otherwise treeless landscape. We were entranced with the seemingly endless vista of interlacing branches hovering above the water.

The canal turned sharply northward to skirt the tiny village of Poilhes and the Roquemalene Hill. Rather than pass Poilhes by, we stopped to buy groceries—more of the local wines, fresh, aromatic bread, and other delectables from the patisserie.

Walking through the little unknown and unspoiled town, we spied a shepherd collecting his sheep near a barn behind one of the old stone houses. He vanished as we reached for our cameras, but later we saw him leading his bleating flock through the quiet streets, on the way to pasture. We were the only people who seemed to pay the slightest attention to him.

From Poilhes the canal swung around to the west again to pass high above the little town of Capestang. From the canal a road led steeply down through narrow streets toward the central square and a great church of ochre stone. So tortuous was the course of the canal here that we practically circumnavigated a farm two miles west of the town.

Near Argeliers we entered the only considerable straight length of the long pound. It was lined with thick bushes interspersed with ancient and twisted parasol pines—a remote and wild-looking scene. Then the canal turned southwest, toward the River Aude, and continued in that direction some ten miles until it reached a position on the north slope of the river valley at Ventenac.

Suddenly, in the heart of the river valley, the waterway widened, and on the left, beneath the arch of the towpath bridge, stretched the Canal de Jonction (opened 1776), the waterway which connects the Canal du Midi with the Aude, the Canal de la Robine (reputedly dug by the Romans), and the city of Narbonne, about half a day's run beyond. Although we passed it by, it would have made an interesting side trip.

La Belle Paule, *a tank barge heavily loaded with wine, enroute from Narbonne to Bordeaux, squeezes through the gates of the Écluse d'Empare on the Canal de Robine near its juncture with the Canal du Midi. Designed just to fit the locks with inches to spare, the barge carries one fender forward and one aft at the turn of the hull.*

Narbonne was the first Roman colony in Gaul; it became the capital of Gallia Narbonensis. In those times it was a grand city with numerous temples and monuments, but hardly any of its ancient heritage remains today, save for some tombs and statuary in the museum and the Canal de la Robine. The canal still runs clear through Narbonne—in one place, under the buildings. Nowadays it is the thirteenth-century Cathedral St. Just that is the beauty and the oddity of Narbonne. One of the tallest buildings in France, it would have been, had it been finished, one of the largest Gothic structures in the country.

A little to the west of the canal junction we crossed the River Cesse over a seventeenth-century aqueduct. From there it was little more than a mile to le Somail, a true canal village that served as the port for Narbonne before the opening of the Canal de Jonction. Here the packet boats once lay for the night and carts brought the produce of the district for shipment.

A high-arched bridge crosses the canal, its gray masonry crumbling from its stone sides, one of which has a small doorway for walkers ashore. Today the stone quay and tile-roofed warehouse of the old port are only reflections in the sleepy brown canal, deserted and, like some abandoned country railway station, watching the traffic pass it by. In the bright spring sunlight soccer uniforms splashed red and yellow over a laundry line before a handsome old row of houses.

It was approaching dusk as we decided to spend the night in Ventenac-en-Minervois, one of a number of villages in this region described by one writer as "a close huddle of pantiled roofs and brown walls as bleached as old bones by centuries of strong sunlight, looking as ancient as that Iberian settlement at Ensérune."

Of Laundresses and Gendarmes Big and Small

We climbed the hilly bank to a winding lane, around the church, and into another lane that took us into the central square. And there we came face to face with Michel, Ventenac's seven-year-old ragamuffin and the hero of our opening pages. He adopted us there, in front of the green bronze statue of Lady Liberty that adorns so many French village squares. Perhaps it had something to do with our gift of French bubble gum (of which our girls had become connoisseurs); in any case, Michel became our host for the evening, only disappearing at intervals to spring upon a cat, chasing it with a stick or making a great deal of noise with his cap pistol.

We woke mid-morning and took another walk up the hill to Ventenac. Sure enough, there was our friend policing the square, clearing it of stray cats and threatening unwary strangers with his cap pistol. We, however, were now numbered among the initiates, and he inquired gently about our night's rest and pointed us to the post office, where we wanted to mail our postcards and letters.

On the boat again, about to pull up our mooring stakes and set out on our fourth day of adventures, we were passed from behind by a loaded commercial barge that was moving slowly and holding to the middle of the channel. Passing these behemoths is discouraged because the suction of their propellers and wash in these narrow waterways makes it a dangerous feat. So we found ourselves maintaining an enforced snail's pace as the canal turned up to follow the Aude's tributary, the Répudre. It followed this detour until, at the apex of the diversion, we crossed the single modest masonry arch of the Pont-Canal de Répudre, Riquet's "premier" aqueduct of 1676. This is the only substantial aqueduct on the entire canal that can be attributed to Riquet himself, and an inscribed stone fixed to it maintains that it was the first pont-canal in the world (a claim that canal historians are still debating).

Returning along the other side of the Répudre toward the Aude, the canal passed Argens and drove around the Rock of Pechlaurier, which falls sharply toward the Aude. When the canal was being planned, Riquet maintained that he could drive his route around the steep flank of this rock and so maintain the canal's position on the high ground above the river. Most of the experts said this was folly. Other routes were proposed that hugged lower ground, and all were rejected. However, Riquet was aware that he would need more than picks and shovels to carve a course along the rocky slopes. But Colbert wrote, "I give orders to Berthelot to supply you all the powder you need," and with this gunpowder Riquet's workmen blasted a course through the Rock of Pechlaurier—one of the earliest uses of gunpowder in the history of civil engineering.

Argens Lock marked the end of the long pound; hereafter, for the next 16 miles, the locks were seldom more than a mile apart. By now we had the process of locking down to a science and were able to negotiate a single lock in five minutes, a double in ten.

Just three miles beyond Argens, at Homps, we cleared a stone bridge under the benevolent gaze of two chunky gendarmes standing back to back—one facing us as we approached, the other eyeing us as we cleared the bridge.

The small town of Homps had a spacious quay, and, on a slope of concrete nearby, knelt a woman with a "large economy size" box of Dash detergent at her side, hard at work pummeling her laundry. We slowed to prevent our wake from splashing her. Communal washing spots are provided at many points along the canal for the benefit of village housewives. They range from the very simple—like this one—to those with roofs and, in some places, a concrete trough in which the women can stand instead of kneel.

Near Puicheric the canal accelerates its climb, moving up steeply in a series of double locks and one triple staircase until the Marseillette pound is reached. It was after 7 P.M. when we stopped for the night between the three-lock staircase of Fonfile and the Écluse de Marseillette. The girls helped Jarrett serve a dinner of lean roast beef, baby spring potatoes, fresh peas from Poilhes, and some delicious Corbières du Roussillon, a simple, hearty V.D.Q.S. wine (one step below A.O.C. standards) grown on the beautiful rolling hills just to the west of us.

Beauty in the Rain

The next morning we were up and off by ten o'clock. The rain that had been threatening us for twenty-four hours began in earnest. We shrugged and counted our good fortune in having had four days on the canal with superb warm, sunny spring weather in April. Rain lent the canal another personality: soft mist rising moodily from the water, the banks shrouded and mysterious, a gauze veil suspended over our boat as the engine throbbed quietly in an utterly silent world around us—no birdsong, no crickets, and no wind to rustle the branches.

This didn't turn out to be our day for making distance. The one-armed, war-veteran lockkeeper at the Marseillette Lock was efficient and friendly and did his work better with one arm than Beverly could with two. We could easily have locked through in our usual five minutes, but there was an unexpected and splendid misty view to the north, across the broad level of the Étang de Marseillette to the heights of the Massif Central, still capped with spring snow. We lingered and enjoyed.

The five-and-a-half-mile pound between Marseillette and Trèbes was one of the most beautiful of our trip. Through the trees of a little château on the left we could see across the valley of the Aude toward the dark Alaric Mountains and, beyond, the vague shadow of the higher Pyrénées. A triple staircase lock at Trèbes would take us up from the Aude to the level of the town. The gates to the first lock were open, but the lockkeeper waved us over to the bank. A loaded barge chugged around the bend behind us, and we were expected to wait. Commercial vessels are given preference since time is expensive to them—and they pay the tolls and dues that maintain the waterways that yachts enjoy free of charge in France.

When the barge had locked through, the *éclusier* signaled to us that he was going in for lunch. By the time he emerged, an hour later, there was another barge waiting to go through, so once again we were "bumped." When we finally left the third lock in the staircase, it was nearly three o'clock. We were beginning to make disturbing calculations about our arrival time in Castelnaudary: we seemed to be a little behind schedule.

In the stretch between Trèbes and Carcassonne the river Aude makes a great loop northward; the canal, in order to keep its position on the north side of the valley, makes an even greater loop, rising through two attractively situated locks at Villedubert and l'Évêque.

We never made it to l'Évêque that day. At three-thirty we came to a standstill before the lock at Villedubert. Five commercial barges were lined up against the banks, including those that had passed us earlier. When asked what was going on, one of the bargees shrugged his shoulders, threw up his hands, and answered *Fermé!* "Closed for repairs. Until tomorrow."

A walk up to the lock itself proved that it was indeed dry and that repairs on the walls were in progress. We were in no position to complain; the commercial barges had much tighter schedules than we, and they seemed quite unruffled.

So we turned around and went back to Trèbes, about thirty minutes away. There we hired a taxi for the four-mile drive to the great medieval walled city of Carcassonne. The Canal du Midi runs through Carcassonne, and we had planned on spending the night at the quay there; none of us could bear the thought of missing it.

Magnificent Carcassonne

Carcassonne, one of the best-preserved examples of a medieval fortified city, has a history that goes back 2,500 years. Writers have described it as "a diadem of towers . . . the king's castle in the fairytale . . . a splendid toy . . . a profusion of turrets, battlements and drawbridges."

Built on a hill, it rises 500 feet over the Aude Valley, a commanding position that the Romans were not the first to recognize. Pre-Roman Gallic remains are built into the existing walls, which through the ages variously hosted or repelled the Visigoths, the Franks, St. Louis, Philip the Bold, Philip the Fair, the Black Prince, the Saracens, the Huguenots, and the Albigensians.

Carcassonne is divided into the fortified Cité (old town) and the much larger and newer Ville Basse (lower town). The Cité has two battlement walls, one inside the other, that enclose an area about a mile in circumference, and it is somberly guarded by more than fifty towers. The curious wooden projections around the tops of some of these towers enabled the defenders to drop boiling oil and molten lead onto the heads of their assailants below.

It was the outer wall that gave the fortress its reputation for being impregnable; built much lower than the more imposing inner wall, it gave attackers no vantage even should they take it. The lower wall also protected the inner wall from "mining," a technique whereby the besiegers burrowed a cavern beneath the ramparts, propped its roof with beams, and at the right moment set fire to the beams so that the cavern caved in and brought the wall down. At Carcassonne, however, any force ingenious enough to break through the outer walls would find itself caught in the deathtrap of the narrow courtyard between the two walls—and suddenly at the mercy of the defenders above and those in the towers behind.

We arrived late in the afternoon to find the western walls and towers bathed in a misty, golden, fairytale light. From the Port d'Aude we walked into the Cité, where a guide took us through some of the towers and into the great Château Comtal of the Trencavels. Built of yellow sandstone, the château was the donjon of the great castle that was Carcassonne, a citadel separated from the city by its own outer defenses, a moat and gates.

Though the city of Carcassonne was able to withstand medieval attack, time became its unconquerable enemy. It suffered neglect after it had been made obsolete by gunpowder and modern machines of war. The city's ancient walls were almost pulled down in 1850; the order to complete the demolition had already been given when Prosper Mérimée (author of the story that inspired the libretto of Bizet's opera *Carmen*) intervened in his capacity as inspector general of historic monuments. He awarded the task of restoring the fortifications to Viollet-le-Duc, whose work has occasioned a great deal of controversy.

Le Duc's self-professed idea of restoration was "to re-establish [a building] in a state of completion which may never have existed at any given moment in the past." This attitude led him to destroy much that was good, to keep much that was not, and to draw on his imagination when he was short of fact. Purists shrink from his interpretations at Carcassonne, though many of his alterations are beginning to mellow and blend with age. We just walked around wide-eyed and gleeful, awestruck at the matchless line of towers against the sky.

The Ville Basse was created in the days of St. Louis, when the Cité revolted under the last of the Trencavels. Louis besieged the city and, having taken it, expelled the inhabitants. He built the Ville Basse, permitted the citizens to return to it, then garrisoned the Cité with royal troops.

Today its encircling green and shady boulevards mark the lines of the old walls. Within the boulevards the narrow streets of the Ville Basse pulse with life. This is the marketplace for the large surrounding district, an area that includes the winegrowing region of Corbières, the largest producer of V.D.Q.S. wines in France.

A famous culinary specialty of Carcassonne and one of the great dishes of southeast France is cassoulet. Though Carcassonne vies with Castelnaudary and Toulouse for the honor of being called home of the "original" (the locals insist fiercely that theirs is the only true and original version), there is no definitive recipe for the dish. It is a marvelous concoction of white haricot beans, garlic sausage, fat bacon, garlic, tomatoes, onions, cloves, and parsley, all of which is cooked for a very long time (Anatole France wrote that the cassoulet in his favorite Paris restaurant had been on the stove for twenty years). Cassoulet usually contains goose when it has Toulouse attached to its name, pork when Castelnaudary, and shoulder of mutton when Carcassonne. According to tradition, the crust that forms in the cooking is broken up and stirred in seven times before serving. And there are many other traditions: the *cassole* (the pot, which gives the dish the name *cassoulet*) must be made of clay from Issel; the beans must be grown on the soil of Lavelanet; the mixture must be cooked in the pure water of Castelnaudary; and the furze (a low, spiny plant with yellow flowers, common in the wastelands of Europe) of the Black Mountain must feed the fires of the oven as the dish cooks.

To sample the cassoulet of Carcassonne, we settled on the Logis de Trencavel on the Avenue Général Leclerc, a restaurant which the Michelin guidebook accorded a rare rosette and one which specialized in cassoulet and the wines of the Corbières and Minervois. We found the cassoulet to be a very substantial dish indeed, the restaurant very pleasant; the prices, while higher than those of our little café in Ventenac, were almost 40 percent lower than those of rosette-rated restaurants we had visited in Paris.

Our touring, wandering, gawking, and dining happily completed, we returned by taxi to our boat in Trèbes. There we retired, looking for a good early start in the morning. We'd have to make tracks if we were going to be anywhere near Castelnaudary when Blue Line expected us!

Hurry Up and Wait

Our sixth morning dawned cold and rainy. We were in front of the recalcitrant Villedubert Lock by eight o'clock, but we had to wait for the last barge to finish going through. When the lock seemed clear, the lockkeeper started down toward us. (It's not a good sign, we had learned, when the lockkeeper wants to chat with you from the towpath.) His message was that he'd been locking boats and barges through since before 6 A.M.; he was tired and was going in for breakfast.

The ramparts and turrets of the restored walled city of Carcassonne. High to the left is the twelfth-century castle and to the lower right the thirteenth-century bridge over the River Aude. The river flows north from the Pyrénées to Carcassonne, then turns to the east and parallels the Canal du Midi past Olonzac before turning to the Mediterranean.

His breakfast finished, we were let into the lock, but the entire morning was slow going; there were delays at every lock because of the backup caused by the Villedubert closing. Everyone—bargees, lockkeepers, their wives and children, crews from the pleasure boats—was working hard, each with his own schedule to make, yet everyone found time to flash a patient smile and to make pleasant conversation.

At about noon we were crossing the Fresquel River via the high and imposing nineteenth-century aqueduct. Just beyond, the canal swung sharply to the south and headed for Carcassonne, skirting the high ground on the right which divides the valleys of the Fresquel and Aude. Approaching St. Jean shortly before one o'clock, we could see that the lock was empty but the doors were closed. The lockkeeper stood stone silent and still, so Jarrett was dispatched to find out what was going on. In her fractured French she asked when he would open the gates.

"*Après!*" he answered simply.

"*Après* what?"

"*Un bateau*" (pointing to the left) "*et deux bateaux*" (pointing to the right).

"Well, about what time do you think that might be?"

"*Après! Après!*"

Un bateau arrived and waited in front of the lock. Then the first of the *deux bateau* emerged from the lock. The bargees apparently knew one another, for there was great waving and laughing between captains and mates, and the two barges met for a half-hour gamming session. We had been told about the barge "grapevine" that extended the length of every waterway; news travels among the barge people with a rapidity that challenges the telephone or telegram, even though the boats themselves move at only four miles an hour. We were witnessing not just a chance meeting between old friends but an event in the routine of the waning barge society.

Completely oblivious of us, the two heavily laden barges blocked the entire canal, wife talking to wife, captain to captain, their boats drifting free most of the time and frequently moving sideways across the canal in front of the lock gates. After a full thirty minutes of enthusiastic and melodious exchange they began to part. But now the eastbound barge had its stern lodged in the shallows of the bank and needed a tow to get off. With a great deal of laughter and joking at his expense, the other *batelier* finally towed him off the muddy bank. Then, with lines flying and hands high in benediction (it might be months or years before they met again), they parted and the westbound barge maneuvered into the lock where the *éclusier* had been waiting, hands on hips and head shaking, for forty-five minutes.

The barge was quickly locked through and the gates opened for us. Beyond the lock of St. Jean the land on the left fell away to give us a superb view of the Cité of Carcassonne, a view quite different from any we had experienced on land.

At the basin in Carcassonne, near the Jardin des Plantes, wine barges were lined up on the left bank filling their tanks. From here it was still 20 miles to Castelnaudary; we were beginning to realize we weren't going to make it as promised by that night.

It was after five o'clock when we arrived at Villesequalande, the next lock. We bought fresh eggs from the lockkeeper's wife, who kept them in a handsome wicker basket; they were to form the central element in our impromptu boatbound dinner. The 7:30 P.M. lock closing obliged us to stop for the night, and soon we were rustling up the best dinner we could with only eggs, bread, sugar, salt, and milk on board. It was somewhat amusing when the girls realized we were actually having "french toast" in France.

Last Climb

On Friday morning, the start of our seventh and final day on the canal, we were off at daybreak and working our way up toward the heavily locked area leading to Castelnaudary. It was raining again. Beverly, who had a cold and a fever, was confined for the day and given little housekeeping chores. These done, she was able to watch the passing scene and the lock activities from the picture windows in the salon. We set her up on the couch, covered her legs with a spare blanket, and gave her a copy of the Canal du Midi guidebook—and she was able to go touring in the warmth of the cabin. We shuddered to think what might have happened had we been hotel-bound in a city; here she could pamper her cold while we floated the French country-side past her admiring eyes.

When we reached the St. Roch quadruple lock, a representative of Blue Line cruisers was waiting for us. He was understanding, having heard about the un-scheduled stoppage at Villedubert. Nevertheless he had to ready the boat for the next charterers, who were arriving that afternoon, so he was anxious to get us to the Blue Line base in the Castelnaudary basin. He helped Laura tend the lines ashore, while the modern electrified machinery did the rest. The lockkeeper monitored our prog-ress from a glass-enclosed control tower set at the top of the flight.

When we emerged from the top lock, we had reached a height of 558 feet above sea level. We were in the Grand Bassin of Castelnaudary, a broad port nearly a mile in circumference. On the north side the old town stood mirrored in the still water, its houses piled in an impressive heap, one above the other, rising almost sheer from the water's edge. Directly opposite stood an old storehouse said to date from the days of Riquet. Our newly acquired guide indicated the Blue Line base next to the storehouse.

A Fitting Climax

Packed and organized, we would summon a taxi to take us to the airport at Toulouse, but first we made a brief detour to the Bassin de St. Ferréol, the main reservoir of the entire canal system, located at the very edge of the Black Mountain. Begun in January 1667 and completed in four years, it was the first dam ever built to supply a navigable canal and was by far the greatest single work of civil engineering undertaken during the building of the canal. Its length is a staggering 1560 feet, its height 105 feet, and its thickness at the base more than 450 feet. Constructed entirely by hand, the dam was built of earth carried to the site in baskets, much of it by women who were paid a penny a load. In the three hundred years of its life it has required no major repairs, and it stands now, still performing the function for which it was built, an impressive monument to the genius and daring of Pierre-Paul Riquet and his engineers.

As we walked along the broad crest of the dam, gazing over the great expanse of tree-lined water that it had created, the fact that it had been built so long ago seemed hardly possible.

Riquet planted trees in the gorge beneath his mighty dam, laid out walks beside the rushing streams, and led the overflow from the spill weir down into these deep green shades by a spectacular series of waterfalls and cataracts. As a final touch in the spirit of the golden age of Louis XIV, he took advantage of the head of water available to place a spectacular fountain near the foot of this man-made cascade. It shoots a single powerful jet of water 60 feet into the air, the water falling as an iridescent white curtain, swaying like a ghostly tree amid the green forest. Dense and very still, there is only the sound of deer rustling through the forest and the water to break the quiet. Wild dianthus glows on the rocks and the brooks flash with trout.

Here was a fitting climax to our trip on the Canal du Midi, the place where the concept was born and made possible—by a genius possessed by an idea, Pierre-Paul Riquet.

The Round Lock at Agde, Canal du Midi. The lockkeeper can tell by the ripples on the water when the next lock has opened or when a boat is approaching.

Some Practical Information

One of the hire boat firms operating in southern France uses the slogan "Come Sunshine Cruising," which very aptly describes waterway cruising through this unique and beautiful region. Here one finds outstanding scenery, ancient historic villages, one of the mightiest rivers in Europe, and perhaps the oldest and most interesting operating canal in the world.

From early spring to late fall the waterways of southern France beckon to the knowledgeable traveler, offering a variety of delightful cruising possibilities, generally excellent weather, superb food and wines, and above all the opportunity to explore the countryside and villages. Here one can really meet the people in face-to-face encounters that are unavailable to most tourists.

Three regions in southern France offer the waterway traveler well-organized and established cruising and excursion facilities: the Midi, the Rhône River, and the Charente-Maritime region.

1. *The Midi,* comprising the Canal Latéral à la Garonne (from Bordeaux to Toulouse) and the Canal du Midi (from Toulouse to Sète) is a 313-mile (504 km) travelers' delight. In the fifteenth century Leonardo da Vinci first proposed a canal linking the Atlantic with the Mediterranean as an advantageous shipping route for heavy goods. After nearly two centuries of consideration and fifteen years of intense engineering and construction, the canal was completed in 1681. Subsequently the Canal Latéral à la Garonne was built, completing the strategic link between France's two coasts.

Today carefree travelers along the two canals are transported back nearly two centuries and are treated to sights of unparalleled beauty and tranquility, from historic sleepy villages, ancient vineyards, fishing hamlets, and ingeniously designed locks to such notable and exciting cities as Béziers, Bordeaux, Carcassonne, and Toulouse, in the shadow of the French and Spanish Pyrénées.

There are two ways to cruise the canals of the Midi:

SELF-DRIVE (BAREBOAT CHARTER) boats are offered by a number of hire firms with bases on the Canal Latéral à la Garonne and the Canal du Midi. These diesel-powered motor cruisers accommodate from four to ten persons and are rented on a weekly basis. The two principal self-drive firms are:

Blue Line Cruisers, Le Grand Bassin, B.P. 67, 11400 Castelnaudary, maintains a fleet of 60 modern cruisers, with hire bases at Castelnaudary and Marseillan.

			June-Sept.	Other
Blue Elysian	27 feet (8 m)	4 berths	$525–600	$250–420
Blue Bermuda	34 feet (10.5 m)	5–6 berths	$560–675	$300–475
Blue Caribbean	39 feet (12 m)	7 berths	$620–775	$350–550

Linen and fuel are extra.

Beaver Fleet, 53 Quai du Canal, 47000 Agen, maintains a fleet of 80 modern cruisers, with hire bases at Agen and Port Cassafières.

			June-Sept.	Other
D'Accord	26 feet (8 m)	4 berths	$500–625	$275–425
New Generation	30 feet (9 m)	4–6 berths	$575–700	$350–500
Bonne Chance	35 feet (10.5 m)	6 berths	$650–825	$400–550

These prices include fuel and linen.

The following central booking agents can furnish information and make bookings for self-drive boats on the Midi:

Floating Through Europe, Inc.
501 Madison Avenue
New York, N.Y. 10022

Blakes Holidays
Wroxham, Norwich NR12 8DH, England

Boat Enquiries Ltd.
7 Walton Well Road
Oxford OX2 6ED, England

HOTEL BARGE. Continental Waterways Ltd., 22 Hans Place, London SW1, England, operates a pair of hotel barges, *Water Wanderer I* and *II,* on the Canal du Midi. The boats accommodate 14 passengers plus 6 crew, with a fare $430 to $460 per person in a twin-bedded room and $470 to $510 for a single; this includes six nights' accommodation, all meals plus table wine, and use of the ship's bicycles. Information and bookings for *Water Wanderer* can also be obtained from Floating Through Europe, Inc., 501 Madison Avenue, New York, N.Y. 10022.

2. *The Rhône River,* flowing from the Swiss Alps through Lake Geneva and then through southeast France to the Mediterranean, is a turbulent, thundering giant of a river that is now being tamed by huge dams and power projects. Its course is 505 miles (813 km) long, 200 miles through Switzerland and 380 through France. Via a series of interconnecting canals, navigation on the Rhône links up with the rivers Saône, Rhine, Seine, Loire, and Garonne, making up the southern section of the vast waterway network that crosses the continent. There are no self-drive fleets on the Rhône, but one French company does offer excursion service on the river:

Compagnie Yacht Le Cygne, c/o M. Couly, 9 rue Fourrier, 30300 Beaucaire, operates the yacht *Le Cygne* between Lyon and the Mediterranean. The boat is 66 feet (20 m) long, 13 feet (4 m) beam, carries 50 passengers, and contains panoramic lounge, solarium, and snack bar. The following prices cover boat passage only; meals and hotel accommodations on overnight cruises are additional:

Lyon to Valence	$10
Valence to Avignon	$14
Avignon to Aigues-Mortes	$12

3. *The Charente-Maritime region,* on the west coast of France some 90 miles (145 km) north of Bordeaux, is an off-the-beaten-path region that has been charming visitors since Roman times. Sometimes called the Atlantic Riviera, it boasts the town of Cognac (world famous for the brandy distilled from local grapes), the lovely Charente River, and three exceptional offshore islands, Oléron, Ré, and Aix. The principal of the three, the Île d'Oléron, connected to the mainland by one of the longest bridges in Europe—nearly two miles (3 km)—is the second largest French island after Corsica. The islands feature mile after mile of deserted and lovely beaches, Roman ruins, historic fishing and seaside villages, sand dunes spotted with pine and oak trees and fragrant with wildflowers, and a host of inexpensive restaurants and hotels.

The Régie Départmentale des Passages d'Eau, B.P. 2012, 17009 La Rochelle-Pallice, operates a fleet of large excursion boats, accommodating from 80 to 230 passengers, along the Charente River and between the islands and the mainland.

For additional information on cruising in southern France, contact:

The French Government Tourist Office
610 Fifth Avenue
New York, N.Y. 10020

Commissariat Général au Tourisme
Service Canaux et Rivières
8, avenue de l'Opéra
Paris 1e

Maps, guides, and books concerning the waterways of France are available from Floating Through Europe, Inc., which maintains an extensive inventory of these publications.

2

*Aboard
the
Jolly
Palinurus*

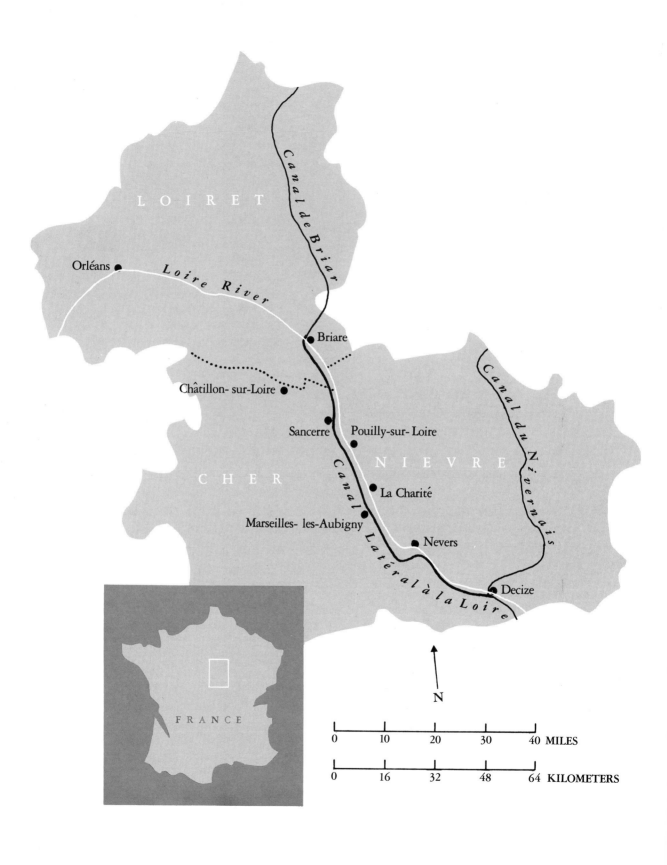

LOIRET

Canal de Briar

Orléans •

Loire River

Briare •

Châtillon- sur-Loire •

Sancerre • • Pouilly-sur- Loire

CHER

NIEVRE

Canal du Nivernais

• La Charité

Canal Latéral à la Loire

Marseilles- les-Aubigny

• Nevers

• Decize

FRANCE

N

| 0 | 10 | 20 | 30 | 40 MILES |

| 0 | 16 | 32 | 48 | 64 KILOMETERS |

The Canal Latéral à la Loire
and a Visit to Burgundy

After our trip across southern France, we decided to move just a smidgen north and to explore the province of Burgundy via the *Palinurus,* a traditional French working barge *(péniche)* that since 1966 has cruised the waterways of central France from early spring until the fall grape harvest, showing small groups of travelers the joys of this region so rich in history, vineyards, and gastronomic delights.

Burgundy's vineyards have brought the region its greatest fame. Reading a map of the province is like dusting off the labels in one of the world's best-stocked wine cellars and discovering names like Pommard, Gevrey-Chambertin, Beaune, Meursault, and Mâcon. But the history of Burgundy can be traced over 2,500 years, and scattered amid the lush vineyards, fields, plains, hills, and valleys are some of France's oldest and most beautiful cathedrals, châteaux, and abbeys, as well as some exceptionally rich museums and picturesque old towns. Many of France's 3,000 miles of canals and 25,000 miles of rivers peacefully wind among these attractions—hidden from the more frequented tourist spots—and provide a unique vantage point for seeing the inside of France.

Our joining instructions from the barge's booking office in London indicated that we would be met at the Hotel California in Paris on Sunday and transported to the barge to begin our cruise. We arrived at the hotel just as the soccer team from Béziers rolled into town amidst great honking of horns, costumed parading, and the general taunts of the Paris populace looking on in fond but haughty amusement from their Sunday places in the Champs-Élysée cafés. Signs and sweatshirts proclaimed that the French contender for the world championship was about to be determined. Paris was momentarily losing its chic, intellectual head!

The invasion of the team from the Languedoc region reminded us that we would soon be far away in still another France, a part of France to be captured and retained on what Emily Kimbrough called a "Floating Island," the barge *Palinurus.*

Bienvenu! Bienvenu à Palinurus!

The lobby of the Hotel California filled slowly, two by two, with British, Canadian, and American couples. It looked as though we would have a full complement aboard the *Palinurus.* Then our host and the co-owner, Richard Parsons, arrived, greeted each of us cordially, and—bag by bag—loaded us into what he called his "beautiful bus." Eagerly we set off toward our presumed starting point, the town of

Sens on the Canal de Bourgogne, some 74 miles southeast of Paris.

"A few preliminary announcements," Richard shouted above the noise of traffic as we lumbered crazily through the narrow streets of Paris. "First, we have a slight change in our itinerary. We just learned last week that the Canal de Bourgogne is closed for its annual cleaning. So we'll be traveling the Canal Latéral à la Loire south from the little town of Briare. That's about three hours' drive from here."

Interestingly, none of our fellow passengers really minded this last-minute switch. One of the joys of canal cruising seems to be the complete abandonment of pressure. The change in plans simply meant that the sights and sounds of the beautiful Loire River valley would replace those of the Yonne; the wines of Sancerre and Pouilly would replace those of the Côte d'Or.

The cuisine, fortunately, would remain the same, for the chef of the *Palinurus* has a reputation for fine provincial cooking. The emblem of the barge is a plump, Pillsbury doughboy-like chef chasing a snail with what looks like a mini-pitchfork. "We think the barge is like a snail," Richard Parsons says, "because a snail carries its home with it, never hurries, and has time to enjoy its rural environment. A snail eats what he finds along the way and takes time to digest." It was apparent that the best of France would be ours, whether in the heart of Burgundy or in the Loire Valley.

As promised, three hours later, after a spectacularly unscenic drive along the highways of France, we arrived on the tiny streets of Briare, a little town best known for its very special kind of ceramic buttons and mosaics. The pier as we approached was alive with a carnival well attended by a milling Sunday crowd of Briarians who eyed us curiously in our "beautiful bus." And there, in the midst of all of the commotion, was the famed barge *Palinurus,* looking flamboyantly unbargelike with its built-up sides for a cargo of voyagers instead of the usual grain, fertilizer, and wine of the French barge trade. The sun was still high at 5:30 P.M. on this mid-May day, and our crew was waving in enthusiastic welcome.

"*Bienvenu! Bienvenu à* Palinurus!"

The Lazy Loire

Born in the Massif Central of south central France, the Loire (known to the ancient Romans as the Liger) defines the western boundary of Burgundy. First it meanders due north; then, like a toddling child, it changes its mind and turns a gentle, graceful right angle westward toward Nantes and the sea. When it reaches the Atlantic, it has traveled some 668 miles, not an extraordinary distance among the world's great rivers. Yet, the English writer A. H. Broderick has said, "no real understanding of the French people is possible without an attentive pilgrimage to the lands watered by this broad, shallow, pale, shifting river, whose ever-changing lights reflect a graceful and subtle sky."

Until the middle of the nineteenth century the Loire was a highway paved with white sails. In times when roads were poor the waterway offered the most practical route for the transport of heavy commercial goods; as early as the fourth century there existed a regular organization of navigators on the Loire.

From the fourth to the eighteenth centuries a tribe of rough, swaggering, hard-drinking rivermen transported the widest variety of articles up and down the river: agricultural products from the Charrolais and Morvan provinces, pottery from Nevers, timber and coal from Forez. Traffic was particularly intense on the downstream leg of the journey, which took about six days at the rate of 18 miles per day. The voyage upstream, however, was extremely difficult because of the fierce current; it took 15–20 days—with a good wind. Following the downriver trip, rivermen often preferred to break up their boats, sell the planks, and return upriver on foot.

In the eighteenth century trade had begun to decline on the river. Then, in 1837, the picture was drastically altered by the opening of the Canal Latéral à la Loire, running 122 miles from Digoin to Briare on the middle section of the river. The opening of the canal infused new life into trade on this section, while the lower Loire succumbed—despite valiant efforts to save it—to the competition of the railroads. On the lower section of the river the final blow occurred when the new railway from Paris to Orléans opened in 1846; by 1892 the last shipping company had ended its passenger service. Today the lower part of the river is totally unnavigable above Angers.

The middle Loire had been saved from such an ignominious end by its canal. Commercial barges still carry coal, iron ore, building sand, fuel oil, wine, and grain from Roanne on the upper Loire to Briare, via this and the Canal de Digoin à Roanne. Today the river that for so long injected pulsating life into the region lies deserted, while the canal throbs with a steady stream of *péniches* wending their way along the manmade cut.

The River Loire continues to give its special character to the countryside: the most beautiful landscapes are those brightened by its long and graceful curves. In summertime thin trickles of water (the *luisettes*) agonizingly advance between enormous golden sandbanks where willows dot the riverbed with green. But from October to June the swirling waters tear along at a fearful rate, a menacing gray-green swelling at Nevers and overflowing at Orléans. The canal, however, remains calm—even sedate—and is consistently navigable right alongside the river's course.

Our Journey Begins

Once we arrived dockside the crew was at work. Luggage disappeared quickly belowdecks. We went down to inspect our accommodations, which consisted of a small and rustic twin-berthed cabin with sink. "Facilities" down the hall were modest and somewhat temperamental in character.

After storing our bags the crew lost no time in casting off from the noisy dock, and almost immediately we found ourselves crossing the Pont-Canal St. Firmin-sur-Loire, which claims to be the longest canal bridge in the world. With a 2172-foot span, it is longer than the Delaware Memorial Bridge. Begun in 1890 by Alexandre Eiffel (of the Tower), this metal aqueduct carries the Canal de Briare over the swirling, unnavigable waters of the Loire, to join the Canal Latéral à la Loire.

The barge was moving so slowly through the narrow aqueduct that several of our company stepped off at the beginning, strolled the entire length, and stepped leisurely back aboard as we reached the end. We preferred to stay on board, higher up, to examine more closely the beautifully crafted old iron streetlamps, now crumbling from disuse, and to look over the sides at the magnificent Loire below.

From the moment we left the aqueduct and joined the Canal Latéral we found ourselves surrounded by woodland and pastures and introduced to the celebrated creamy white Charrolais cattle on their home turf. The Charrolais are known the world over; they are exported to some fifty-eight countries because they readily adapt to all climates, fatten on a minimum of feed, and yield an unusually large amount of high-quality beef.

The landscape in the late afternoon light was a startling green, luxuriant in daisies and cherry blossoms; the canal banks were full of friendly wild iris and bullrushes, lily of the valley and buttercups. Mistletoe hung from stately old trees. We passed an

In March of each year a list of "chomages" appears showing which locks on the canals of France will be closed for maintenance and the dates of closing. Here at Houard a section of the Canal Latéral à la Loire, usually filled to its grassy banks, is almost empty, giving a clear view of the lock gates and the open sluices at the bottom.

ancient château that was dug into the hill near the canal and tried to imagine it in its more glorious days, when it possessed its own moat and drawbridge. Today it is just one of hundreds of châteaux the tourist will never know because it is privately owned and overshadowed by the more popular and well-known château grandeur on the lower Loire to the west.

On the right bank stood an orchard in full bloom and, lounging under the trees in the fading light, a small group of picnickers. The birds came alive in the twilight, and the trees in which they mingled hovered so close over the *Palinurus* that the birdsong was in stereo. Looking back, we could see a curve of the Loire through the evening mist and the swaying boughs of the trees.

Little more than three miles beyond the aqueduct at Briare the *Palinurus* softly nestled up to the grassy bank and was secured to some nearby trees for the night. We had arrived at Châtillon-sur-Loire, a village that prides itself on abundant fishing—whitefish, perch, pike, carp, and sandre—in both the canal and the river. All sixteen passengers discreetly sniffed the aromas of dinner wafting from the galley, and cocktail hour was announced promptly at seven o'clock. If there was a ritual aboard the *Palinurus,* it was the cocktail hour, during which passengers whipped up an appetite taking in all those tempting galley smells while soaking up whatever new scene surrounded us at the moment.

Our second day out found us up early and inspecting *les bicyclettes de la Loire,* a collection of motley, not-very-confidence-inspiring relics from past *Palinurus* voyagers, who had supplied them with a copious quantity of dents, scratches, knicks, and bent handlebars and a rickety, uncertain look. This may have turned out to be an advantage, for there were only seven bicycles for sixteen passengers. Due to the rugged appearance of the sport, we usually had little competition for the limited supply of "wheels."

We struck off on the towpath, up the little hill to the narrow road, and into Châtillon. The first thing we noticed about Châtillon was that there were no postcard vendors, no souvenir shops, no boutiques. It was, very simply, a living, working survival of the fifteenth century. It has kept its old church, some of its fifteenth-century houses, and its picturesque wobbly streets. Women opened their shutters on second-floor windows and looked out; shopkeepers arranged brightly colored fruits and vegetables on the streetside stands. We passed yards filled with vegetables and flowers in profusion, and sleeping dogs awoke to bark as we appeared. Townspeople paused to smile and turned to watch us as we departed. It is not exactly a town accustomed to visitors; indeed, most tourists never see little hamlets such as this.

A quick turn around the main square on our trusty rusties and we headed back toward the canal. This time we pedaled right on past the canal, over a suspension bridge spanning the Loire, which looked like a mighty river but was actually a shallow pussycat whose swirling currents and eddies were caused by sandbars and old logs. In the center of the river was a narrow, thickly arbored islet, a haven for birds and wildlife and the source of much of our precious evening's birdsong.

Returning along the towpath, we were greeted by the unmistakable aroma of French-brewed coffee and warm croissants, and we joined the rest of the ship's company for a leisurely breakfast. While we sipped our chicory coffee the crew was already casting off lines for the day's adventures.

Six miles beyond Châtillon, Maimbray Lock took us up a level. Up was where we would be heading through almost all the locks for an entire week—up, up, and up toward the mountain sources of the precocious Loire. Up, that is, in everything but lock numbers—we would work from No. 38 to No. 15 at Decize, 82 miles south from Briare.

We moved slowly through peaceful plains and pastures, past tiny walled cemeteries, farms with rich soil and hay-pitching farmers, and masons working bricks in time with the tuneful call of the cuckoo. Suddenly we were in flower-studded Belleville, a lettuce-patched, woodpiled, apple-blossomed, belilacked village—aptly named and beyond appreciation from any vantage save our barge on this bright and warm spring morning. Brown goats grazed before distant cypress trees. The lockkeeper here kept morning doves, rabbits, and curious dogs who poked their noses into the barge windows as we rode up on our slow but dependable elevator. Entire families stopped their field work to stare at us and wave. We were a curious sight, a barge with a cargo of blue sun umbrellas and multicolored lounge chairs, but we gazed and waved back with just as much curiosity as they.

For the entire morning we had the canal to ourselves; it seemed to have been built for this barge, this cruise, this week alone. But now, up ahead of us and bearing down fast, was a monstrous piece of machinery that appeared to be an empty barge. Suddenly the canal seemed too narrow and too shallow for two full-sized *péniches*. Only after some fancy maneuvering were we able to get by the huge steel hulk.

We were mopping our collective brow in sympathetic relief for our helmsman Howard when we became aware of the activity in the dining room. Lunch was being set up, and—as would soon become routine—we prepared for a short stop by the side of the canal. This lunch was to be typical of all our lunches on board: two or three types of cold meat, deviled eggs, salads, crunchy fresh bread, and a bottomless pitcher of red wine at every table. We were invited to serve ourselves as much and as often as we wished but were cautioned to leave room for the ubiquitous groaning tray of local cheeses and fruit. Refreshing, not *too* sinful, and delicious!

Our "First" Château

After a brief rest following our lunch, the barge resumed its southerly climb through several more locks. At one of these Guy (our captain and guide) suggested we step off and take the bicycles to the little Château of Buranlure nearby. We did, and we found the stately, well-preserved château in a lush hollow filled with great woods and a flock of sheep. But what was this sign? CHÂTEAU PRIVÉ, PAS D'ENTRÉE. Thoroughly insulted, we decided to pretend we hadn't seen it.

The family who lived in the farmhouse behind the château appeared to be glad to see us. The woman even sent out her three growling dogs to greet us, then moved forward cautiously herself to tell us in French, and in no uncertain terms, that we were welcome to look through the bars across the moat and then to depart. This we did, not without haste, because the dogs, like their owners, didn't understand English and seemed bent on escorting us back up their driveway.

Pedaling frantically to escape the dogs of Buranlure, we headed for the lock and there found the *Palinurus* waiting for us. Despite the fact that we were somewhat later than expected, there seemed to be no hurry, no worry, no schedule missed, no impatience—just a warm welcome.

A few hours and a leisurely ten miles later, at the Port of St. Thibault, we were guided toward a tiny, shaded side-canal for the night. The *Palinurus* nosed in cautiously, squeezing through the tunnel-like eye-of-the-needle space beneath a bridge. The spot suited the captain, but the barge itself balked and settled about 13 feet from

The Ancien Abbaye de Fontenay founded in 1118 represents a change from earlier ornate architecture toward simplicity of design, emphasizing the humility and simplicity of monastic life. The Abbaye includes a church, cloister, dormitory, infirmary, fish hatchery, garden and a wonderful canopy of great old trees.

the bank (our gangplank was just 14 feet long). We were aground (but it was no problem).

Under a late afternoon sun we enjoyed a casual walk through the tiny village of St. Thibault, the seat of an old priory that in the thirteenth century had become the proud owner of the relics of St. Thibault. To preserve this heritage, the town built a remarkable church with an elegant, five-sided chancel and a doorway that is said to be among the most beautiful pieces of carving in Burgundy.

In the morning, after having disentangled ourselves from the canal bed and backed through beneath the tiny bridge, we glided south along a magnificent promenade of poplars and green fields abloom with dogwood. Enormous crows nested high in the trees, and, a mile south of St. Satur, we caught our first glimpse of vineyards —reaching right to the canal banks. There were tamarisk trees, wisteria in bloom, long vines topping fences and surrounding walls, and lilacs. The morning was filled with the sounds of mockingbirds and cuckoos, the sight of terns swooping over the canal in loose formation, the smells of fern-carpeted woods bordered with wild poppies and nasturtiums.

Mid-morning, near the seventeenth-century Château de la Grange, we moored to some trees at a little spot widened just for the barge. We were surrounded by the most incredibly green meadows, backed by the heat-haze shrouded foothills of the Morvan Mountains. Saluting us were straight, stately rows of tall poplars. A stream nearby was filled with schools of trout that swam carelessly beneath our feet as we perched on a tiny footbridge. Our reflections gently rippled in the crystalline water as it carried the trout effortlessly downstream. And so we passed the middle of the day, some of us walking through the fields, some bicycling along the towpath and venturing into nearby villages, and some just lolling about the barge and soaking in the sunshine.

After lunch a chartered bus took us up a long, slow hill and through the vineyards surrounding the history-rich and wine-bountiful village of Sancerre. The village is the major marketplace of the Loire Valley, famous for its delicious white wine (with its "gunflint" dryness) and for the little round goatsmilk cheese made in nearby Chavignol.

Land of the Goat and the Vine

If the wines of the Loire Valley are not instantly recognized, like those of the Côtes du Rhône, it is because none of them are sold under their regional name. Wines of the region, like Sancerre and Pouilly, are far better known by their town names.

Yet the wines of the Loire are almost invariably considered as a group because they all share a certain character that marks them as Loire. They can best be described as "charming." If they lack some of the magnificent breed of the great Bordeaux and Burgundies, they have nevertheless a special style, a grace and gaiety that makes them wonderfully refreshing.

Caesar's wine-drinking legions may have introduced the vine to the shores of the Loire, or the vine may already have existed when they arrived. Here as elsewhere, it was the Church that was responsible for the growth of the wine industry as we know it.

Sancerre wine can have great finesse, being dry without pronounced acidity and full-bodied without losing its crisp appeal. A good Sancerre, they say, can smell like a mountain meadow when the snows are melting: cool, with a floweriness in the background. Louis XIV is said to have drunk Sancerre in great quantities. Today, while it is not considered one of France's greatest wines, it is still very popular throughout the world; no wine cellar is considered truly complete without at least one bottle of it or Pouilly-Fumé.

Sancerre is also noted for its special goatsmilk cheese, the *crottin*—whose name demonstrates one of the more lighthearted twists of the French language. Referring surely to the shape of the small round cheese and not to its delicious taste or its mode of manufacture, the name means literally, "little turd."

At the crest of the hill in Sancerre we found the Promenade of the Caesar Gate, a lookout point offering a vast panorama of the vineyards of the Loire Valley—mile after mile, as far as we could see, of vineyards planted on the sunny, exposed slopes, interrupted only by the twelve small towns of the Sancerrois, among them St. Thibault and St. Satur.

Just behind us was one of Sancerre's most noted landmarks, the round Tower of the Fiefs, which was built at the end of the fourteenth century and fiercely defended during the Hundred Years' War. The town's strategic position gave Sancerre an important role in this war as a stronghold of Protestantism against the royal forces of Charles VII. Now, six violent centuries later, the Tower of the Fiefs is the only trace of the original castle of the earls of Sancerre.

The narrow, winding streets of the old town invited us to wander, past historic houses bearing plaques that drew our attention here to a special gable, there to a turret, a portal, or a carved ornament. Charming little alleys led nowhere, tortuously climbing or descending the steep hill on which the town is perched.

Touching the Heart of the Loire

A short bus ride took us to the mountain town of Chavignol, known to produce the best of both the Sancerre wine and the *crottin.* Here we were to learn firsthand about one of the major pleasures of the wine regions of France: the sign DÉGUSTATION, which hangs over some very unlikely-looking doorways. It means "Come in and taste our wine," and whenever wine lovers see that sign, they cease all other activities and knock on the door. The proprietor, of course, hopes you will order some—an often inconvenient practice for foreigners, for wine typically has more difficulty crossing borders than do people.

In these cellars—often former quarries cut into the white chalk of the hillside

—the true character of the Loire country can best be discovered. The galleries sometimes extend for several hundred yards underground, opening into great halls that are used for meetings and celebrations of local societies, such as that of the winegrowers, who carefully preserve the traditions of fine drink and fine drinking in the Loire Valley.

Our bus stopped before a sign proclaiming the cellars of a maker of fine wine: R. BOURGEOIS—VINS FINS, BLANC ET ROSÉ. Monsieur Bourgeois guided us cordially into the ancient, hand-dug cellars where the A.O.C. Sancerre wines are aged.

"These cellars," he explained, "are some of the oldest in France." Picking up some lifeless-looking twigs from the dirt floor, he told us that they would someday produce the grapes from which the Sancerre wine is made. The only grape allowed in wine bearing the A.O.C. Sancerre label is the Sauvignon, which acquires a special flavor from the mineral in the local limestone soil; this gives the wine its flinty quality —markedly dry, with a crisp, refreshing tang.

And here we were, in the temple of Bacchus, facing the barrels of the latest vintage firmly fixed in their stands! The vigneron's wife and children arrived bearing trays full of small glass goblets which M. Bourgeois lined up on his counter before the vats of a 1974 rosé. This was *vin ordinaire* (common wine, without the mark of distinction of the A.O.C.); it ran into the goblets as the plug was carefully withdrawn from the vat.

The etiquette of *dégustation* demands that wine not be swallowed in a gulp. First we tested the bouquet: sniff! we could tell it was dry, and the color was very pale. After testing the bouquet and noting the color, one must give one's host an appreciative glance, then drink the wine in sips, pausing to enjoy the lingering aftertaste and to chat and share the impressions of those most knowledgeable (or most articulate) in the group.

Taking an enormous key from a pocket in his gray apron, the winegrower invited us to follow him down some earthen steps to another, deeper cave complex. A lock grated, and the cellar—*la cave,* the sanctuary of his finest whites and prize vintages —was open. Here we would see exactly what *mis en bouteille au château* meant, as M. Bourgeois surveyed pridefully his best stock. He chose a series of bottles and passed among us as host, pouring the 1974 white Sancerre and explaining some of the finer distinctions between similar grapes planted in different types of soil (often at the same château).

By the third vintage, the group from the *Palinurus* was having an absolutely marvelous time. Shyness had fled as M. Bourgeois continued to replenish every glass that was less than brimful. He had a bottle in each hand, and he replaced each of them several times before we reluctantly had to take our leave.

We might never have left had we not been expected at the Fromagerie Dubois-Boulay for cheese-tasting. Here the little *crottins* are received fresh from the farms of the surrounding countryside and aged—turned into little round cakes of deliciousness covered with a healthy variety of furry mold. The process takes about fifteen

The bridge over the Loire River and the church of St. Étienne towering over the city have been painted for centuries on Nevers' famed faience pottery. In the old pottery drawings the sky is filled with birds, and the river is covered with shallow-draft sailing craft headed downstream and skiffs rowing upstream.

days, beginning with the loose, milky lumps of freshly made cheese and ending with a small, round, rather tall cheese covered with a fuzzy gray beard, ready to be shipped throughout France and Europe—and to be tasted by wine-livened groups fresh from M. Bourgeois' caves up the street.

There were still more gastronomic treats of the Sancerrois for us to experience, so we headed for the nearby village of Fontenay-sur-Loire and its festive center of *dégustation,* the caves of Clos la Perrier. Built into the steep hillside, this commercial drinkerie was enormous. It had seating for hundreds of wine lovers, an ancient winepress enshrined on a stage, and balustrades of old, craggy vines. The caves were so huge and cold that the furthest reaches were filled with a mysterious fog. It seemed a true shrine to the vine, complete with everything from ambiance to an ambulance —a white handdrawn cart decorated with a red cross that provides a special service to patrons whose *dégustation* goes a bit too far.

Our last stop was in the nearby village of Pouilly-sur-Loire, the center of the production of the famed Pouilly-Fumé wines. Here we had a rendezvous with winemaker Georges Guyot, whose wind-toughened hands were still covered with the limestone soil of his vineyards when we arrived. He led us into a musty, 200-year-old cave filled with both wooden casks and modern vats and surrounded by ancient sweating stone. Here a plaque advised us, in French, to "Think of the efforts that have been made to bring this to your glass."

Considerable effort was apparent in his gold medal 1974 Pouilly-Fumé vintage, which was not yet fully mature but was nevertheless deliciously smoky. We were invited to refill our glasses with the 1973 growth, winner of six gold and four silver medals, a fully mature and wonderfully dry vintage.

Our visit with M. Guyot was not yet ended; he had consented to take us into his vineyards. We had all seen vines before, but never as a close backdrop to their windburned, handsome, proud owner as he pointed out Chasselat vines that had been producing since his grandfather planted them in 1895. The old vines, which produce the sweetest grapes, were just then coming into flower. Their roots reach so deep into the soil that they can survive an entire summer without rain. We marveled to think that they had been producing fine wines, oblivious to the invention of the automobile, the airplane, and two world wars.

It had been a full and glorious day, and we could feel the wines of the Loire coursing through our veins. For all our foggy vision and uncertain stride, we felt we had touched the very heart of the region.

The *Palinurus* was alive with activity as the crew prepared an open fire for a shish kebab feast; after a day of wine-tasting, this promised to be a rare treat.

The sun set, the group grew suddenly quiet. We stood and gazed and felt the wonderment of all travelers of the ages who have just heard their first nightingale serenade. We saw the silhouette of one of our shipmates against the campfire: She stood stock still, arms limp, chin jutting, ears cocked, with the look of a privileged pilgrim allowed entrance to a private shrine. The serenade continued for nearly an hour, and even the bullfrog was inspired to join in with an out-of-tune obbligato.

On the morning of our fourth day the sun continued to dominate the cloudless sky, warming the skin to a bronze pink. Bicyclists left the barge to ride ahead and wave back from bridges and farmhouses. The more sedate of our company had their books and sketch pads open but were continually distracted by the smell of fresh-cut grass and green blooming things and the sight of poplar avenues backed by church steeples. White Charrolais cattle grazed in velveteen fields of blooming clover, and a cluster of old stone farmhouses passed as our diesel purred softly, echoing our progress off the low banks in a slow chug-a-chug.

We stopped for lunch near the village of Herry, where we took a walk on the Rue du Paradis, listened to children sing their *Ave Maria* in the old stone church, watched an aged woman push a baby carriage full of dishes (!), and returned to the sounds of a Mozart woodwind quartet on the *Palinurus* stereo, serenading the lazy bodies of our comrades lounging on the grassy bank.

The Charity of the Good Fathers

In the afternoon we reached the city of La Charité, a mad jumble of red tile roofs clustered in terraces on a slope bathed by the Loire, which stretched here in a majestic curve and was crossed by a picturesque sixteenth-century bridge. Dominating the scene was the famous basilica of Notre Dame, whose history goes back to a monastery founded in the eighth century. The present building, constructed in 1107, drew the attention of travelers, pilgrims, and the poor—who, knowing the hospitality and generosity of the pious fathers, came to solicit their charity. "Go to La Charité" became a common expression throughout the region in those times, and the town became known by that name.

At the time it was built the basilica was the second largest church in all of France. Now, of the original building, which was 400 feet long and could hold five thousand people, only one of the two great towers that once framed the magnificent central door remains, and the facade stands alone, separated from the vast body of the building.

We parked our bicycles in Fishermen's Square, in front of the basilica, and sat down at a little café to study the facade and to quench our thirst. After a walk around the elegant but bare interior, we followed a series of arrows up a short hill to the Promenade of the Ramparts, the crumbling twelfth-century ruins of the original city walls. These were the walls that turned back Joan of Arc and her raggle-taggle troops in 1429, during the Hundred Years' War.

At the top of the ramparts we enjoyed one of the most spectacular sweeping views of the entire trip, graced by the lovely Loire, the sixteenth-century cambered stone bridge, and the red tile roofs of La Charité densely clustered in ringlets on the hillside. The bells of the basilica told the hour with a stately, dignified B-O-N-G . . . B-O-N-G . . . B-O-N-G. . . .

The Long Way Home

It was six o'clock and the *Palinurus* was some two miles down the canal, so we started off on our bicycles. We had just crossed the old stone bridge when Jarrett heard an ominous explosion beneath her feet. She had a flat tire (not just flat; destroyed). Since the only gas station we had seen had closed at six o'clock, it looked as though it would be a long walk. To add to our worries, there was some confusion in our minds about just how we might reach the *Palinurus,* which had moved down the canal after we cycled off. We knew it would be tied up to the right bank, yet the towpath ran along the left. We're pretty good swimmers, but with bicycles in tow we thought we'd best find our way along the local roads on the right bank of the canal.

It was a long trip on foot, our bodies hunched over the small, balky bikes. The road had led us quite a distance away from the canal, and when we saw a dirt track leading back in that direction, we decided to follow it. Greeted by the traditional ferocious watchdog, we came quickly to the conclusion that we were in someone's back yard. Alerted by the barking, the entire family emerged from the now visible farmhouse, and we told them in our stammering French just how lost we were. Mercifully, they restrained the dog and directed us to take the "first left" off the main road. Undone by the dog and our somewhat uncertain situation, we neglected to ask how far that might be—and realized too late that it might be miles. We were *very* far out in the country, it seemed.

Back on the main road, we could see the canal stretching out parallel to our course, about a mile down a long, gentle hill covered with pastureland. We were so frustrated at seeing it so close below us and yet so inaccessible that we discarded the laws of propriety and cut down, bikes and all, through the fields. There was the barge, behind some trees around a gentle bend. All that separated us from seven o'clock cocktails was some tall grass, a vast green meadow, and three barbed-wire fences.

We'd come this far; we decided we might as well climb those fences. We kept expecting to hear the report of a rifle in the arms of some irate farmer, and we were grateful to get into the shoulder-high grass for a little cover. Stan was just testing the first fence with a foot when Jarrett spotted a herd of Charrolais bulls, creamy-white and curious, silently studying us from the far end of the pasture. Aghast, she pulled Stan from the fence he was about to climb. Before he could ask what the hell she thought she was doing, he saw from the corner of his eye the movement of the bulls. They were bounding—the young ones kicking up their heels, the old ones bellowing—down the hill in our direction.

Stopped by the fence, they hung their heads, sides heaving, nostrils flaring. Foiled! We stood behind the safety of the fence—and our bicycles, for good measure—and contemplated the dozen 2,000-pound snorting animals—who in turn were contemplating us.

While the bulls followed our progress with interest from the other side of the fence, we found ourselves another fence and another field. Shortly thereafter, covered with mud, bicycle grease, brambles, and smiles—oh yes, we were smiling—we arrived, bikes in tow, at the *Palinurus* in time for dinner.

In Pursuit of Nevers

The next day's program ambitiously called for us to travel 35 miles (56 km) through twelve locks from La Charité to Nevers, capital of the Nivernais. After lunch we stopped for an hour in Marseilles-les-Aubigny, at the headquarters of Loire Line cruisers, where we took on water and repaired a balky part of the old diesel. The Loire Line is a British-owned fleet of hire boats giving self-drive cruisers access to the Canal Latéral à la Loire, the Nivernais, and the Canal du Centre. Their yard seemed a little oasis of the English, the Union Jack flying proudly over such boats as *Lady Grace of Hornsea* and *Trader-Cheltenham.*

Bathed in the warm evening light of the western sky, the Quai du Gai Le Clerc at Joigny is reflected in the still waters of the River Yonne. The low quay makes convenient dockage for the cruising yachts, and shops for provisioning are easily accessible.

Late afternoon, about 12 miles before Nevers, we crossed the Allier River on an aqueduct after climbing a series of tall locks. Known as one of the best trout streams in France, the Allier was verdant, rich, and beautiful, rushing along between banks shaded by tall trees. At another lock further on the lockkeeper received a small "thank you" from the *Palinurus* chef in the form of a carboard box full of leftover bread for his chickens, ducks, and geese.

Just at dusk we turned into a two-mile branch canal leading into Nevers, a historically important crossroads at the junction of the Allier and Loire rivers. In 52 B.C. Caesar turned this town into a strategic storehouse for food and fodder for his army before starting his campaign against the surrounding towns. When his enemies eventually set fire to the town, Caesar found his position in Gaul extremely precarious.

Today Nevers is best known for its pottery, introduced in 1565 by Louis de Gonzague, duke of the Nivernais, who brought artists and craftsmen here from Italy. Gradually, as local craftsmen learned the techniques from the Italians, the form, colors, and decorations of the faience (clay pottery covered with a tin-oxide glaze) acquired a distinct Nivernais style. The pottery industry reached its height about 1650, when a dozen factories employed a total of 1,800 workers. Later the French Revolution almost entirely destroyed the art of faience in Nevers, leaving just three factories, two of which are small craftsmen's workshops.

Friday morning, our sixth day aboard the *Palinurus,* we took the bicycles into Nevers, crossed the bridge, rode along the lovely Loire promenade, and left the bikes at the beautiful fourteenth-century Porte de Croux, a vestige of the original city walls. A short walk up the hill brought us to the Cathedral of St. Cyr and St. Juliette, a vast and curious building embracing architectural styles from the sixth to the sixteenth centuries—a strange combination of pillars, flying buttresses, pinnacles, romanesque towers, niches, statues, and art work from many different periods. The range of styles boggled our minds.

Winding through the tiny streets, we found the lovely Renaissance-style Ducal Palace, once home to the Nivernais princesses who became the queens of Poland from 1645 to 1696. A modern bas-relief recalls the legend of the swan knight, said to have inspired the legend of the Lohengrin.

Down one of the twisting little streets stands a grand indoor market, its colorful and beautifully arranged fruits and vegetables, meats, fish and shellfish, flowers, and local cheeses a riot of design expertise and careful placement—a veritable still life from a Renaissance painting or a banquet for kings.

We continued through the town, visiting the eleventh-century St. Étienne Church, awesomely simple and massive in its Romanesque purity. We walked through the eighteenth-century Porte de Paris, a triumphal arch commemorating the victory of Fontenoy, and up the hill to St. Gildard Convent, which houses the miraculously preserved body of St. Bernadette of Lourdes, who died in 1889.

A leisurely walk back down the hill to the Porte de Croux returned us to our bicycles and thence to the *Palinurus* in time for lunch. Soon the barge was under way, bound for the castle of Chevenon some five miles distant.

A Funny Thing Happened . . .

. . . to us on the way to Chevenon. A suspicious leak in the engine room drew the attention of the entire crew, with the exception of Howard at the helm. In the confusion Howard steered us past Chevenon (the château was hidden from the canal), and we continued innocently on our way. The engine problem was solved as we approached the village of Uxeloup, five miles further on, but there was no question about turning the barge around on the narrow canal—it was impossible. A night at Uxeloup would do no one any harm, we decided. Besides, Uxeloup boasted its own small thirteenth-century château which, if not as grand as Chevenon, was charming nonetheless.

After a peaceful evening filled with stars and crickets and the serenading of birds, we began the final day of our journey. The canal widened beyond Uxeloup to grand proportions, then, after two miles or so, trimmed again to its old tree-lined, tunnellike self. The sun warmed us as we passed through lush green countryside where blackberries grew wild, villages were rare, and beautiful old homes could be discerned in the distance, lording over vast pasturelands filled with Charolais cattle.

We approached Decize, our final destination, where a branch of the Canal Latéral entered the town, which is perched on a craggy knoll on an island in the Loire. In this village of twisting medieval alleyways stands the eleventh-century Church of St. Aré. It has a rare, seventh-century Frankish double crypt built to hold the remains of its patron saint, the Bishop of Nevers. Legend holds that when the bishop died in Nevers, his body was placed on a funeral barge and floated *up* the Loire, running aground at Decize.

The most impressive sight here is the Promenade des Halles, a majestic, nearly 3,000-foot long promenade of four straight rows of plane trees (or sycamores) planted in 1771. Some of them reach a height of 200 feet. Situated in a quiet park between the village and the river, the promenade provided a peaceful place to contemplate our week aboard the *Palinurus*—a week of windbrowned hands and rich, fertile lands . . . grand châteaux and mistletoe . . . nightingales and snails and seven o'clock cocktails . . . mad dogs and bullfrogs . . . cuckoo calls and crumbling walls . . . trout streams and moonbeams . . . Voltaire and alleys leading nowhere . . . wine cellars, poplars, and picnickers . . . white bulls and old cathedrals . . . poppies and daisies and blackberries and deep green valleys . . . dogwood and sainthood . . . and feeling good. . . .

Some Practical Information

If you enjoy sights and experiences that can only be described in superlatives, you will want to cruise the waterways of central France, the wine capital of the world. The area abounds in medieval towns and Roman remains nestled within rolling, sun-drenched hills and valleys. You can leisurely float down quiet waterways past twelfth-century basilicas and abbeys and ancient Roman aqueducts, go marketing or antiquing in forgotten villages of just a few hundred inhabitants, ooh and aah your way through the royal grounds at Fontainebleau with its incredible palace, or, for a change of pace, explore the little-known and delightful waters of Brittany. The list is long; you must see and feel northern France for yourself.

The two regions in central France which are of particular interest to the waterway traveler are the Burgundy/Loire Valley region and Brittany.

1. *Burgundy and the Loire Valley.* Try this word-association quiz: Burgundy? Wine. Loire Valley? Châteaux. It's that simple.

Even in a world as complicated and accelerated as ours, Burgundy still "means" wine and the Loire Valley still "means" châteaux—just as they have for centuries. The roster of Burgundy's renowned wine towns reads like a who's who of vintage labels: Beaune, Chablis, Pouilly, Beaujolais, and Côte de Nuits; many of them have been famous since Roman times. By far the best way to visit these vineyards and their caves and to sample their bounties is by slow boat along the rivers and canals, where proud and patient vintners have been cultivating and producing their fine wines for generations. The small boy or girl you see trooping through the vineyards behind their father may one day be proprietor of some distinguished label.

Although most of the important medieval châteaux and abbeys of the Loire Valley lie somewhat to the west of the navigable waterways, they can provide exciting side excursions for the waterway traveler.

The tourist has the option of cruising these regions in either a self-drive, diesel-powered cruiser or a captained and staffed *péniche,* a traditional canal barge converted for use as a hotel boat. There are several hire firms offering self-drive boats; the two most established firms are:

Loire Line, L'Equerre, 18550 Marseilles-les-Aubigny, maintains a fully staffed and well-equipped English-speaking base on the Canal Latéral à la Loire, adjacent to the Canal du Nivernais. In addition to offering a fleet of 30 modern diesel-powered cruisers, it maintains service and repair facilities for private boats, offering skilled mechanics, engine work, boat and gear storage, haul-out and drydocking, and deposit of customs documents with French authorities.

			June 15–Sept. 15	Other
Calypso	29 feet (9 m)	4 berths	$520–575	$305–470
Bermuda	34 feet (10.5 m)	5 berths	$575–625	$360–525
Bermuda RS	34 feet (10.5 m)	6 berths	$650–800	$425–575

These are weekly rates for an entire boat. Also, fuel is not included in the above prices.

Burgundy Cruisers, 89650 Arcy-sur-Cure, operates a small fleet of diesel-powered cruisers on the Canal du Nivernais, from its base at Vermenton.

			June 15–Sept. 15	Other
Seamaster	27 feet (8 m)	2–3 berths	$430–510	$300–400
Caribbean	39 feet (12 m)	6 berths	$675–825	$400–550

The above prices include diesel fuel.

The following central booking agents can furnish information and make bookings for self-drive boats in Burgundy:

Floating Through Europe, Inc.
501 Madison Avenue
New York, N.Y. 10022

Blakes Holidays
Wroxham, Norwich NR12 8DH, England

The rivers and canals of Burgundy contain the most hotel barges of any region in France. Three major operators offer hotel barge service:

Floating Through Europe, Inc., 501 Madison Avenue, New York, N.Y. 10022, has scheduled the *Janine* for service commencing in June 1979. A luxury hotel barge 126 feet (38 m) long, it will carry 24 passengers and a crew of 8 between Dijon and Lyon, the gastronomic and wine capitals of France. Facilities will include large staterooms each with private toilet and shower, a high standard of gourmet food, bicycles, and a chauffeured minicoach to take passengers on sightseeing and shopping excursions.

Inland Voyages Ltd., Guildford Boat House, Millbrook, Guildford, Surrey GU1 3XJ, England, operates the 96-foot (29 m) hotel barge *Secunda.* Carrying 14 passengers and a crew of 5, the boat has been converted from a Dutch cargo barge. The following rates per person include 6 days accommodation, all meals, and table wine:

	June 15–Sept. 15	Other
Twin cabin	$420	$400
Single cabin	$500	$470
Entire barge	$5,500	$5,100

Continental Waterways Ltd., 22 Hans Place, London SW1, England, operates two hotel barges, the *Palinurus* (100 feet—30 m—long, carrying 18 passengers and a crew of 6) and *La Guêpe Buissonnière* (120 feet—36 m—long, carrying 28 passengers and a crew of 8), on fully inclusive six-day cruises, with the following rates per person:

| | May, June, Sept., Oct. | | Other | |
	Palinurus	*La Guêpe*	*Palinurus*	*La Guêpe*
Double cabin	$470	——	$410	——
Twin cabin	$450	$475	$390	$425
Single cabin	$510	$470	$645	$595

2. *Brittany.* Occupying the peninsula in northwest France between the English Channel and the Bay of Biscay, Brittany provides the visitor with a very different view of France than that of Burgundy or the Loire Valley. The entire region is punctuated with charming and rustic centuries-old fishing villages, and the countryside is covered with rugged hills and serene farmland and pasture. Brittany is bisected by two little-frequented rivers, the Vilaine and the Erdre, and by several peaceful nineteenth-century canals. Wonderful cruising, fishing, and swimming, unique seaside and inland villages with delightful and hospitable hotels, restaurants and cafes, and unusual shopping opportunities await the waterborne visitor to Brittany.

The several self-drive hire firms located here all offer diesel-powered cruisers.

Caravans Sur La Mer Ltd., Station Road, Cowfold, West Sussex RH13 8DA, England, has a small fleet of diesel-powered, steel-hulled cruisers available from April through November. An English-speaking staff operates their hire base at La Roche Bernard, and Caravans' cruisers come furnished with linens and towels, heated cabins, and fully equipped galleys and private facilities. The following prices per week are exclusive of diesel fuel:

		June-Sept.	Other
38-footer (11.5 m)	5 berths	$550–675	$350–475
45-footer (13.5 m)	8 berths	$800–875	$450–600

Ladbroke Travel S.A., avenue du Port, 35480 Guipry Messac, is another English firm that offers a fleet of diesel-powered cruisers for weekly hire. The following prices per week are exclusive of diesel fuel:

		June–Sept.	Other
28-footer (8.5 m)	3 berths	$440	$240–310
30-footer (9 m)	4 berths	$550	$300–390
30-footer (9 m)	5 berths	$590	$325–410

Ripplecraft Ltd., 56130 La Roche Bernard, offers a small fleet of fine diesel-powered cruisers from their base at La Roche Bernard. The following prices per week are exclusive of diesel fuel:

		June-Sept.	Other
30-footer (9 m)	5 berths	$585	$270–400
34-footer (10 m)	5–6 berths	$610	$300–420
38-footer (11.5 m)	7–8 berths	$680	$365–500

The following central booking agencies can furnish information and book self-drive cruises in central France:

Floating Through Europe, Inc.
501 Madison Avenue
New York, N.Y. 10022

Blakes Holidays
Wroxham, Norwich NR12 8DH, England

Maps, guides, and waterway books are available from Floating Through Europe, Inc., which maintains an extensive inventory of such publications.

For additional information concerning cruising in central France, write to:

The French Government Tourist Office
610 Fifth Avenue
New York, N.Y. 10020

Commissariat Général au Tourisme
Service Canaux et Rivières
8, avenue de l'Opéra
Paris 1^{e}

3

The Proud and Noble Rhine

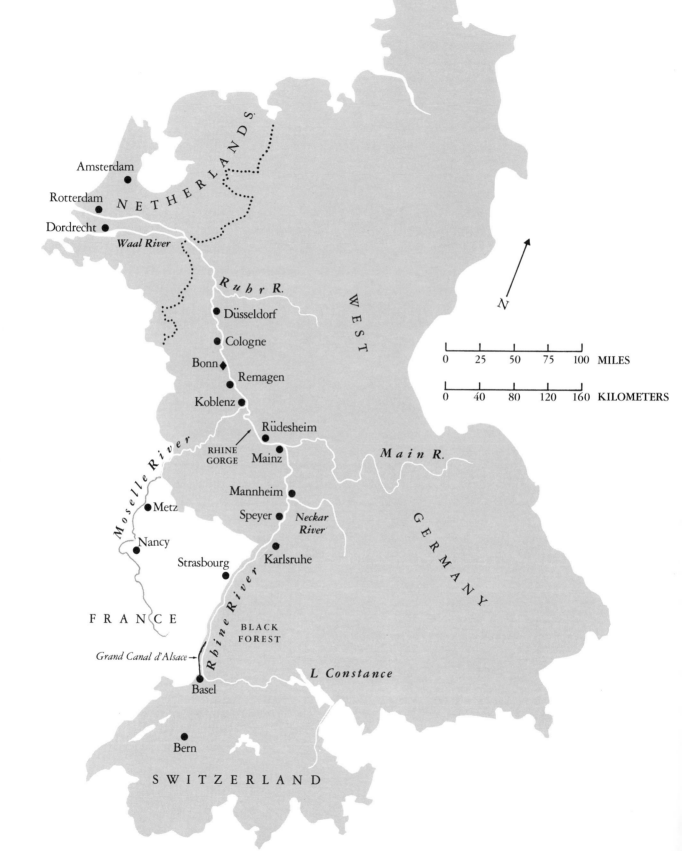

Amsterdam

Rotterdam

Dordrecht

Waal River

NETHERLANDS

Ruhr R.

Düsseldorf

Cologne

Bonn

Remagen

Koblenz

RHINE
GORGE

Rüdesheim

Mainz

WEST

Main R.

Mannheim

Speyer

*Neckar
River*

Metz

Moselle River

Nancy

Strasbourg

Karlsruhe

GERMANY

FRANCE

Rhine River

BLACK
FOREST

Grand Canal d'Alsace →

L. Constance

Basel

Bern

SWITZERLAND

N

| 0 | 25 | 50 | 75 | 100 | MILES |

| 0 | 40 | 80 | 120 | 160 | KILOMETERS |

A Steamer Trip Through the Rhineland:
Switzerland, France, Germany, the Netherlands

O, the pride of the German heart is this
noble river! And right it is; for of all
the rivers of this beautiful earth there
is none so beautiful as this.

LONGFELLOW

Eleven thousand feet above the sea, in the Alps of eastern Switzerland, the crystal meltings of the massive Rheinwaldhorn Glacier quietly spill down the steep trough of the Hinterrhein Valley. The Rhine is born.

Like a vast root system, feeder streams unite with the newborn river as it forms Switzerland's frontier with Liechtenstein, then Austria, and finally West Germany at Lake Constance. Here it rushes from the lake's western rim, thunders impressively over the Rhine Falls, divides the port of Basel, and turns north, leaving both youth and Switzerland behind, to become a giant among rivers.

Some time later and half a continent away the trickle has swelled to a flood, passed through six countries, connected with scores of other major rivers and canals to form the vast circulatory system of the inland waterways of Europe, and surged into the North Sea at the rate of 146,000 tons of water per minute.

Throughout its 820-mile (1,320 km) journey the river defines what is known as the Rhineland—a land with no flag, no capital, no coinage, no real geographic boundaries. It traverses the vicinity of the Neanderthal cave and the Heidelberg castle, the Eifel, the Odenwald, and the Palatinate. It encounters the ghosts of Constantine and Charlemagne, Gutenberg and Beethoven, Erasmus and Holbein.

More than twenty peoples have been shaping and changing the Rhineland for more than twenty centuries, and they have left in their path their festivals, songs, stories, legends, and myths, revealing what has preoccupied men and women through the ages.

We made our first breathtaking acquaintance with the Rhine as it emerged wide and proud from a sharp bend leading into the Swiss city of Basel, where we would begin our 600-mile (965 km) journey downstream to Rotterdam. From our perch on the steep, 200-foot cliffs that define the city's riverfront, we admired the panorama of the Jura Mountains to the west, Alsace to the northwest, and Germany's Black Forest to the north.

We had arrived in this chic, sophisticated, truly international city, situated at the junction of Switzerland, West Germany, and France, early enough to spend the afternoon getting to know it. Dating from 44 B.C., Basel earned its chic and sophistication by enduring a series of rulers from the Romans, the German tribes, the Frankish Empire, the Burgundians, and the Holy Roman Empire before it finally joined the Swiss Confederation in 1501. It was here, in 1515, that Erasmus first published the New Testament in Greek.

We walked the streets of the old quarter, from the twin-spired Munster Cathedral (housing the tombstone of Erasmus) to the open market in the central square, past the colorfully decorated City Hall, down medieval lanes, and past sculptured fountains to the most beautiful city gate in Switzerland, the Spalen Gate. A ferry took us across the Rhine for a spectacular view of the late-medieval heart of the city, then back to the world-famous Kunst Museum, a Michelin three-star attraction and one of 23 museums the city boasts.

For us, however, all paths led to the Rhine port. The harbor is situated near the convergence of the three nations' frontiers, just two and a half miles from the heart of the old city. Here the steamer *Nederlander* lay, gleaming white in the rushing currents like a Caribbean sun cruiser—long, low, streamlined—the last word in supersophisticated, neatly understated, long-distance river travel. Porters hurried forward to take our bags, and we were soon being shown our rosewood-paneled cabin with its broad picture window, plaid sofa, easy chair, and a cocktail table offering a sweet little plate of ripe fruit. There was an adequate private bath, with stall shower and toilet, and very limited stowage space.

It was about eight o'clock by the time we were settled on board, and on the salon deck tables were laden with a cold buffet. We were assigned to a private table and introduced to the waiters who would serve us during the four-day voyage. Tables sparkled with fresh linen and pink carnations. Forward of the dining salon lay the large, glass-walled observation lounge, soon to be the scene of champagne parties, speeches of welcome, and mid-morning snacks. A walk around the sundeck discovered the heated swimming pool and dozens of deck chairs. Sauna, barber shop, hairdresser, and gift shop assured that most needs would be answered. Full of food and tired after our day of touring, our eyes and our minds boggled by the luxury, we fell into our neatly turned down bunks, planning to be up and about when the crew cast off the next day at 6 A.M.

The Trip Begins

The next morning we were surprised at 5:50 A.M. by the sounds of the four powerful engines cranking up, and by the time we had scrambled up on deck we were already steaming downriver at our cruising speed of 16 miles an hour. We had begun our 600-mile journey north to Rotterdam.

The Grand Canal d'Alsace, running parallel to the Rhine for 75 miles from Basel to Strasbourg, carried the rushing waters (and us) safely down from 800 feet to 420 feet above sea level in a series of nine gigantic locks. One of the most modern waterways in Europe, its lockkeepers' stations looked like airport control towers, standing high above the water, with huge, button-covered control panels to open and close the mammoth lock gates.

The lack of immediate scenic interest along the canal gave us the opportunity to ponder perhaps the most storied river on earth, one of the very axes of civilization since the time of Neanderthal man, whose home was here. Its story begins twenty centuries ago, when the Romans marched across the Alps and discovered a marvelous waterway that led them a thousand miles north and deep into the country of the barbarians. Surrounding the river was a wide, fertile plain running north from what is now Switzerland to the environs of Frankfurt and Mainz, an area considered today to have the mildest climate in Germany. Bringing with them their Mediterranean civilization—including the cultivation of the vine—the Romans colonized the Rhineland with the polyglot population of the empire.

Following the age of the Romans and the Great Migrations, the region was dominated by Charlemagne, whose vast empire was divided after his death into several kingdoms that evolved into France, Germany, and Austria.

Division begat subdivision; by the height of the Middle Ages every mile along the river's commanding heights was claimed by a rival robber baron, some of whom had the temerity to erect their toll houses smack in the middle of the river. While the barons fought over gold and honor, the princes of the Church went about building the magnificent cathedrals at Cologne, Strasbourg, Mainz, Worms, and Speyer, awesome structures that house the greatest collection of ecclesiastical art works outside Italy.

The dawn of modern times found the Rhine become a prize contested by kings and emperors; it also saw the birth and education of geniuses like Goethe and Beethoven and the efflorescence of the Rhenish character, in a type of hedonism and joyousness that erupts yearly—now as then—in the madness of carnival all along the Rhine.

The Romantic Age hallowed the river in the golden light of myth. Richard Wagner's *Ring of the Nibelungs,* the last great European epic, is the apotheosis of the Rhine. Founded on Rhenish legends, set beside and even in the river, the tetralogy culminates in a sublime passage in which the sacred stream rises and extinguishes the fires of divine and mortal strife, thereby re-establishing the harmony of the universe.

The earthly Rhine is a volcanic caprice whose craggy shores form a shadowy frontier between Roman and Celtic civilizations. Silted with legend and the startled rapturous responses of travelers who, like Byron, came to moon over its ruined castles and fortresses, the Rhine remains one of the world's great sights.

We had plenty of company; the Rhine, legend or no, is one of the major arteries of transportation in Europe and the world's busiest river. Its 15,000 deep-bellied ships, many of them the largest in Europe, haul some 220 million tons of cargo every year—a figure nearly equal to the combined total for those two North American giants, the Mississippi River and the St. Lawrence Seaway.

And so we took our leisurely "elevator" ride down, down, down the canal, the long, dark crests of the Black Forest facing, mirrorlike, the Vosges Mountains across the Rhine. The two ranges approximate in altitude; both are densely wooded and both drop steeply toward the Rhine plain.

Queen City of the Upper Rhine

Soon after our sumptuous lunch we pulled into the city of Strasbourg, capital of Alsace. Strasbourg is the fifth largest French port, a center of the Reformation, the seat of the Council of Europe, a university town, and a city where red sandstone buildings of great taste and beauty appear on all sides. It is also the most picturesque and well preserved of the larger cities along the Rhine, offering medieval cobbled squares, quiet canals, carved half-timbered houses wearing their windowboxes like cherished campaign ribbons, and places like the Marché au Cochons-de-Lait (Market of the Suckling Pigs) and Rue du Jeux-des-Enfants (Street of the Children's Games).

Here in Strasbourg one of the most stirring of all national anthems had its birth. In the Place Broglie, on the site of the present Bank of France building, Rouget de Lisle composed the words and music of the *Marseillaise* in a fever of patriotic excitement following a public dinner in 1792. The composer called it the *Chant de guerre de l'armée du Rhin* (War Song of the Army of the Rhine); its familiar name was later given it by troops storming the Tuileries in Paris.

Yet for all its charm and sophistication, Strasbourg has taken for its symbol a rather curious animal: the common barnyard goose. The reason for this is a somewhat less common epicurian delight known as pâté de foie gras, of which more than 50 percent of the domestic supply and 80 percent of exports are produced here. The industry is imbued with two centuries of tradition and something approaching military secrecy. The basic ingredients are goose liver, pork, lard, and usually a core of truffle (that highly prized subterranean fungus). But the distinguishing difference between the various brands, and the reason for the shroud of secrecy, is the spices. In one leading firm, only the president holds the secret to the particular blend of spices, and he is reputed to mix them himself—once a year, at night, in a room locked and bolted.

Above the sunlit and colorful orange-tiled roofs of Strasbourg, the single off-center spire of the Gothic cathedral rises 466 feet in dark, rose-colored perfection. We disembarked and headed toward it.

Perhaps the most famous sight of the cathedral is its sixteenth-century astronomical clock. The list of ingenious complications built into the clock is almost endless. Every day at half past noon the cock crows and the apostles pass before Christ, turning toward him and bowing while Christ lifts his hand to bless each in turn. When the fourth, eighth, and twelfth apostles pass, the cock beats its wings to remind us of the

Below Münster Cathedral at Basel, Switzerland, the fast-flowing current of the Rhine powers a little red ferry through a small free-wheeling trolley riding a cable suspended above the river. When the captain flips the pole and painter over the port gunwhale, the ferry swings around and rides on the current. A flip of the pole and painter over the starboard gunwhale starts the return trip.

denial of St. Peter. Death, with a bone in his hand, strikes the hours, and the Four Ages of Man pass before him on every quarter hour, while an angel turns an hour-glass. Each of the statues strikes the quarter hour with the help of an angel. A figure of the moon tells the exact phase of the moon over Strasbourg, a model of the solar system loses only eleven seconds every thirty years, and the chariots of the gods and goddesses show the days of the week. Finally, Apollo indicates the date with his arrow on a great gliding circle. Not bad engineering for the sixteenth century!

After leaving the cathedral we enjoyed a taste of that sumptuous pâté de foie gras, then strolled the cobblestone streets. These paths offer many fine views of the old town and comfortable outdoor cafes. Then we were off to meet the *Nederlander* at Drusenheim to continue our downstream trip.

Some 25 miles north we enjoyed the sunset as it cast its golden light eastward over the industrial town of Karlsruhe. We were entering the region known as the Rhineland-Palatinate, a former German state founded in 1100 and then ruled by a member of the German imperial family assigned to govern the area under the title of archduke or prince elector. The Palatinate owes its name to the title *palatine* given to the highest officers in the Holy Roman Empire, who were in the confidence of the sovereign. Through the wise government of these princes, or palatine-electors, the Rhineland-Palatinate became one of the most advanced states in Europe.

Today the Palatinate is the greatest wine-producing region of Germany, accounting for almost one-third of the total national output. Along the foot of the Haardt Mountains, protected from harsh winds and facing the sun, extends a long reach of good vinegrowing country. The almost flat land produces fruity, sweet red and white wines of rather high alcoholic content.

Just 24 miles north of Karlsruhe is one of the most important centers of the German wine trade, the city of Speyer. Here we would berth for the night within view of the magnificent eleventh-century cathedral, the largest Romanesque basilica in Europe and the final resting place of generations of German Holy Roman emperors. With its boldly conceived lines, the cathedral is an early example of the golden age of Rhine architecture.

Speyer is believed to have originated some 3,000 years ago, when prehistoric settlements were taken over by Celtic tribes. The Romans and Huns swept over it, then the Franks came to stay. In the sixteenth century the town became famous for the printing of books, the Imperial High Court of Justice, which sat in the city, and a number of Diets (the word in German means "popular") that were convened here. The most famous Diet of Speyer, held in 1529, confirmed the Edict of Worms' ruling against Martin Luther's innovations in the Christian faith. The Lutheran reaction to this Diet gave rise to the term *Protestant.*

Some towns of undisputed historic interest are not much fun to stroll around; others have an immediate appeal. Speyer is one of the latter, and our evening stroll revealed many wonderful attractions. A fine, broad main street had charming modern shops tucked in among baroque houses with steep gables. At one end of the street was the lofty tower gateway, an old entrance to the town built in 1230; at the other end, backed by gardens, were the two domes and four austere towers of the cathedral.

South of the cathedral we came upon the remains of the medieval Jewish ghetto —remnants of a twelfth-century synagogue and underground baths. Nearby the old quarters of the fishermen (Hare's Pool) and shipmen (Donkey's Dyke) contained the old fish and timber markets. In the gardens behind the cathedral was the Pagan Tower, a thin slab of a monument that was part of the old city walls, and a stone basin in the Cathedral Square marked the limit of the zone of sanctuary on the edge of municipal territory. The Brezel Fountain stood in the Konigplatz, where a market is held. The *brezel,* that tasty bit of deliciousness that is twisted and lavishly sprinkled with salt before baking, has been a specialty of the city since the fourteenth century; the annual summertime Brezelfest is accompanied by processions of floats, bands, and dancers.

We strolled until our feet and our bodies told us it had been a long day since our 6 A.M. reveille 140 miles away. Yet it hadn't been the kind of "hard touring" day we remembered from our pre-waterway travels; it had been filled with restful hours and leisurely five-course meals. We made our way slowly back to the *Nederlander* and our neatly turned-down beds with the fluffy down quilts—and settled our heads happily for the night.

Romance and Ruins

Our second morning found us up early for breakfast as the boat made its way to Mannheim, a city boasting the largest baroque palace in Germany. Once there we stepped ashore to hop a bus to travel 11 miles east of the river to Heidelberg, the heart of the Romanticism celebrated by German poets and the political center of the Rhineland-Palatinate (and the home of its electors until 1700). With its translucent skies and the outline of its austere ruined castle, Heidelberg also offers the oldest university in Germany. It is this university, dating from 1386, that provided the setting for the operetta *The Student Prince.*

The Roman army had its northern headquarters in Heidelberg from 56 B.C. to about 300 A.D., and around the fort grew up a small town. In 1100 the Palatinate state was formed, and the archdukes chose Heidelberg as their residence. They began building the castle in the middle 1300s and continued for 250 years, adding more and more watchtowers, fortifications, and moats. The result was not one but seven enormous palaces joined together in a nearly impregnable fortress. The Thirty Years' War (1518–1548), between Protestants and Catholics, was a great tragedy in German history; it reduced the population from 18 million to 6 million. Heidelberg, the center of Protestantism at this time, suffered greatly.

Even worse for the city was the War of the League of Augsburg (1688–1697), with the French. A princess of the state, daughter of the archduke, had been married to the prince of Orléans, a brother of Louis XIV, in order to solidify relations between the two countries. This worked until the archduke died in 1685; then Louis XIV claimed half the Palatinate as the princess' inheritance. After three years of negotiations Louis XIV ordered his troops to march on the Palatinate, and many of the cities along the Rhine were completely destroyed by fire during the invasion. Heidelberg was brutally laid waste, its castle sacked. Total disaster followed in 1693 when the town—built almost entirely of wood—burned to the ground.

The city of Heidelberg stands on cliffs overlooking the Neckar River, a small river that brings to the Rhine its own offerings from the Black Forest and the Odenwald Mountains. Heidelberg castle thrusts its jagged ruins bleakly skyward, crowning and guarding the city at its feet and presiding paternally over the wide and winding Neckar below. It has lain mostly in ruins since the War of the League of Augsburg, though clumsily restored here and there.

Arrived at the castle, we set out to explore its vast interior. We descended stone steps to one of several enormous cellars and a visit to the Great Vat. In medieval times winegrowers in the Palatinate vineyards were obliged to bring a percentage of their grapes to the archdukes as tribute. Here the grapes were pressed and fermented; this cellar alone was filled with 420,000 liters of Palatinate wines in ten enormous, wooden, hand-coopered casks—including one that holds 200,000 liters. With a permanent household population of more than 400 people, they needed every drop!

Aboard our bus again, we set off for Gernsheim, 20 miles to the north, to rendezvous with the boat. One deep turn toward the riverfront gave us a view across the Rhine of the famous city of Worms, one of the oldest towns in Germany. At the time of the Great Migrations, Worms was the capital of Burgundy. Then, in the year 437, the town was overrun by the Huns and the ensuing battle formed the historical foundation for the *Song of the Nibelungs.* By the time Charlemagne celebrated his two weddings in Worms (not simultaneously, and not in the present cathedral) the city was already very old. During the Middle Ages, Worms became known as the Mother of Diets, for the Imperial Diet was summoned to meet there on almost a hundred occasions.

In 1521 Martin Luther appeared before one of these Diets on being ordered to defend or recant his criticisms of the Church. He responded: "Without any subtlety and with simplicity . . . I cannot and will not recant, for it is neither secure nor advisable to do something against one's own conscience. Here I stand, I cannot act otherwise, so help me God. Amen." This testimony led to his being banned from the Empire by Charles V and his works' being burned.

Worms claims the largest and oldest Jewish cemetery in Europe, in use since the eleventh century. Within sight of it is the eleventh-century St. Peter's Cathedral, with its six great towers from the golden age of Romanesque architecture on the Rhine. A smaller church is far more famous, however: the little Gothic church of Liebfrauen, whose vineyards produce the original Liebfraumilch wine.

The Vines of Charlemagne

When we reached the *Nederlander* at Gernsheim, luncheon awaited us on linened tables decorated with fresh flowers. As we ate we floated by Oppenheim, a dream village nestled into a hillside crowned with a stately old cathedral and backed with acres and acres of vineyards. This was the real beginning of our tour through the Rhine wine district, our introduction to the famous triad of names that are household words to connoisseurs of fine German wines: Oppenheim, Nierstein, and Nacken- heim. The hills of Oppenheim and Nackenheim faced each other at a distance on the left bank of the Rhine, forming a gentle curve around Nierstein. The vineyards were every imaginable size and shape, the rows of vines running up and down the slopes, seeking the sun.

It is said that the great Charlemagne once stood on the balcony of his castle (now long gone) at Ingelheim and, seeing how warm the sun lay on those south-facing

The towers of the eleventh-century Cathedral of Speyer reach into a golden sunset over the Rhine. On the river, with hatches open and holds empty, a barge bucks the current. A modern radar antenna spins over the pilot house aft, but the blue flag on the starboard spreader of the foremast is still used on the Rhine to signal the vessel intends to overtake or pass another.

slopes, sent men to Orléans for grape vines. "Ere the moon had gone round her course" the men returned, and Charlemagne "planted with his royal hand the French vine on German soil." Now, when the fragrance of the grape blossom fills the air in spring, "a tall shadow wanders about the vineyards at night, a purple mantle hanging from his stately shoulders, and a crown upon his head." It is Charlemagne coming to bless the grapes.

Soon, beyond the splendor of the vineyards, we were moving past the city of Mainz, more than 2,000 years old, the Roman capital of Germania Superior and now capital of the Rhineland-Palatinate. In the twelfth century Mainz was so prosperous that it became known as Golden Mainz; here, early in the fifteenth century, Johann Gutenberg, the inventor of movable metal type, was born. And it is here that the Rhine gets a push from the River Main as it prepares to conquer the Taunus Mountains.

Five miles ahead on the right bank appeared the first slopes of the Taunus. The peaks, reaching a height of nearly 3,000 feet, are wrapped in wonderful forests and fringed with famous mineral springs, spas, and sun-seeking vineyards. On the southern slope lies Wiesbaden, a famous watering spot for 2,000 years, resplendent with gardens and trees more than a century old.

Here the Rhine is compelled to make a great sweep around the Taunus hills, a sweep that has been called a "respectful bow to the beautiful landscape of the surrounding Rhenish district." On both banks are charming little towns with names famous in the wine trade: Schierstein, at the very beginning of the Rheingau district; Eltville, the tiny town of wine, champagne, and roses; Erbach, since 954 devoted almost exclusively to the cultivation of fruit and wine; Oestrich, with its neat little brown and white half-timbered houses amid gardens and vineyards at the foot of the Taunus foothills; Winkel, whose very name derives from *vinicella,* or vineyard; and Geisenheim, with its Gothic church pealing the wonderful bells mentioned by Longfellow. On the right bank, in the distance, we could see the Johannisberg castle, a long, yellow, eighteenth-century palace surrounded by world-famous vineyards.

In mid-afternoon, 14 miles beyond Wiesbaden, we approached our final destination for the day, the celebrated tourist center of Rüdesheim. Here we had a wide choice of things to see in the afternoon. We might take a chairlift over the vineyards to the Niederwald Memorial, a statue of gentle Germania, a lady of "considerable" weight (35 tons), measuring 23 feet around the hips and towering 738 feet above the confluence of the Nahe and the Rhine. Or we might taxi to the dark, cubic, fortified castle of Bromserberg that commands the northern exit of Rüdesheim and houses a wine museum. Or we might take the ferry that crosses the Rhine between Rüdesheim and Bingen, a town dating from the twelfth century B.C. and whose Klopp Castle is built on the foundations of Drusus' Roman fortress.

We opted for a fourth possibility: a twin-engine airplane excursion above the Rhine Gorge. The "airport" was a long, grassy field bordered with pony stables

(PONY RIDES, 3 DM) and a quaint old half-timbered building. One small plane was tethered in the field; there was no paved runway. With the engines roaring in our ears, the plane started slowly forward. As it gathered speed, its up-and-down momentum was nearly as powerful as its forward drive. We didn't just "take off," we bounced off in a series of amazing lurches that ceased just short of a line of tall pine trees.

The dramatic gorge below looked forbidding: the darkness of the slate rocks, the swiftness of the confined current (six knots is not unusual here), the concealing curves and unheard echoes all conspire to furnish a landscape that for centuries has fostered legends of violence. We would be following its treacherous path aboard our steamer the next morning.

Returned to the ground and to the *Nederlander,* we had a leisurely dinner and then slowly made our way through the streets of Rüdesheim to the famed Drosselgasse, the lively, narrow, and picturesque street of the wine taverns. Both Rhinefolk and touring merrymakers gather here for festive evenings of wine and song and dance. Lively bands send their oompah strains wafting through the streets, inviting one to join in the fun. Our evening was spent wandering happily from one inn to another, sipping in cellars and learning that on the Rhine song is the medium that brings people together. The spirit of song—the Rhine melodies that have been sung here for generations—grew more expansive as the evening progressed and the wine flowed. Soon perfect strangers were raising their glasses and bellowing the verses at one another. Young danced with old, ladies with ladies, and laughing—oh, there was a great deal of laughing! People were laughing together who couldn't even understand one another's language—laughing and drinking, drinking and singing, singing and dancing.

In one tavern the dancing took on a snake format; it looked as though the line of dancers would continue to twist between the crowded tables all night. Occasional figures resigned (in exhaustion or thirst?) from the long, skinny human chain, yet the line quickly closed up without the dancers' missing a step. Invitations to join in were freely given, and we readily accepted; in this atmosphere it was no use standing on our dignity—nobody else did—as the mood became more and more merry with wine.

The Wild and Haunted Gorge

And so it happened that, on the third day out, the day we sailed through the most memorable portion of the Rhine, we awakened a little fuzzy-headed and limp-limbed. The all-knowing chef of the *Nederlander,* however, seemed to have anticipated this turn of events and had prepared an enormous breakfast that soon put us back on our feet.

The ship pulled quietly out of its slip at 8 A.M. on a Sunday. We were entering the Bingen Gap, the most storied stretch of any river in the world. Here the Rheingau vineyards cease and the Rhine becomes a different river. Faced with a solid block of rock in the Taunus Mountains but getting a shove from the tributary Nahe on its left bank, the startled Rhine pulls in its belt, puts on pace, and claws its way through the mountain walls. It then hurls itself northward again over rapids that are the sill of the superlative 38-mile Rhine Gorge, over which we had flown the previous day. Half the shipping accidents on the entire river occur in this dangerous stretch.

Just off Bingen, on a mound of inhospitable-looking quartz, stood the Mouse Tower. It is said that the tower got its name from the legend of the cruel Archbishop Hatto of Mainz. The archbishop, in order to put an end to the plaints of a people half starved after a hard winter, had the beggars rounded up and placed in a barn. The barn was set on fire, and Bishop Hatto, looking on, gloated: "Listen how my mice are squeaking in the corn!" The "mice" had their day, according to legend, when they came pouring out of the barn, chased the cruel bishop to the tower off the Bingen shores, and devoured him. There is a much more prosaic explanation for the name Mouse Tower: the word *Mause* derives from the German *Maut,* meaning a customs toll.

It was customs tolls that built the castled Rhine between here and Cologne to the north. In the Middle Ages, during the period of the Holy Roman Empire in Germany, the law decreed that the territories of the nobility should each be divided among all heirs (rather than pass intact to the oldest son). This created, in time, a growing number of increasingly small feudal estates. Lacking a powerful king, they set themselves up as independent rulers. And each feudal lord tried to cash in by extorting wealth from the commerce passing through his lands.

Consequently every square foot of precious ground was hotly contested and had to be carefully defended. So, out of necessity, the castles were built—simple structures at first, then enlarged bit by bit until they became the elaborate fortresses that stand today.

Feudal lords of every rank jostled with each other in their eagerness to secure possessions on the Rhine, the main artery of European commerce. As Rhine traffic increased, so did the number of toll stations, until 62 had to be passed between Basel and Rotterdam. More often than not the stations were the castles of robber knights who sometimes stretched chains across the Rhine to hold up the ships. Wrecking activities were common. Captains unable to pay the tolls risked losing not only their cargoes but their lives. In time Prussian supremacy and confederation of the German states put an end to despotism on the Rhine; the practice of collecting tolls ended in 1868 with the Treaty of Mannheim.

In the 96 miles between Bingen and Cologne we'd be passing more than thirty castles, each carefully situated for preying on everyone within reach—peasants, townsfolk, merchants, and travelers. Every tower, keep, and battlement reeks of legend: ghosts of robber barons, of knights who returned too late or too early, of ladies who waited in vain or had to fend off unwanted suitors—all have been known to gibber and twitter and curse and moan between the water and the walls as the wind rises. Once known to the poet Byron as "chiefless castles breathing stern farewells," the fortresses now breathe a warm welcome—as public museums, restaurants, hotels, and youth hostels.

North of Rüdesheim, with the skies a pale blue and the sun shining low in the morning sky, we looked up at the narrowest part of the gorge and the ruins of Ehrenfels Castle, which stood for four centuries before it was destroyed by the French in 1689. At the end of the narrow gap, stretched out along the right bank, was Assmanhausen, a colorful village of half-timbered houses. On the left bank three more castles succeeded each other. Rheinstein, 260 feet above our heads, rose right out of the ragged cliff face. Burg Reichenstein, more than a thousand years old, looked gray and sinister against the dark forests on the mountainside—a distinct contrast to the pert and quaint village of Trechtingshausen below, at the river's edge. The last castle, Burg Sonneck, just as old as Reichenstein, seemed a maze of staircases, platforms, and terraced gardens, impressively situated high over the Soonecker Grund.

The Krone Hotel at Assmannshausen near the southern end of the great gorge, where on the vine-covered terrace tourists, lovers and poets linger over their wine and watch the boats on the Rhine where the current runs fastest. Goethe stayed at this five-hundred-year-old inn built between the vineyards and the Rhine.

Three miles downstream on the left bank is the village of Niederheimbach, dominated by the castle of Heimburg in a romantic setting. Directly opposite, on the right bank where the River Wisper brings its secret treasures from the Taunus Mountains, is the town of Lorch. This community and its twin, Lorchhausen (a bit further downriver), were steeped in vineyards and centered around St. Martin's Church, known for its beautiful bells, and the eleventh-century castle of Nollig, which once formed a part of the town's fortifications. Across the river, on the west bank, the ruined towers of Furstenberg stared mournfully.

The sweet little town of Bacharach appeared on the left bank, deserving in every way the description picturesque. Its walls and towers enclosed a cluster of red-roofed, flower-decked, half-timbered houses surrounded by climbing roses, gurgling brooks, and an air of vigorous lushness. One of the most famous villages in the Rhine Valley, it was a busy commercial center in the days when Bingen Loch was still unnavigable for shipping and the wine from the surrounding Rhenish district was brought here by horsedrawn wagons. Long before the fiery local wine became famous throughout the world, it was the delight of connoisseurs. Legend tells us that the wine was so beloved that some of the villages' first consumers erected here an altar to Bacchus, the god who provided them so liberally with wine, and the god's name soon became that of the town.

Rising above the town are the ruins of the once-magnificent red sandstone Gothic Werner Chapel. Through its high arches and around its flying buttresses we could see the vineyards beyond, perched precipitously on the wild mountainside. Nearby Stahleck Castle, one of the most famous of Rhine fortresses, was given by Emperor Frederick Barbarossa to his brother Konrad.

Just beyond Bacharach we passed a small island on our left and found ourselves in a narrow channel. Then, on a continuation of the narrow islet, Pfalz Castle rose defiantly from the center of the riverbed, its powerful five-sided keep encircled by a turreted castle wall, one of the most interesting fortresses in the world. Built at the beginning of the fourteenth century on this island in the narrowest part of the river, it was impossible to pass without paying the toll demanded by its owner, Lewis the Bavarian.

On the east bank, glaring down from high above the little town of Kaub, and surrounded by vineyards, is the well-preserved thirteenth-century Gutenfels Castle. With its stately three-story palace and majestic 95-foot belfry, it's a magnificent example of Rhineland architecture.

Just north of Kaub on the left bank, at a sharp easterly bend in the river, stands Oberwesel, with its fourteen original watchtowers from the thirteenth and fourteenth centuries, conjuring visions of life as it must have been in the Middle Ages. High above, the towers of Schönburg Castle rise boldly from the cliff. It was here, according to legend, that seven maidens taunted their suitors and welshed on their promises. As punishment for their heartlessness, they were turned into stones and placed in the riverbed just downstream from Oberwesel. To this day, the story goes, the maidens still await deliverance. The Seven Maidens Rocks enable rivermen to check the level of the river when they appear above the surface, one by one, as the water level drops.

As the river continued to snake its way northward, we approached the Lorelei, perhaps the most legend-haunted rock in the world. Even now it is said that one can recognize the marks of the devil's claws when, full of envy, he tried to prevent God from creating this beautiful valley. Rising almost straight up from the water to a height of 417 feet and yielding at its base a magnificent sevenfold echo, it is reputed to have been the burial place of the treasure of the Nibelungs. Poets have portrayed the Lorelei as a sorceress, a witch, or a mermaid. Rivermen were repeatedly warned in folklore about the magic wiles of the golden-haired siren, clothed in white and with a wreath of stars in her hair, who would try to distract their attention in order to lure them to their death against the dangerous cliffs. In fact the channel narrows dangerously here, turning the waters into deep, treacherous whirlpools.

Seventeen miles from Rüdesheim, on the left bank, appeared the town of St. Goar, once a place of religious pilgrimage. Here, in 611, St. Goar, a hermit of Aquitania and converter of heathens, produced miracles so great that he was summoned by his bishop and called to account. In answer, the story goes, the gentle monk simply took off his cloak and "hung it on a sunbeam."

The small, typically Rhineland town of half-timbered and slate houses is overlooked by the vast ruins of Rheinfels Castle. Perched 377 feet above the river and originally the strongest fortress on the Rhine, it withstood the combined forces of twenty-six Rhenish cities who tried to storm its walls. The castle only succumbed to the zealous forces of the French Revolution—who laid the castle in ruins.

A ferry runs from the town of St. Goar to its sister village across the river, St. Goarshausen. There, standing guard over the pretty village, is Castle Katz, built by Count Katzenelnbogen at the end of the fourteenth century. Just downriver from Castle Katz is Castle Maus—supposedly named that by Count Katzenelnbogen, who used to say with playful malice that the mouse of the Trier electors was soon to be "devoured by the cat."

Across the river, nestled in the shelter of the valleys like a pearl in its shell, is the lovely town of Boppard, famous for its vineyards. In Boppard the landscape became less wild; fruit trees appeared and the vine-covered hills came into view. Soon we saw the magnificent Marksburg fortress towering on a high crag 492 feet over the town of Braubach.

Nine miles beyond, the waters of the Lahn River merge with the Rhine. At the crossroads of the rivers sits Lahneck Castle, which occupied an important strategic position for the trade routes of the Middle Ages. Just across the Rhine still another grim-looking castle, Stolzenfels, stared back vacantly through its restored pseudo-Gothic windows. Upstream from the Stolzenfels was the Konigstuhl zu Rhens, the medieval meeting place of the electors for the selection of the German emperor. The choice of this ground as a gathering place was by no means accidental; the "call of the heralds" could actually be heard from the castles of four electors: Rhens, belonging to the bishop of Cologne; Stolzenfels, to Trier; Lahnstein, to Mainz; and Braubach, to the Palatinate.

From Burgs to Beethoven

Three miles downstream, we were passing Koblenz, a charming city situated at the confluence of the Rhine and the Moselle, separating the Eifel in the north from the Hundsruck Mountains in the south. The Romans were the first to discover this spot, and here they constructed the *Castellum ad confluentes* in 9 B.C. Around this castle grew a flourishing city that became the residential seat of the electors of Trier during the Middle Ages. In 1815 the Prussians recognized Koblenz' great strategic and military importance, and the stronghold of the archbishops was converted into one of the greatest fortresses in Europe. High on a hillside commanding a sweeping view of the city across the Rhine, the old Roman castle, now called Ehrenbreitstein, yields in size only to Gibraltar.

From the Rhine promenade along the Koblenz waterfront, visitors can watch operettas on a floating stage and view the spectacular illuminations and fireworks displays of the "Rhine in Flames." On a tongue of land marking where the Rhine and the Moselle actually meet stands the ruin of the once grand Deutches Eck statue; all that remains today is the great base, 107 steps high, on which used to stand an enormous equestrian statue of Kaiser Wilhelm I.

Less than five miles further downstream, on the east bank, stands the little town of Rheinbrohl. At this spot, in the first century A.D., the Roman frontier, or *Limes,* was laid out with stakes from the Danube to the Rhine. Today, high above the village, crowning the towering Grauwacken Rock, brood the ruins of Hammerstein Castle.

Bad Honnigen was next, with its "castle of many windows" (an estimated 365), a converted pseudo-Gothic hodgepodge; across the river was Bad Breisig with its chairlift to the 64-foot tower and Romanesque chapel, all that remain of Burg Rheineck. Then, as though the river knew we were ready for more cheerful scenes, the friendly village of Linz appeared, its gaily painted yellow, white, pink, and brown half-timbered houses ajumble with flowers in windowboxes.

At Remagen the volcanic action that produced the steep cliffs on either side of the river also created the town's mineral springs. Yet legend offers a more imaginative explanation for the springs: When St. Apollinaris, bishop of Ravenna, died in Italy, his head was sent bobbing down the Rhine as a present for the archbishop of Cologne. It landed short of the city, however, and at the spot where it landed in Remagen, the medicinal springs began to flow. The present church of St. Apollinaris was built in 1839 to replace the original pilgrim shrine.

Remagen has another story, one less deeply buried in the mists of time. The former Ludendorff Bridge of Remagen occupied an important strategic position across the Rhine during World War II. On March 7, 1945, American troops marched unopposed over the bridge even though the Germans had mined it and ordered it blown up. The Americans owed their good fortune to a splinter from a grenade that had severed one of the fuse cables leading to the explosives. Blind destiny? The Germans thought not; four German officers were court-martialed and shot. The heavily damaged bridge collapsed shortly thereafter, but its capture greatly aided the American advance and hastened the war's end.

The four miles between Remagen and Rolandsbogen is widely regarded as one of the finest portions of the Rhine—the last magnificent stretch of the gorge, where its banks plunge from a height almost as great as the width of the canyon. On the right bank the stumps of the Seven Mountains (Siebengebirge) jut out, only to be replaced by the great cliffs of the Erpel. Ivy-covered Rolandsbogen (Roland's Arch) is all that's left of the citadel that Charlemagne's favorite knight ordered built at the foot of the Roddersburg, an extinct volcano of the Eifel range.

The Eifel is the greatest of the Rhineland mountain ranges. Once the hunting lands of Charlemagne, its hills rise to well over 2,000 feet, covered with forests of beech and spruce, trout streams, lakes, and romantic castles. Paris' Eiffel Tower was

Castles that live in legend, fairy tale and opera line the banks of the Rhine. Rheinstein, rising out of a steep cliff of live rock, is a beautiful one, with a fine view of the river from its crenellated watchtower. The number 533 on the shore marks the kilometers from a source of the Rhine at Lake Constance.

built by a man whose family came from this region—Gustave Eiffel, born Alexandre Bonickhausen at Dijon, France, in 1832.

It is the Siebengebirge, or Seven Mountains, that captures the hearts of lovers of the romantic Rhine. The entire region has compressed into its seven small peaks the loveliness that makes the Rhine so unforgettable. The road to the seven peaks passes through Nightingale Valley, and each of the hills has its legend, its fairy princess. Overlooking the Rhine, across from Bad Godesberg, the seven rounded volcanic hills were once crowned by castles. Today thick forests soften their outlines, and the whole massif forms a national park of some 10,000 acres (4,000 ha).

The slopes of the 1,000-foot Drachenfels peak are the northernmost place in Germany where vines can be cultivated. Here the best-known vintage is the Drachenblut (Dragon's Blood), a name that is indeed appropriate. In a cave on the hillside, legend says, lived a ferocious, winged, fire-spitting dragon who met his end at the sword of Siegfried, hero of the Nibelung saga. When Siegfried bathed in the blood of the infamous dragon, he became invulnerable. The practical Germans don't suggest that you bathe in their modern-day Dragon's Blood; you need only drink it in quantity to achieve the same effect.

Commanding a sweeping view of the Rhine and the Siebengebirge is the city of Bad Godesberg. One of the historic meetings between Chamberlain and Hitler in 1938 took place here. Other places of interest include the ninth-century Muffendorf Church and the famous thirteenth-century castle of Godesberg. Only the castle's battered round tower and shattered defenses remain from its spectacular destruction in 1583 by a mine weighing more than 1,500 pounds. The ruins sit atop the basalt crag above the parks and gardens in the center of the residential city. The crag was once the place of sacrifice for worshipers of Odin, the ancient forest god. Now, within their crumbling, ivy-covered walls, the Godesberg ruins house a modern restaurant and hotel of international reputation.

Five miles downstream, on the west bank, loomed the city of Bonn, capital of the Federal Republic of Germany since 1949, with a population of 300,000. Bonn is best appreciated as the birthplace of Ludwig van Beethoven. The house where the composer was born in December 1770—a charming building that miraculously escaped the almost total destruction of the war years—is now the site of the best of all Beethoven museums. Beethoven Haus is positively crammed with memorabilia of the great man. Here we studied his famous portraits and the fascinating life and death masks, shook our heads over the bizarre hearing horns with which he contrived to combat his deafness, pored over his letters and music manuscripts, admired his pianos, and, finally, paused with more than a little awe at the door of that rough little upstairs room—hardly better than a garret—where Beethoven was born. Though the room held only a wreathed bust placed upon a pillar, like everything associated with the colossal composer's personality it produced a palpable effect even in those disposed to scoff at simple acts of piety.

Bonn has honored its famous son with a special festival hall, Beethovenhalle, surrounded by gardens on the Rhine front. The modern festivals tend to be less eventful than the first one, held in 1845, when a statue of Beethoven was unveiled for the king and queen of Prussia and a former student of Bonn University, Prince Albert, who attended the event with his wife, Queen Victoria. (Spohr and Liszt had organized and directed the festival, and Berlioz and Meyerbeer were in the audience.) When the unveiling took place, the guests of honor were surprised to find that the statue faced away from their vantage point. The king of Prussia called out, "Ah, he's turning his back on us!" And Alexander von Humboldt, the naturalist and explorer, who was standing nearby, remarked quietly, "Well, all his life he was a very rude fellow."

Approaching the Lower Rhine

It's an old and slow-moving Rhine that flows past Bonn and moves out onto the sandy sea floor to the north. Becoming broad and majestic, the waterway overcomes its last impediment, the Rhenish-slate mountains near Bonn, and heads north toward the vast lowland region stretching from Cologne to the sea at Rotterdam. We were entering the lower Rhine Valley.

Just three miles north of Bonn the tiny, thousand-year-old fishing village of Mondorf appeared. Its local fishermen's fraternity grants membership on the basis of heredity—and membership carries fishing rights on a fixed stretch between the rivers Rhine and Sieg.

At four o'clock we pulled into Cologne, one of the most remarkable of German cities, ancient capital of the Rhineland, whose history spans 2,000 years. The city's name originated with the Roman Colonia from 50 A.D., when this frontier outpost exported the earliest eau de Cologne, a perfumed oil. The eau de Cologne of today is said to have been devised here in 1709 by Giovanni-Maria Farina from twelve drops of five essential oils (bergamot, citrus, neroli, orange, and rosemary), a drachm of Malabar cardamom, and a gallon of rectified spirit.

The view from the riverfront is almost rhythmic in its belfries, bold cathedral spires, and groups of bridges. The Rhine curves from St. Severin's Church northward past the cathedral to the botanical gardens, then bends back again. This sweep of riverfront remains among the most vivid memories of Cologne.

Cologne has perhaps the most extensive "old town" in all of Germany; running along the left bank of the river, it is outlined by the four-mile "ring" that follows the lines of the twelfth-century fortifications. The remainder of the town, with its Höhenstrasse and Schildergasse and fashionable shops, forms concentric circles around this kernel and is known as the "new town," though it is now more than a hundred years old.

As we slid in under the benign old bishop whose statue blesses all incoming craft, we feasted on the majestic sight of Cologne's celebrated cathedral. Begun in 1248, it was built to house the relics of the Three Magi, brought back from Milan to the archbishop of Cologne by Frederick Barbarossa. The cathedral took six centuries to build and was completed in 1880. Fortunately, Allied bombadiers in World War II managed to spare the Gothic masterpiece when they devastated the city.

Cologne's citizens are famous for their outspokenness and wit. In the darkest days of 1945, when the city lay in a honeycomb of ruin, an anonymous resident posted amidst the rubble a sardonic sign quoting a speech by Adolf Hitler during his catastrophic rise to power: "Give me five years and you will not recognize Germany again." Hitler, for one, would not recognize postwar Cologne; it is prosperous, gay, and inviting and has lost none of its gift for humor. In one of the local beer halls hangs a telling sign, mixing Latin and German in verse, to proclaim: IN VINO VERITAS; IN BIER IST AUCH ETWAS (roughly, "In wine there is truth; in beer there is also a little something").

Shortly before dinnertime our ship glided smoothly out under the great modern A-shaped piers of the St. Severin Bridge and headed for naughty Düsseldorf, some 25 miles (40 km) to the north.

Düsseldorf is variously called the "daughter of Europe," a reference to her international character; the "new art capital of Europe," because of her many art galleries; and the "desk of the Ruhr," because the industry of the Ruhr and the stock exchange residing here have made it the richest city in the Federal Republic. The industrial parks beside the Rhine are spectacular with their painted smokestacks, twisted piping labyrinths, and colored smoke drifting in the breeze.

The presence of a great many Deutschmark millionaires has made Düsseldorf an important fashion center. The city's famed Königsallee, affectionately called the Ko, is an elegant and lively boulevard—the heart of modern Düsseldorf—with large banks up the west side and cafes, restaurants, and luxury shops along the east.

One famous product of Düsseldorf was Heinrich Heine. Born in 1797, the son of a Jewish shopkeeper, he became a great poet, literary critic, and social satirist. His poem set to music, "Die Lorelei," was so famous the Nazis couldn't ban it, so they listed it as "author unknown." Other greats associated with Düsseldorf are Felix Mendelssohn, who directed the Rhine music festival in the city, and his friend Robert Schumann, who conducted the municipal orchestra for four years.

Not far from the city is a region made famous by—and subsequently renamed after—the seventeenth-century hymn writer, composer, and poet who was fond of the solitude he enjoyed in the valley of the River Düssel. The man's name was Neander, and in Neanderthal, as almost everyone knows, the bones of an Ice Age man were discovered by quarrymen in 1856.

When we docked for the night at Düsseldorf, we were offered our first nightlife tour of the trip—and politely declined. From the Bingen Gap to Düsseldorf, some 70 miles, 30 castles, 2,000 years of condensed history, and innumerable romantic legends later, we were so saturated that an intellectual digestive seemed more appropriate. In other words, we "crashed."

Windmills on the Rhine

On the morning of our fourth and final day out, we watched the mighty Ruhr River basin, industrial heart of Germany, glide past our breakfast table. Full of towering blast furnaces and smoke-blackened chimneys, known as Germany's Coal Bucket, or the Iron Rhine, this district produces most of the country's industrial coal and 75 percent of its iron and steel.

As we passed through customs at the German-Dutch frontier, we left the Rhine to join the River Waal in its westward journey to Rotterdam. The landscape was already becoming flatter, the light softer, and seagulls were seen more frequently.

We passed ancient Nijmegan, where dairy cattle wandered freely into the waters of the Waal and creampuff clouds drifted above. A carillon pealed in Tiel, a quiet little town of rivermen and shippers some 34 miles beyond the Dutch border. Soon after Tiel we came upon a setting like that of a classic Dutch painting, the landscape dotted with lazing, grazing cattle on the lowlands.

Thirteen miles west, at the convergence of the Meuse and Waal rivers, is Gorinchem, a beautifully landscaped old Dutch river and sea port. High on the opposite bank of the river stands Castle Loevestein. Here, when the famous moated fortress served as the state prison of the Netherlands, Hugo Grotius, founder of the doctrine of international law, made his renowned escape, smuggled out in a wooden box that is still on display in the town's orphanage.

Leaving Gorinchem on the Merwede River and crossing the nearby dikes, we arrived at the famous Dutch town of Kinderdijk, which has the most magnificent windmill terrace of the Netherlands. The landscapes of the area justified the dreamlike vision we had of Holland.

The silhouette of Dordrecht, some 14 miles from Gorinchem, stood out against the gray horizon like a lovely fretwork, with the square tower of its Grote Kerk, a twelfth-century landmark, above. Founded by the Franks and the Frisians, Dordrecht once occupied the position of importance in waterborne commerce now held by Rotterdam, only 14 miles downstream. Dordrecht still claims more navigational activity than any other place in western Europe.

It was mid-afternoon when we began seeing in the distance ahead the vague outline of a steel forest of 400 towering cranes and thousands of ships' masts. This was Rotterdam, home to nearly a million people, kilometer 1,000 of our Rhine journey, and our final destination. By now we had begun to appreciate that Holland and her waterways were another, wholly different story. We looked forward to devoting time exclusively to the Netherlands—and, fortunately, we wouldn't have long to wait; it would be our very next trip.

In the meantime we reflected on our four days aboard the handsome Rhine steamer, tracing the path of the Roman legionnaires in their quest for a greater empire, hearing the ghosts of knights and ladies from the Age of Chivalry, and seeing perhaps the most awesome landscapes ever formed by the hands of the Creator.

Some Practical Information

The Rhine River, 820 miles (1,320 km) long, is considered by many the most important river in the world, both politically and economically. From its modest beginning in the heart of the Swiss Alps, the Rhine thunders through Switzerland, France, Germany, and Holland and into the North Sea, swollen throughout its course by numerous tributaries. Geologists believe that the Rhine was originally much longer, at about the time the British Isles were connected to the Continent, and that the Rhine's outlet extended far northward, to somewhere between Norway and Scotland.

Present-day Rhine travelers, following in the wake of Caesar's and Napoleon's legions, will be delighted to find extensive and highly efficient cruise services operating throughout the entire 550-mile (885 km) navigable portion of the river. However, because of the heavy commercial traffic, the swift current, and the uncertainties of navigation, self-drive hire boats are not available.

The principal cruise service along the Rhine is operated by the Köln-Düsseldorfer German Rhine Line (KD German Rhine Line). Founded in 1826, it is the oldest and largest shipping company on the river, with twenty-three ships in service on the Rhine and the nearby Main and Moselle rivers. It offers a variety of cruises and excursions, ranging from one-day steamer and hydrofoil trips to seven-day and eight-day Rhine and Moselle cruises.

The prices shown for the following excursions are per person, one way; the upstream trip is one day longer than the downstream trip in each case.

	Upstream	Downstream
Two-Country Rhine Cruise Between Mainz and Rotterdam (2–3 days)	$180–245	$109–175
Three-Country Rhine Cruise Between Strasbourg and Amsterdam/Rotterdam (3–4 days)	$304–327	$272–294
Four-Country Rhine Cruise Between Basle and Amsterdam/Rotterdam (4–5 days)	$342–409	$325–392

	Upstream	Downstream
Five-Country Rhine Cruise Between Basle and Antwerp (5–6 days)	$471–500	$417–446

Rhine-Moselle Cruise

From Basle to Trier and return (8 days)	$548–602
From Rotterdam to Trier and return (7 days)	$475–530

The KD German Rhine Line also offers special cruises, including four-and-a-half-day Christmas and New Year's cruises. In addition, it runs regular day-excursion service on the Rhine, the Main, and the Moselle and a hydrofoil service between Düsseldorf/Cologne, Koblenz, and St. Goar (Lorelei).

The Line extends discounts for round trips and for large groups traveling together, and it has facilities for cruise-combined conventions and seminars. Passengers can arrange for their car to be shipped from embarkation to disembarkation points for a fee (it will be shipped free for those buying four or more steamer tickets).

As the handsome white Rhine steamers do not sail at night, upon arrival in port each evening, passengers may go ashore and either take the organized tours arranged by the company or tour independently.

Additional information about cruising the Rhine may be obtained from the U.S. representative for the KD German Rhine Line:

Rhine Cruise Agency
170 Hamilton Avenue
White Plains, N.Y. 10601

Floating Through Europe, Inc., 501 Madison Avenue, New York, N.Y. 10022 —as well as other travel agents—can furnish brochures, handle bookings, and arrange travel to and from the Rhine cruise.

National tourist offices of the respective countries can furnish tourist information:

French National Tourist Office
610 Fifth Avenue
New York, N.Y. 10020

German National Tourist Office
630 Fifth Avenue
New York, N.Y. 10020

Netherlands National Tourist Office
576 Fifth Avenue
New York, N.Y. 10036

Swiss National Tourist Office
608 Fifth Avenue
New York, N.Y. 10020

4

Dutch Odyssey

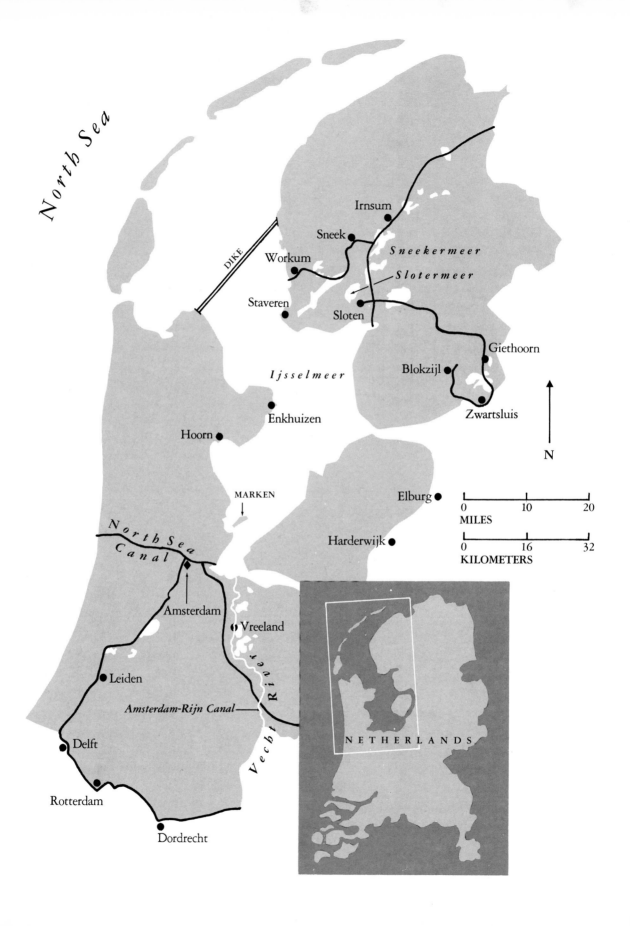

North Sea

Irnsum

Sneek

Sneekermeer

Workum

Slotermeer

Staveren

Sloten

Giethoorn

Blokzijl

DIKE

Zwartsluis

Ijsselmeer

Enkhuizen

Hoorn

N

Elburg

MARKEN

North Sea Canal

Harderwijk

Amsterdam

Vreeland

0   10   20
MILES

Leiden

Vecht River

Amsterdam-Rijn Canal

0   16   32
KILOMETERS

Delft

Rotterdam

Dordrecht

N E T H E R L A N D S

On a Private Clipper-Bowed Yacht Through the Lakes and Canals of Holland

Early one July morning, a number of unsuspecting travelers along the road paralleling the Winkel River, south of Amsterdam, encountered a most incongruous situation.

Here in this tiny waterway, no more than 50 feet wide, was a lovely old 56-foot clipper-bowed steel yacht heading neither upriver nor downriver but crossriver, with her crew on either bank hauling on the lines like beasts of burden, grunting and pulling, cursing and puffing. The man at the helm was shouting encouragement, but getting out of the predicament appeared an impossible task.

"What's going on?" the arrival inquired of a bystander on the riverbank.

"Bunch of crazy foreigners, I guess," the bystander replied, shaking his puzzled head. "How they got this far upriver is beyond me. Barely water to float a duck."

This is the story of how a couple of crazy foreigners managed to get themselves too far up a Dutch river, couldn't turn around, and loved every minute of it.

If you close your eyes and conjure up your personal images of Holland, you may see profusions of tulips and daffodils, rich dairy farms with men in baggy pants and wooden shoes, windmills, flat fields dotted with plump livestock, flavorful old cities with demure humpbacked bridges built over quiet canals, carillons pealing a thousand different melodies from a thousand church steeples, herring stands, cheese markets, a sudden glimpse of a woman in ancient regional costume.

A Dutchman would tell you that the Netherlands is more than these lovely images; Holland is a modern, dynamic nation that boasts some of the boldest engineering wonders in existence. Rotterdam, for instance, is a forest of space-age architecture—all new since World War II.

Yet the old endures, though you must search for it here and there. Of one thing you can be sure: If you travel through the large cities on the museum route traditionally followed by organized tours, you will not see the old Holland. The best way to see it, appropriately enough, is by boat.

One-quarter of the Netherlands lies below sea level. This geographic circumstance is responsible for centuries of struggle against the sea. Holland has more than a thousand lakes and over 3,400 miles (5,500 km) of canals—in an area barely twice the size of New Jersey. Nearly every town and village is either on the sea, at a lakeside, or crisscrossed by canals.

Our Dutch odyssey began at Amsterdam's Schiphol Airport. We drove north, headed for the little village of Irnsum, passing reclaimed seabeds of the old Zuider Zee and looking forward to joining the 56-foot motor yacht *Sirene,* our home for the next fourteen days, whose classic clipper bow we had so admired in photographs. Built in 1893 as a steam yacht for the president of a Dordrecht shipyard, the *Sirene* was said to be the fastest yacht in Holland when she was launched. We were anticipating meeting her captain and owner, George Van Dam Merrett, an experienced yachtsman who was proud of the *Sirene*'s low-slung sheerline, twin masts, brass and mahogany wheelhouse, and a character that had survived intact 83 years and several engine changes. We had been corresponding with Captain Van Dam for months regarding our proposed itinerary and plans, and we had been impressed with his intimacy with the whole of Holland and his excellent command of English.

It was nearly ten o'clock when we arrived in Irnsum, where the *Sirene* was moored before a lovely old farmhouse on a tiny island in the middle of the Kromme-Grouw Canal. The night was still; the lights of the farmhouse glistened on the water of the canal. We could dimly see the aristocratic profile of the *Sirene* as Captain Van Dam hailed us and then hopped into a small launch to meet us. After a tour below-decks we quickly began to feel at home in the two forward double cabins furnished in the original varnished teak and mahogany, with shiny old-fashioned brass fittings.

Our arrival in Irnsum had put us square in the middle of the province of Friesland, least crowded of all the Dutch provinces. The Frisians have clung stubbornly to their own language and customs throughout the centuries, though they are passionately Dutch. The Frisian language shows the influence of the North Sea, resembling English more than Dutch, with a good helping of Norwegian and Scottish.

Having found that Friesland is last-mentioned in the guidebooks, we proposed to make it first on the itinerary of our two-week tour of the Netherlands—a wending through the lakes and ponds and tiny, winding canals that shake hands with each other in a nearly unending chain.

The Ubiquitous Windmill

The next morning George introduced us to the pleasures of a traditional Dutch breakfast: pumpernickel, ginger, and honey breads, paper-thin ham, a hunk of aged Gouda, sweet butter, and eggs, along with several kinds of jam. After this first meal, we would be in charge of our own galley.

At about ten o'clock the sun beckoned us to begin our voyage. We cast off and floated past the reed-lined banks of the Princess Margriet Canal as herons and gulls, diver ducks and moorhens continued uninhibited in their morning activities. Less than an hour later we arrived at the village of Grouw on the shores of the Pikmeer, one of the eleven original Frisian towns.

Here George took us on a whirlwind shopping tour that included a busy, out-of-the-way butcher shop ("best one in town") that we would never have found by ourselves. It needed a near-native to break the code of those little alleyways and footpaths among the old brick walls.

Crossing the long Pikmeer through a narrow connecting canal, we found ourselves on the Wijde of Peanster Ee, second in the daisy chain of Frisian lakes. Here we tied up to the grassy bank to enjoy our first Dutch lunch—open sandwiches of cheese, meat, sausage, fish. The only concession we made to our foreignness was a bottle of wine; a real Dutchman would have preferred a good Dutch *Pils* or a cup of strong coffee with the noonday meal.

After lunch we headed into the Jansloot, a canal so tiny as to be insignificant even on the large-scale official waterway chart. Then, navigating a narrow, hull-scraping lock, we entered the Modderidge Bol, an ever-so-slight widening in the water-road, well characterized by its name, the Muddy Bowl.

"Look!" Stan shouted excitedly, "our first windmill!" He was wrong; it was our first *two* windmills, one nearly behind the other. I wondered how many scores of tourists have felt the same excitement at seeing their first Dutch windmill.

In spite of the destruction of some 220 windmills during World War II, nearly a thousand remain, many of them still active.

Windmills have been used since the eleventh century to reclaim land from the sea, to grind corn and spices, and to make paper.

Windmills even have their own sign language, a "code of the vanes" that has been used by millers for centuries. When the vanes form a Greek cross ($+$), it means the mill is ready to go; when they form a St. Andrew's cross ($\times$), the mill will not be running for some time. Various other positions can indicate that the miller has just become a proud father, that his daughter has become engaged, or that he is in mourning. During festivals the mills are ablaze with garlands, baskets, heart shapes, and figures representing the sun, love, music-playing angels, or the Dutch flag.

Tall Reeds and a Private Pond

Soon after leaving the windmills of the Muddy Bowl, we entered the sprawling Lake Prinsenhof, a maze of channels and islands. Once the hunting grounds of Prince William of Orange, it is now a wildlife preserve filled with a matchless variety of waterfowl hidden among its tall reeds.

Later, as dusk approached, we pulled up before the Prinsenhof Hotel just in time for cocktails. One of our purchases in Grouw, selected with George's expert guidance, had been a bottle of yellowish Oude Jenever (old native Dutch gin). This, George advised, was to be drunk well chilled and straight in a small shot glass made for the purpose, "preferably with a bit of smoked Zuider Zee eel." With George's coaching, we set upon initiating ourselves in this most Dutch of Dutch customs.

A delightful setting, the Prinsenhof Hotel boasts old-style architectural lines, thatched roof, and meandering rooms and hallways that contrast with the large, elegantly modern windows overlooking the harbor. After a delicious dinner, we returned to the *Sirene* and cast off, to anchor for the night on what George fondly called his "private lake." This lake, duly noted on the waterway charts as the Holstmeer, shows a depth of just under three feet. Since the *Sirene* draws four feet, one would assume the lake was inaccessible to it. George, however, knew better.

So, at dusk, we were motoring down the Princess Margriet Canal, a commodious but quiet waterway lined with pleasure craft tied up for dinner or for the night. Here and there we saw a barge secured to a stately old tree, laughing children rowing small rubber dinghies, and the warm glow of oil lanterns in tiny cabins with families gathered around their coffee. We seemed lonely travelers amidst this peaceful scene, and we didn't have far to go when George announced, "Oops! We missed the turn!"

Like a racing-car driver, he peeled off in a semicircular left turn for the Holstmeer. Tiny and overgrown with lush vegetation, it hardly looked like a turnoff at all. But in we went, George noting that here there was a sandbank to avoid, there it was silted up, and that we would be "making our own channel" into the lake. Soon we were laying comfortably to anchor in the middle of a small pond surrounded by reeds, with not another boat in sight. It was truly our own private anchorage that calm, cool, windless night. Crying of gulls and singing of frogs were the only sounds we heard.

Snaking Through Sneek

The misty-morning screeches of gulls over sleeping water awakened us, and then we heard the drone of fishermen trolling nearby. A vigorous swim followed by a hearty breakfast started us off on our second day.

The *Sirene* took us into the Sijtebuurster Ee, a small lake that connects with the Wijde of Peanster Ee—which meant that we had completed an almost perfect circle since leaving Grouw the previous day. Traveling in circles, we decided, could be quite pleasant if done in the proper spirit.

Here we turned south, zigging and zagging along the Zijlroede Canal until it flowed into the village of Nes, where it turned decisively west—and the entire character of the canal changed. Now we wandered along mere triflings of water, lined with houseboats, their lace curtains in perfect order and their picture windows a jumble of houseplant greenery.

The canal twisted through a tumble of red roofs that randomly described the two towns of Nes and Akkrum. Children with tousled blond hair fished off the banks, and people went about their business just as they would have if we hadn't been there. Low bridges opened in response to our horn, and occasionally we were ever-so-gently accosted by a miniature wooden shoe swung down from a bridge to request payment of a small toll. Then civilization slowly fell behind, leaving us in the midst of endless grassy fields where the tousled heads of small boys popped up among the reeds.

We were heading southwest for the Sneekermeer, home to a famous round of Frisian sailing regattas known as Sneek Week, the occasion of great revelry during the third and fourth weeks in August. The town of Sneek, one of the best-known

At Sneek, the twin-turreted Watergate Towers of red brick and sandstone rise over the Gieuw near Lemster Bridge. Sneek is the center of trade and commerce in southwest Friesland, and Sneek Lake is a yachting center with one of the largest yacht basins in Europe.

yachting centers in Friesland, presents its prettiest, most interesting, and historic face to the canal. We floated past the nave of the early Gothic Reformed Church, then the seventeenth-century Town Hall with its rococo facade. As we admired the cherubs flying on the balustrades, George was trying to wend our way between the barges that were tied four deep along the banks.

We turned a right corner and headed toward a bridge and the red-brick Water Gate, a last vestige of the town's original thirteenth-century fortifications. As its name implies, the Water Gate once stood guard over the canal at the town's entrance. Today it was crowded with tourists—sitting, climbing, munching snacks, and watching us as we slipped under the raised bridge and negotiated a quick turn past some red-brick, red-roofed seventeenth-century houses.

Nearly two miles west of Sneek we passed the village of Ijlst, famous for its hand-carved wooden ice skates, toys, and tools. Then we turned south toward the town of Heeg, where men still fashion the classic Dutch *boyiers* (sailboats) by hand at the rate of three per year. At the workshop in Heeg we saw these flat-bottomed, beamy, traditional craft taking shape: skilled hands worked the enormous leeboards to a perfect finish and carved delicate ornaments on their carefully fashioned tillers.

In the gray, flat light of the misty afternoon we approached Workum, a town surrounded by velvet pastureland, a simple windmill in the distance, and sheep grazing the banks of the canal. We ventured through the streets past the lovely old houses, fine Town Hall, and seventeenth-century St. Gertrude Church to find a charming old tavern full of warm candlelight and red-checkered tablecloths. Just across the way was the Market Square, in the frenzy of festival. Local food specialties were offered piping hot at a long, covered booth; there were carnival rides full of brave and laughing children, balloons, cotton candy, hot roasted chestnuts.

Hindeloopen Heritage

The morning of our third day we took a short jaunt south, down the coast of the Ijsselmeer to the thirteenth-century fishing village of Hindeloopen. There the harbor is nestled comfortably in the heart of the town. Under a lovely old clock tower, and in front of a seventeenth-century lock, we found the Liar's Bench, the time-honored spot where the old fishermen gathered to tell favorite stories. The clock tower carried the symbol of the town: three fishermen in an open boat, pulling in their heavy nets.

Nothing we had read had prepared us for the charm of this little village with its winding, twisting alleyways separating the neat front yards with their trim little houses built by the captains of bygone days. Here and there we spotted an old commander's house, recognizable by the two stripes of yellow stone over the facade and a cast-iron hook near the door. (When the captain returned from the sea, he hung a little anchor on the hook to show that he was ready to take on new cargo.)

As we cast off from the harbor, a bright blond boy in a hand-knit red sweater was fishing off the gate of the little lock at the head of the harbor, and an old man in baggy pants and wooden shoes rode his bicycle past the Liar's Bench. The Liars were comparing notes on George's prowess as a captain, pointing out the *Sirene's* classic lines as we disappeared through the narrow opening into the old Zuider Zee.

The Little Woman and the Skutsjes *of Stavoren*

In the harbor of the town of Stavoren a stone statue stares forlornly out over the Zuider Zee. The Little Woman of Stavoren was erected in honor of the legendary wealthy young widow of a shipping magnate who is said to have ordered her captains to bring back the most costly cargo on earth. When one returned with a shipload of corn, the widow was so angered that she ordered him to throw the whole lot into the sea. Slowly the seed grew and silted up the harbor, making passage impossible for ships. According to the chronicles, the prosperity of the town—once so rich that the steps of the houses were "paved with gold"—came to an abrupt end.

There was no provision in this dismal legend for what happens to the place when you fill it with a fleet of enormous Frisian *skutsjes*. The whole of Friesland seemed to have burst into life on this particular day, and the normally sleepy old town was a ball of activity by the time we arrived. The reason for the excitement was the impending annual *skutsje* race.

The *skutsje* is the national Frisian cargo sailboat, varying in size from 30 to 50 tons. With its blunt bow and stern, formidable beam, and precious little draft or ballast, its telltale leeboards and grand spread of canvas, the *skutsje* is the quintessential Dutch sailing vessel. It was used commercially on the Zuider Zee until just after World War II, when it fell victim to the faster powered cargo ships.

Since 1946 the eleven towns of Friesland have been competing each July for the *Skutsjeseeilen* speed crown. The Frisians look upon the vessels as a remnant of their former seapower, and their egos become deeply involved in the races. The owners of the vessels are ingenious and inventive in pouring on more and more sail, and captains take great pride in their speed and daring. Young Frisians can see in the flash of an eye at a distance of hundreds of yards just how the races are progressing, and the spectators work themselves into a frenzy.

Like racing sailors everywhere, the skippers of these tremendous yachts seem kindhearted enough on shore but show themselves to be anything but that when behind the helms of their boats. A favorite *skutsje* racing maneuver is to slip up behind a competitor, tack right into the leading boat's stern, and smash the big outboard rudder off!

We joined the sizable spectator fleet just in time to have a bite of lunch before the races began. (Newspapers later reported 15,000 spectators on the beach and in the spectator fleet.) The spectators around us were as colorful and interesting as the race itself. On our left were three old sailing barges with rust-brown sails. On the other side was an old tar-painted warhorse of a sailing barge covered with a raggle-taggle of hanging laundry. Further down was a beautiful old black sailing barge with bright red trim on its proud topsides. And all around us were children swimming off their boats, flags flying briskly in the fresh wind, families eating picnic-style, women sunbathing, and men fishing, looking like lazy truants and twice as happy.

From our vantage point near the second mark, the parade of these stately and handsome yachts as they raced past and headed proudly downwind, starting their great, gaff-rigged mainsails and setting whisker poles to keep their jibs out and full, was something quite regal.

Passing through the little lock at Stavoren after the race, we retraced our wake over the Heegermeer and into the Slotermeer, to the town of Sloten.

With a population of just 700, Sloten qualifies as the smallest—yet one of the prettiest—towns in Holland, filled with many lovely old houses, ramparts, and water gates and a delightful old mill. The banks of its tree-lined canals offer fine views of the countryside, where windmills reach above the gabled roofs of tiny houses.

When we arrived in the early evening, Sloten was alive with festival. Lights illuminated the footbridges over shimmering canals, and there were the clamor of ducks and the chatter of children. We dined in an old converted barn that provided simple, inexpensive service and delicious food; we sat in a wooden booth near a window offering a view of the world at jack-rabbit level.

After dinner we wandered through the streets gay with carnival atmosphere, visiting the eighteenth-century Town Hall and the seventeenth-century Reformed Church. We were intrigued with the little Frisian Museum of Magic Lanterns, which was full of hand-painted slides, those wonderful predecessors of moving pictures. The moon was full, the night warm, and the laughter from the fair seemed centuries away.

Peat Bogs and Thatched Roofs

The fourth morning brought drizzle and gray skies as we left Friesland and entered the province of Overijssel, an area of lakes, canals, and dreamy towns whose livelihood until World War II depended primarily on two local resources: peat and reeds. Since the Middle Ages people have been digging peat from the bogs—literally digging the soil out from around their villages, leaving the water to occupy the vacant space and thereby create new waterways. The reeds provide the basis of the second local industry; they are cut in great quantities for thatching, wickerwork, and caning.

Along the fascinating stretch of waterways from Ossenzijl to Zwartsluis, one can still see signs of the reed and thatching industry. All along the Kalenburgergracht Canal the banks are heaped with specially baled reeds drying in the sun, leaving room only for a jumble of flowers and houseplants and picture windows under traditional thatched roofs and neatly trimmed lawns.

We were heading for Blokzijl, a town which in 1600 was a famous and prosperous port on the old Zuider Zee. Although the Northeast Polder has been interposed between the little town and the sea, Blokzijl remains essentially a water town. The village clusters around its lively harbor, now full of pleasure boats

The winding River Vecht is a connection between Muiden on the Ijsselmeer and the Amsterdam Rijn Canal. It makes a delightful short cruise past windmills, old villas, tea houses, gardens, swaying poplars, herring stands and attractive inns.

Yachts moored along the canal that leads from the Slotermeer to Sloten share the banks with grazing sheep and cows. In the low land, boats, both power and sail, seem often to be gliding through the fields. To the right is the little town of Sloten with a busy yacht harbor usually bustling in the early evening with preparations for dinner.

where there used to be great cargo ships laden with peat for worldwide export.

The lock at Blokzijl was typical of most locks we found in the Netherlands. Situated in the middle of the village, it seemed designed to provide both villagers and tourists with much of their outdoor entertainment. A dozen or more boats jostled for a spot, owners and crew working to fend off the next craft. Colorful costumes, picturesque old buildings, the chance meeting of friends in the same lock, dozens of assorted dogs wandering between pairs of legs on the quayside, and children—scores of blond-haired, blue-eyed children—laughing, playing, working, and watching.

We found a berth along a quiet residential street, opposite a cluster of sixteenth- and seventeenth-century gabled houses. Then we took off on foot to spend the rest of the day exploring the grand Dutch Reformed Church (full of Renaissance furnishings) and to wander the narrow lanes past aromatic bakeries and curtainless picture windows.

On the fifth morning we made our way out the other side of the harbor, through the Vollenhovermeer—a long, narrow spit of water—and into the village of Vollenhove. This former fishing town still devotes itself to eel smoking, as our nostrils soon detected.

Just before lunch we arrived in Zwartsluis, where barges congregated three and four deep under old trees along the canal. Jarrett headed for the shops to stock up on food, and Stan set out to rent a sailboat for the day. We were bound for the "fairytale" village of Giethoorn.

Although the trip to Giethoorn would cover a scant seven miles, it involved negotiating a canal that was just 70 feet wide and was totally congested with ponderous yet swift-moving barges, pleasure craft of every shape and size, and enormously long fishing poles poking from the muddy banks every few feet. To top it all off, the wind was directly in front of us. What a scene! And the madness continued until we entered Giethoorn.

Lying in marshes near the inland sea, the town has no streets at all. Every house has been so thoroughly harvested of peat that it stands on its own tiny island completely surrounded by water. All traffic here is that of punt or motor launch: housewives shop and husbands visit the local tavern by boat; wedding and funeral processions float through the maze of broad and narrow, straight and winding canals and streamlets that separate the dwellings from the outside world and from one another. Punts piled high with vegetables move slowly along the lazy waters. Every wooden cabin has its own humpbacked timber bridge over the green water to the cabin opposite.

The next morning, in strong winds, we skirted the Ijsselmeer and worked our way south to the town of Elburg, where we found old facades and cobbled sidewalks worn smooth by the centuries, and the remains of bastions and gates gave off a medieval flavor. We passed under the Elburger bridge, keeping a close eye on our watches—we still had 15 miles to go to reach Nijkerk Lock before it closed at 7 P.M. We might just make it—but we hadn't figured on the lock at Harderwijk.

Hard Work at Harderwijk

The lock at Harderwijk was a storm lock, used only to hold back high water during heavy winds; at other times it stood open and unused. But a full day of 35-knot winds had pressed it into service, at a rate slower than normal. When we arrived, we found about twenty yachts, some anchored and some drifting about, trying not to hit each other. We moved alongside a 35-foot, double-ended sailboat, found its crew convivial, and, several Oude Jenevers and a good deal of laughter later, watched the lock gates open to reveal a chamber big enough to take perhaps fifteen boats.

"You think we'll fit, George?"

"Have to. The lock closes in thirty minutes. At the rate this lockkeeper moves, this may be his last load for the day. There's no harbor on this side of the lock for 20 miles—and nothing in the refrigerator for dinner." By now George had cast off from the other boat and was headed full speed toward the lock. Threatened with being deprived of his dinner, George was prepared to risk all.

"George, I can't understand their Dutch, but these people seem to be yelling at us. And the screamer on the brown powerboat looks pretty mad."

"When you see them shaking their fists like that, you don't need to understand Dutch. Matter of fact, you're better off if you don't."

In the lock now, our bow was pressed against the next boat's transom, yet our stern was hanging some distance out the rear gates.

"How are we in front?"

Our anchor was hanging *into* the stern porthole of the next forward boat. "You're in about as far as you're going to get, George."

"Sorry. Give me another three feet. My stern is hanging out the gates."

"Another three feet? There isn't another foot in this whole lock, George! I don't know where you're going to get it."

George, unflappable, hung a fender off the stern just in time to ward off the closing gates. Then, while we fended off the three boats at our bow, the gates slowly pushed us—with all the other boats in the lock—three feet forward. We were in.

We dined in the town of Harderwijk (whose pronunciation in Dutch is almost "harder work"), an old harbor town with a university distinguished by such names as Boerhaave and Linnaeus.

After dinner we walked through Harderwijk's fourteenth-century gate to the fishmarket, through the old streets and past the medieval churches. After a day of gale-force winds, occasional crises, and a goodly portion of the remedial Oude Jenever, we turned in early, glad to be alive and glad to be in a place known so aptly as Hard Work.

On the seventh morning of our journey, we cruised through the Veluwemeer, passing Nijkerk, a city which sent many of its inhabitants to the New World—among them, two founders of New York, Kiliaen van Rensselaer and Arent van Culder.

A little further on we came to the twin towns of Bunschoten and Spakenburg. Both have been faithful to their traditions and costumes, yet they are far less commercialized than Marken or Volendam, the favorites of the Amsterdam bus tours. Although merged by a single long street, the two towns have quite different personalities. Bunschoten is the village of the milkmaids, Spakenburg that of the fishergirls; Bunschoten is in the meadows, Spakenburg is down on the old Zuider Zee. Arriving on a Wednesday, we were treated to the sight of the village washing hung out across the streets to dry. The women of the town were a beautiful sight, dressed in starched and glazed yokes of chintz and white lace caps, each with a tight roll of hair over her forehead and a scarlet and white checked cotton scarf around her neck.

Along the River Vecht

Continuing westward toward Amsterdam, we arrived in the harbor of Muiden, with its thirteenth-century toll fortress at the mouth of the River Vecht. As the lock leading to the river was closed for repairs, we would have to make the grand tour through Amsterdam, down the Amsterdam-Rijn Canal and through the town of Weesp (home of Van Houten, the oldest chocolate company in Holland and one famous throughout the world).

Passing under a very low bridge at Weesp, we joined the river that in the eighteenth century was one of the glories of Holland. On both sides were splendid villas and gardens belonging to the nobles and rich burghers of Amsterdam and Utrecht. Owning a home on the Vecht at that time was comparable to having a town house on the Champs-Élysées or Fifth Avenue today.

Above the town of Vreeland, where the concentration of teahouses and famous old mansions and gardens begins, the Vecht is a delightful, tree- and houseboat-lined, windmill-dotted river. The banks, with their low-hanging weeping willows, gave the river a feeling entirely different from that of the reed-lined waterways of Friesland or Overijssel.

In Vreeland, just beyond the hand-operated bridge, we looked up at the Hotel de Nederlanden, rated by the Alliance Gastronomique Neerlandaise as one of the twenty best restaurants in Holland. Here we would spend the night before passing down the famed stretch of river that lay beyond, and we looked forward to a candlelit gourmet dinner preceded by cocktails carried on silver trays to the decks of the *Sirene*.

The stopover at Vreeland did not disappoint us. We fell asleep that night filled with the joys of the previous days' discoveries and the expectations of the next day's trip down the fabled Vecht.

On the eighth morning of our venture, the start of our second week, the sun peeked in and out of grand billowy clouds and the wind blew crisp and cool across the river as we reached the cluster of teahouses that stretched from Vreeland to Zuilen. The Vecht's giant willows, which usually languish gracefully down to the water, danced and swayed; we could almost see the ladies in their long white dresses carrying parasols to tea in the octagonal wooden teahouses at the river's edge. Nowhere else in Holland will you see such a magnificent parade of eighteenth-century graciousness than here, in and around these willowy, thatched garden spots.

Loenen's lovely church filled the foreground as we reached a slight widening of the river. Poplars and teahouses presided over the water's reflections of swans and the small white sails of village boys on their tiny skiffs. Bicyclists clothed in purple, blue, and yellow rode along the towpath as we passed the peaceful town of Breukelen's castle of Nijenrode. We were a world away in every respect from Brooklyn, New York—to which this pretty town gave its name in the seventeenth century.

Zuilen, trim and neat, looked like something from a forgotten dream, sporting a pair of windmills as unmatched as any two windmills could be—one stout and thatched, the other a miniature red wooden barn on a graceful pedestal. A field of black sheep lay in the background. Then appeared the best-known castle on the entire river, the twelfth-century castle of Zuilen. We had reached the end of our trip on the River Vecht.

Utrecht to Arkel to Dordrecht

From here it was just a fifteen-minute journey to Maarssen and the Amsterdam-Rijn Canal. The enormous Princess Beatrice Lock lifted us about five feet—the most drastic altitude change we had experienced in this flat country. At Vreeswijk we crossed the River Lek and reached tiny Vianen, whose church bells serenaded us as we turned south onto the Merwede Canal between rows of 120-foot poplars. We were again in fertile farm country full of cattle, sheep, orchards, and sleek horses.

Dinner aromas emanated from boats moored alongside the banks, reminding us it was getting late. We found a slip in the little marina at Arkel, tied up for the night, and walked to an intimate canalside pub whose young owner proudly showed us pictures of him and his bride beaming honeymoon smiles before the Statue of Liberty.

The Linge River is a curious, meandering stream that intersects with the Merwede Canal in the very heart of little Arkel. It goes nowhere; rather, it ambles along, hardly spoiled by villages—a peaceful country stream flowing through open fields lined with livestock, reeds, and wildlife—definitely one worth traveling.

Friday morning was another uncertain, windy day with big, puffy clouds and periods of hot sunshine interlaced with sudden downpours of rain. We took the Linge to Leerdam and back to Arkel before setting off again toward Dordrecht and Rotterdam. It was a very green retreat, and we could picture a family spending their entire vacation tied up along the bank of this clean, fresh stream, taking walks, swimming, cooking, pitching tents.

The village of Heukelum, nestled under steeples and among trees, was a jumble of green houses, red tiles, and thatched roofs. Its river banks were lined with boats, and around a quiet bend near the town bridge were fishermen wearing wooden shoes.

After a brief stop in Leerdam, renowned for its artistic glassware, we returned along the now-familiar Linge to Arkel. Here we rejoined the Merwede Canal and soon reached Gorinchem (pronounced "Gorkum"), a fortified town built in the thirteenth century by the Count von Arkel. Its grim and somber-looking fifteenth-century Castle Loevestein stands on a spit of land between the Maas and Waal rivers just opposite the town, its mighty walls encircled by murky-looking moats. Beyond Gorinchem the Merwede splits into two branches; we followed the North Branch to Dordrecht, the oldest town in Holland.

Dordrecht is full of delightful, typically Dutch canal vistas. Its ancient houses rise directly from the rushing waters and lean toward each other at picturesque angles. Situated at the busiest intersection of rivers in the world, this city has a large shipbuilding industry (its Koopman Yard built the *Sirene* in 1893), and its large fleet of yachts makes it one of the main watersports centers of the Netherlands.

Exploring Dordrecht on foot, we found waterways everywhere and pearls of

Volendam, known for its old houses, costumes and fisheries, is also a good harbor of refuge when the Ijsselmeer turns stormy. Along the quay, pounds are filled with squirming and slippery eels, a local delicacy and a substantial part of the fishermen's catch.

architecture scattered along the winding alleys that serve the city as streets. Dordrecht is very much a living piece of history: small children run through the streets in wooden shoes past long-haired teenagers revving up their motorcycles. The tempo and sounds were distinctly modern, busy, and powerful.

In company with the huge tugs and commercial barges that churn their way up and down the Merwede, we and the *Sirene* headed toward Rotterdam and Delft. The clouds formed puffy mountain ranges that marched briskly across the sky, while the sun's gold filtering through a silver-heather crevice gave us a classic luminescent Dutch sky.

Just beyond Kinderdijk we floated past one of the most famous spots in all Holland. Here, far below sea level, was a field of nineteen picturesque windmills built to collect excess water from the neighboring polders.

Rotterdam and Delft

We were approaching Rotterdam, with a population of more than one million the largest city of Holland and the busiest seaport in the world. The city was destroyed by bombing in 1940, so while it is ancient (700 years old) it is also the home of a super-modern complex of glass sheathed skyscrapers, an immense, gleaming-white observation tower, shining mosaic streets, contrasting pavements, gushing silver fountains, and an air of almost raw newness. Within the central 500 acres of the city there is virtually no such thing as an old structure—except one very fine old windmill that miraculously escaped German bombs and the ensuing fire.

Rotterdam has been called a harbor with a city attached, but this ocean port actually lies 20 miles inland, connected with the North Sea only by a long channel. Nevertheless, every year some 32,000 oceangoing ships find their way into the harbor to exchange their cargoes with 260,000 smaller craft that ply the rivers and waterways into Germany, Switzerland, Belgium, and France. This truly colossal armada accounts for the breathtaking forest of cranes, funnels, and hoists that dominates the skyline of the port. Ashore and afloat, all is a noisy bustle of smoky efficiency.

The furious activity of the harbor, with its giant ships setting up a wash in every direction, made the *Sirene* roll madly. It was no place for a pleasure cruise, so we scurried into the calmer waters of the Delftsche Schie Canal and headed for Delft.

As we rounded the corner there appeared a lock gate so narrow we feared the *Sirene,* with her modest ten-foot beam, wasn't going to make it. Just under the low bridge the walls narrowed suddenly to pincerlike proportions, and George used every skill he had to keep the *Sirene*'s paint off the walls.

Delft, a city of quiet canals shaded by lime trees, peaceful convents with picturesque courtyards, high towers with magnificent carillons, finely worked facades mirrored in smooth water, the pastel skies of Vermeer, and the special brand of blue known the world over as Delft Blue, surprised us as we entered through her "back door"—via the canal. Displayed along the banks was a thriving chemicals industry and miles of electric cables. The epitome of dreamy Dutch memories of a glorious past was vibrantly alive with 80,000 people and an active heavy industry.

However, the rugged, modern industrial section soon melted into the old Dutch quaintness we had sought, and we tied up in front of the Oosterport (East Gate), the only remnant of the original thirteenth-century fortifications and a structure that appears in many of the oldest paintings, prints, and tiles of Delft.

Arriving at sunset, we were able to make our acquaintance with Delft in the quiet twilight, after the departure of the tour buses and day-trippers from Amsterdam. Our walking tour took us along old canals with white wrought-iron bridges, past beautiful Dutch Renaissance houses in perfect repair—completely restored with enviable stuccowork encircling their huge doors and Belgian glass windows. Houses rose right out of the tiny canals, and some of the oldest canals were so full of houseboats as to be completely inaccessible. Gradually the lights of the town flickered on, and soon the buildings and towers were regally illuminated.

A Race to Leiden

The next morning, a Saturday, we planned to tour the lake district; we would go through the heart of old Amsterdam on Sunday. But first we would need to pass through the final bridge at Leiden, some 25 miles away, before it closed at two o'clock today—or we would spend the weekend in Leiden instead.

At Rijswijk, our first stop early that morning, we admired the perfectly manicured lawns of the large estates. Willow trees leaned far out over the waters of the canal, sleeping ducks and swans tucked their heads under a wing to sleep, herons standing at alert attention pointed their beaks proudly skyward, their necks gracefully arched. It was near Rijswijk that we came, totally by surprise, on what declared itself to be the Tower of Hofwijk, bearing a date of 1641 and decorated on every side with "fool-the-eye" paintings depicting classical sculptures of the goddess Diana, Cupid, and other mythological figures. The marvelous building, in pale gray and white, was surrounded by a moat and formal gardens.

At Leidschendam—halfway to Leiden—we pulled up to a lock just as the doors banged shut. George calculated that we had a long wait, so we tied up to a pier and had a chance to admire the charming little village, dominated by its imposing church. Jarrett scampered ashore to buy supplies and look around the town, and Stan walked over to the lock.

A full hour later the lock doors reopened. We were first in line, followed by an armada of pleasure boats, among them an old flat-bottomed, tar-painted, open barge of the kind used to haul cows, manure, and milk on the canals. It was loaded with a number of young men who had fashioned an extraordinary figurehead: a dime-store mannequin wearing a blond wig, a chiffon scarf billowing from her neck—and absolutely nothing else. Behind this piece of feminine pulchritude stood a tall flagstaff proudly flying the Heineken beer flag. Cases of the golden liquid lined the floorboards, much of the cargo already consumed by the young crew.

We cleared the lock ahead of the other boats to find clear sailing. It was nearly one-thirty; were we going to make that bridge at Leiden by two o'clock?

Leiden is one of the most beautiful of the old water towns of Holland and the site of one of the most beloved stories of Dutch history. In 1574, during the Eighty Years' War for independence from Spain, the superior Spanish army tried to take the city by storm. But the city would not surrender, even when its people were forced to eat rats and chew leather belts and boots for sustenance.

Meanwhile, Prince William of Orange pressed forward from Delft with his ragged army of patriot-rebels to help the city. The progress of the "Beggars" was painfully slow. Finally, the prince took the most extreme measure known to the Dutch: He had the precious sluice gates opened, thereby flooding a large area of southern Holland. When the wind was right, the Beggars sailed over what had once been meadows and pastures to rescue the besieged town. The arrival of the relief boats loaded with bread and herring is celebrated every year on October 3, when the burgomaster distributes white bread and herring to the entire population.

Leiden has another story that is of special interest to Americans. When the Pilgrims fled England in 1609, they sought asylum in Leiden. There they lived until 1620, when they made up their minds to go to the New World. They boarded the *Speedwell* in Rotterdam to begin a voyage that joined the *Mayflower.* Everyone knows the outcome of that story.

Leiden edges the southern end of Holland's important bulb-growing region, which stretches from Leiden northward to Haarlem. The entire region is studded with bulbfields, nurseries, gardens, and parks that, every spring, explode into dazzling color. Windmills abound here more than almost anywhere in Holland, and so do lakes. We were headed for the Kagerplassen, a large, shallow lake divided into six smaller areas by four uncrowded islands.

Our tour of the Kagerplassen was a leisurely joy. Flotillas of small yachts sailed before the wind, cows grazed in the pastures of the surrounding farmlands, windmills vied for our attention, wildlife was abundant in the reed-lined banks. Everywhere we turned we saw sails passing behind low hills and barns and spinnakers floating over old wooden sheds.

The absolute ultimate was the Dutch version of the hayride: waterborne on an old barge, a group of bathing-suited youngsters sprawled atop an enormous stack of hay. The old farmer, wearing wooden shoes, stood placidly back at the tiller.

Leaving the Kagerplassen on the shallow riverlet Ade, we joined the Ringvaart van de Haarlemmermeerpolder, which leads to the Westeinder Lake. Surrounded by reed fields, the Westeinder is dotted with reed-covered islands in the shallows and filled with hundreds of sailboats. The city of Aalsmeer lies on the shores of this charming lake, hiding its houses behind a foliage of green plants and greenhouses with tall chimneys. Half the flowers grown in Dutch greenhouses—as well as many of the outdoor flowers—are raised here in Aalsmeer.

We pulled into the little harbor of Kudelstaart nearby and had an enormous dinner brought to the *Sirene*'s table from the shoreside restaurant.

Sleepy Old Amsterdam

Sunday morning, already the eleventh day of our journey, we set out after breakfast on the Ringvaart for Amsterdam. We passed a community of houseboats that looked just like any large residential development—except for two minor things: all the homes were afloat and no two houseboats were similar, save for the large picture windows filled with plants and flowers that hung from the ceiling or rested on the window sills inside. There were two-story houseboats, split-level houseboats, boaty-looking houseboats on old barges. And every one of them was topped by a tall television antenna.

We were in no hurry this morning. We looked forward to seeing bustling, modern Amsterdam step out of character, her streets deserted but for her pajama'd citizenry leaning out their windows to stretch a long, Sunday-morning stretch.

The houses on the banks of the Schinkel of Kostverloren Vaart Canal are typical of the seventeenth- and eighteenth-century homes for which Amsterdam is known. In these houses with their gabled and carved facades and wrought-iron staircases, where emblazoned balconies embellish the homes of rich merchants or important magistrates of the Golden Age, the heart of Amsterdam still beats. Modern offices have been installed in many of them, but the buildings have the familiar old pullies at the roof, still used for hauling furniture because the staircases are too narrow.

The North Sea Canal connects the Ijsselmeer with the North Sea and embraces the harbor of Amsterdam. This port is second only to Rotterdam in the Netherlands. And yet, for all the weekday activity in the harbor of Amsterdam, we found with pleasure this quiet Sunday morning that the *Sirene*'s was virtually the only wake in the entire harbor.

We made our way into the legendary Ijsselmeer, placid this morning with a precocious, fickle breeze, and steamed northward at eight knots across a stretch of water that would soon disappear. We may have been among the last sailors to cross this part of the Ijsselmeer; it was soon to be drained and turned into the new, 120,000-acre Marketwaard Polder.

We rounded the island of Marken, known for its costumes and picturesque wooden houses, all tarred and covered with tiles, and past the simple old fishing hamlet of Volendam on the mainland. The harbor was alive with fishing boats, and men in baggy trousers carried casks of smoked eels. Shortly thereafter we passed the home of one of Holland's great cheeses, Edam. Finally, in mid-afternoon, after a pleasant crossing, we arrived in the once-busy seaport of Hoorn.

Plenty in Hoorn

Hoorn's circular brick Harbor Tower dating from 1532 promised us a town full of treasures from a glorious past. For it was from here that hardy sailors once set out to venture to the East, the Baltic, and the Indies. In those days Hoorn was one of the world's great seaports (with Cape Horn its namesake).

For Hoorn, as for so many other Dutch cities, the seventeenth century was the beginning and the end of the Golden Age. Today she has closed her eyes on the edge of that old sea that used to be the Zuider Zee, a sleeping beauty lost in nostalgic dreams of her former glory.

We arrived in Hoorn with the afternoon to meander through its maze of streets both wide and narrow, lined with old brick houses that lean toward each other at every angle—many of them as much out of the perpendicular as the leaning tower of Pisa. Many houses are graced with truly beautiful sculptured panels; notable is a bas-relief running across three seventeenth-century houses, showing the defeat of the Spanish naval forces that took place in 1572 just outside the harbor—complete with attendant winds in the form of naked ladies holding sails or wind scarves. It was from the top-floor windows of these houses that the furious battle was best observed, as it continued day and night until the Spanish admiral Bossu surrendered on board his galleon, *The Inquisition*.

The fishing harbor was alive with boats, the docks lined with strollers and with children who periodically threw themselves into the cool water. The focal point of the harbor is the Harbor Tower, surmounted by its elegant campanile which dates from 1651. Once a part of the medieval city walls, the tower was later the head-quarters of the North Company, which specialized in whaling. Mounted on the adjoining wall are "The Cabin Boys of Bontekoe," sculpted in bronze by Jan van Druten. Padde, Hajo, and Rolf were the leading characters in the popular boys' book by Johan Fabricius, inspired by the famous world traveler from Hoorn, Willem Bontekoe.

Just behind the Cabin Boys stood a large and busy herring stand, emanating irresistible aromas of fried, smoked, and fresh herring and attracting a crowd of its own. We elbowed our way in to taste the Dutchman's Delight: fresh, raw herring smothered in onions. The native way to eat this national snack is to pick it up by the tail, lower it into your mouth, and chomp your way up.

On summer Wednesdays the streets of Hoorn are filled with market stalls manned by net menders, spinners, and weavers, clog-makers, flower arrangers, potters, saddlers, woodcarvers, basket weavers, blacksmiths, laceworkers, and calligraphy artists, who keep their ancient trades alive from the Golden Age. The collection of costumes and crafts is a spectacle that attracts people from all over Holland.

We dined on local specialties in the tavern near the harbor and contemplated the old horn-shaped harbor through wavy, antique windowpanes.

Enkhuizen and Monnikendam

The next morning we headed up the coast toward Enkhuizen, which seemed in many ways to be a sister city to Hoorn. Like Hoorn, the town looks back nostalgically on a proud maritime history and has preserved many of its old treasures—the bastions and gates, the churches, the facades from the Golden Age. But here the most compelling sight was the famous Zuider Zee Museum, housed in the former warehouse of the East India Company. We could have spent days wandering there.

It had been our plan to travel back down the coast to Monnikendam in the afternoon, but we spent so much time in the Zuider Zee Museum that when we arrived the sun was sinking in a great red ball behind the dike.

We tied up at the old wooden pier before the Hotel and Restaurant Stuttenburg. Entering the restaurant, we discovered a treasure trove of old music boxes and gramophones lining the walls and scattered at unlikely spots between the tables. As we accustomed our eyes to the candlelight and our comfortable surroundings, we were struck with the charm and grace of this wonderful place, its outstanding warmth and hospitality, and—as we were soon to discover—its fine kitchen.

The next morning, day thirteen, we struck out through the Stuttenburg aviary, which is filled with peacocks, parrots, and a host of other exotic birds. Then we moved on to the village of Monnikendam—just six miles from Amsterdam, but a world apart. This lovely region between Amsterdam and the northern part of Holland is known as Waterland. Rembrandt used to travel here a great deal, sketching the pretty girls of Rummsdarr, the scenery, and especially the light and the sky.

Trousers in the Water

Broek in Waterland ("Trousers in the Water") is a delightfully minute, quiet old village. It grew up around the small harbor at the junction of two canals, and its overly modest people soon came to call it Holland's most beautiful village—as they filled it with cheesemongeries, model farms, tiny wooden houses with painted white shutters and handkerchief-size gardens. The interiors as well as the exteriors of most of these Golden Age homes are decorated with Louix XVI rococo shapes, and behind the tiny windows gleaming copper bowls were filled with flowers. The one small bridge had a white balustrade, and the village hall had a swan painted on it. Boats bobbed up and down in the Havenrak pond, and ducks swam in and out of a small floating house, decorated with red and white diamond shapes on miniature shutters under a thatched roof, built especially for them.

The *Sirene* continued past a Huck Finn raft, homemade from boxes and crates with a jury-rigged mast made from a broomstick and a thwartships-rigged squaresail from one of mom's old sheets. And, suddenly, we were back in Amsterdam and headed for the Vinkeveense Plassen, a forgotten bit of water within an area not covered by tourist literature even though it lies just a few miles south of Amsterdam.

We joined the Angstel River, which flows through incredibly rich farmland whose bright summer-green pastures were full of sheep, plump cows, and sleek riding horses. Here and there we saw small boats with their bows buried in the reed banks, an anchor thrown out off the stern. Some impish Dutch boys were swimming with their inner tubes, their wet blond hair flattened in points on their dripping faces.

At the entrance to the Vinkeveense Plassen, we were lowered six feet in the tiniest working lock we had ever seen. The *Sirene* just fit within its mossy walls. The gates of this dollhouse lock were operated not by geared handcranks but manually —by pushing with a long boathook.

The Plassen was punctuated with tiny islands the size of a single large tree, looking like exclamation points, as well as little drips of reeds popping up out of the lake. We glided along past pretty villages, picking out boats we liked, memorable churches, and other small joys. We pulled into a little yacht harbor for a quiet dinner, then right back out again to anchor for the night in the shelter of a small island.

The Amazing Turnaround Rag

Wednesday morning we found the opening of the tiny Winkel River, one of the funniest little rivers in all of Holland. With a width of just 50 feet and a depth of three feet in places, it was a river in which we had to make our own path.

Rounding a hairpin turn in the river, we came suddenly on a tiny footbridge operated by a pink-cheeked nine-year-old girl, who pulled a handle that spun the bridge around to let a boat pass. But before she finished opening the bridge, there appeared from the right, coming from a junction waterway at terrific speed, what looked in these close quarters like a GIGANTIC barge. On any other stream it would have seemed insignificant, but its proximity and speed magnified it a hundred times.

Engine hard astern, the *Sirene* seemed to stop on a dime before the bridge. The barge, operated by a lone bearded bargee, managed skillfully to squeeze itself around the bend and through the bridge. But then he had to contend with us. Our starboard side was in the reeds on the right bank, yet the barge had a tight squeeze to get through. When he had passed, we broke into spontaneous applause, and the bargee poked his head out the wheelhouse door to take a bow.

Once past the little bridge, the river grew both narrower and shallower. It wasn't until we were nearly two miles beyond the "bridge of the skillful barge" that George announced, in a very Georgelike way, that—Oops! we had missed an essential right turn. Where? Back where we had met the barge. *Two miles* back.

And here we were on the 50-foot-wide Winkel River with a 56-foot boat. At first it seemed like an interesting intellectual exercise: How can you turn around in a space shorter than your length? Well, we agreed, a river's not exactly regular; there are wide spots. At the next one, we'll take lines ashore and pull the *Sirene* around.

And that's how we got ourselves crosswise on the tiny Winkel River, our bow poking over the left bank, our stern nearly unbudgeable on the right. Spectators soon began arriving—by Volkswagen, bicycle, and on foot. One old man suggested that just beyond the next little footbridge there was a wide spot where we might have better luck. (Naturally, he then disappeared.)

Jarrett ran to the farmhouse near the footbridge to call the bridgekeeper; having just awakened, he looked out his window at the masts of the enormous *Sirene* on his tiny river and decided we were all a bit crazy. He suggested that not only could she open the bridge herself but she could also pay herself the toll he usually collected.

After some fumbling, Jarrett succeeded in opening the bridge, and the *Sirene* plowed its way through the mud to a slightly wider spot, where we attempted again to swing the boat around with lines ashore. It was a hot morning, and the bugs in that reedy, weedy riverbank area were out in force. Was this what George had meant in his brochure by "light crew work"?

We held a summit conference with George and, after a lot of head-scratching and bug-slapping, concluded that there was nothing to do but back the boat the two miles downriver to our "essential right turn." Since most of the time the *Sirene*'s rudder and screw would be buried in the mud, it was logical to assume that George would have no steerageway. This would necessitate getting a tow to drag the helpless, hapless, 22-ton boat through the muddy bottom and down the river.

"And where are we going to get a tow?" we asked. George just looked at us, each holding a line—one to the stern and one to the bow—and laughed. Jarrett looked at Stan incredulously, but he wasn't moved by her femininity. She scurried over the footbridge to the other bank, and we both began grunting and pulling, pulling and grunting. The sun rose higher, the bugs got thicker, and the cursing from the banks (both sides) grew louder and meaner.

Numerous groundings and considerable huffing and puffing later, we were back at the "essential right turn," where George took over the steering—and almost hit a houseboat. By this time, of course, we were aground again, and George took the long boathook down to pole our 56-foot gondola around the corner. With every bit of progress he made came the gloppy sounds of the mud suction as the bottom of the river tried to hold the *Sirene* in place.

We sat back and enjoyed the pleasant sight of George in his plight, feeling more like guests again. This was our last day aboard the *Sirene,* and soon we would be clean again, laundered again, and rested again. Soon we would be sitting back in comfortable chairs, happily reminiscing about George, the *Sirene,* and our Dutch odyssey.

In our two weeks afloat in the Netherlands we had passed through nine of her twelve provinces and had experienced joyfully and personally her tulips and daffodils, windmills and moorhens, *skutsjes* and *boyiers,* dunes and dikes, thatched roofs and peat bogs, Oude Jenever and smoked eel, houseboats and houseplants, water gates and picture windows, wooden skates and milk cans, carillons and communal washlines and country-fair locks, teahouses and willow trees, history and heresy, huge barges and humpbacked bridges, reed banks and Rembrandt—and, most important, her people: earthy, real, proud, and free.

Some Practical Information

The beauty and charm of the Dutch waterways are matched by the scope and variety of available facilities, services, and information. Nowhere else in Europe will you find such hospitable, well-organized, and efficiently executed tourist services.

Nearly every village and town—including the tiniest—is located on a canal, a river, or a lake. All the elements, from the local quayside to the harbormaster, the village tourist information office, and the wonderful hospitality of the people, combine to make waterway cruising in Holland an unqualified joy. The Dutch themselves fully utilize their own waterways (in contrast to many other European countries, where the waterways are used principally by visitors), so you will have the opportunity to live and travel among the people in their leisure times.

Travel costs for self-drive boatspeople are modest. There are no charges for canal cruising other than an occasional request, in the form of a wooden shoe swung on a string from a lock or bridge, for a small coin. Docking charges at quayside, collected by the harbormaster, are minimal, and there are opportunities to anchor all along the waterways.

There are three principal organizations at your service for information and advice, each competently staffed by knowledgeable, multilingual personnel:

The Netherlands National Tourist Office is the official government tourist agency, handling all types of tourism in Holland. Upon request, they will furnish a listing of available boat rentals, as well as excellent maps and pamphlets. Three pamphlets are of particular interest to waterway visitors: "Holland, Watersports Paradise," "Holland—the Dutch Coast," and "Friesland Watersports."

Netherlands National Tourist Offices are located in five countries:

17 Mauritskade
The Hague, 2005

143 New Bond Street
London W1, England

576 Fifth Avenue
New York, N.Y. 10036

91 rue de Richelieu
Paris 2^e, France

651 Market Street
San Francisco, Calif.

Schildergasse 84
5-Cologne, West Germany

Royal Dutch Touring Club ANWB is the principal tourist organization in the Netherlands and the best source for excellent, detailed charts of the Dutch waterway system. The ANWB Waterkaart (waterchart) series consists of sixteen large folding charts, drawn on a scale of 1:50,000, with each chart covering a specific region. ANWB also sells, at modest cost, two waterway guides: one (published annually) lists hours of operation and other pertinent details for all locks and bridges; the other sets forth the navigational rules of the road, waterway signals, and so on.

In addition to the above materials, ANWB offers pamphlets that list boats available for charter and camping areas accessible to the waterways. It also offers a list of sailing schools, some of them world famous, with courses ranging from a single day's instruction to comprehensive programs lasting several weeks.

The main office of the Royal Dutch Touring Club ANWB is at Wassenaarseweg 220, The Hague. Regional ANWB offices are located in all Dutch cities.

The Tourist Information Office (VVV), with branch offices in even the smallest towns and villages, serves the tourist on a more local level. Once your itinerary has been established, you can write to the VVV of each town along your route for specific information about that town or region. One VVV publication of particular interest to the waterway tourist is the "Touristic Guide to Friesland," available from the VVV, Friesland-Leeuwarden, Stationplatz 1, Leeuwarden. The VVV will also assist with reservations and other specific needs throughout your trip.

One can cruise the Dutch waterways in three different types of boats:

SELF-DRIVE CHARTER. Motor and sailboats, from 16 to 46 feet, are available throughout Holland. A list of self-drive firms is available from both the ANWB and the Netherlands National Tourist Office.

One of the oldest established self-drive firms, operating since 1960, is *Vijn Yacht Charters,* with a modern and efficient base at Sneek, in Friesland. Their fleet of 18 boats (14 motorboats and 4 sailboats) is diesel-powered and well maintained, and their personnel speak fluent English.

Approximate costs are:

		June-Sept.	Other
35-foot (10.5 m) motorboat	6–8 berths	$540–675	$400–525
30-foot (9 m) motorboat	5 berths	$350–425	$250–350
30-foot (9 m) sailboat	5–6 berths	$320–400	$225–300
22-foot (6.5 m) sailboat	4 berths	$210–250	$130–195

Fuel is not included in the above prices.

LUXURY HOTEL BARGE. Traveling on a newly converted barge offers you a more carefree and relaxed way to cruise the Dutch rivers and canals.

Floating Through Europe, Inc., 501 Madison Avenue, New York, N.Y. 10022, operates the *Lys* along the fabled rivers and canals of Holland. Carrying 12 passengers and a crew of 4, its fully inclusive rates include 6 days on the barge, all meals plus table wine or Dutch beer, large staterooms each with private facilities and showers, a high standard of Dutch-Continental food, and a chauffeured bus to take passengers on sightseeing and shopping excursions.

	June-Sept.	Other
Double cabin	$460–490	$420–460
Twin cabin	$440	$400
Single cabin	$520	$480
Entire boat	$5,200	$4,800

PRIVATE CAPTAINED YACHT. Here's a very individual and personal way to cruise the waterways, suitable for a small family or a group of four to six persons—guided by a knowledgeable, experienced skipper (usually the boat's owner). The craft range in size from 35 to 60 feet. It is essential that pre-trip correspondence discuss fully the subjects of costs, itinerary, the guide services the captain will perform, and the crewing services expected of you. Fees for a skippered yacht can run as high as $1,800 per week for a party of four, excluding food. Information concerning captained yachts is available from the ANWB and from Floating Through Europe, Inc.

Waterway maps and guides are available from the Netherlands National Tourist Office, the Royal Dutch Touring Club ANWB, and from Floating Through Europe, Inc., which maintains an extensive inventory of maps and publications.

5

*Adventure in
Schleswig-Holstein*

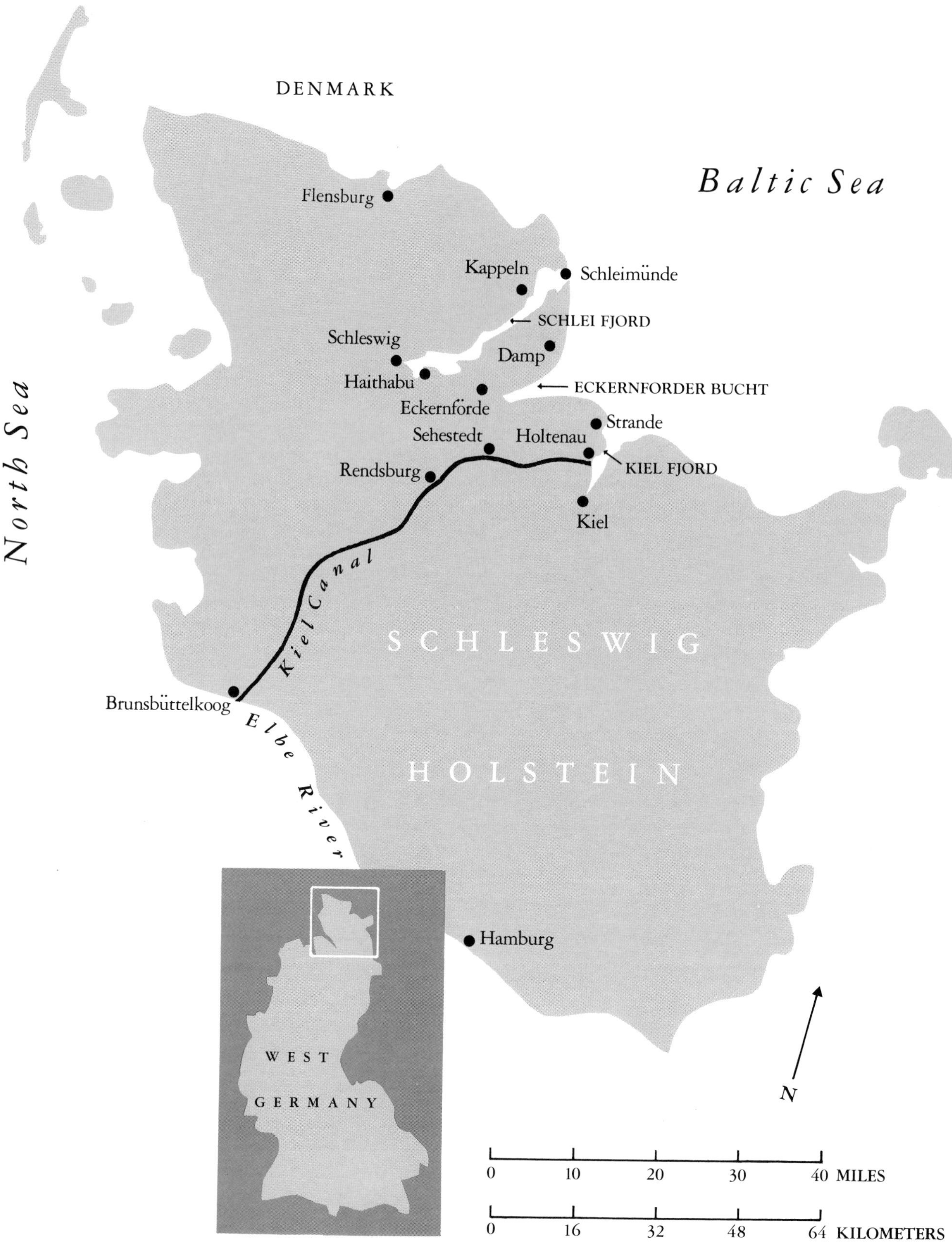

DENMARK

Baltic Sea

Flensburg

Kappeln   Schleimünde

← SCHLEI FJORD

Schleswig   Damp

North Sea

Haithabu   ← ECKERNFORDER BUCHT

Eckernförde   Strande

Sehestedt   Holtenau

Rendsburg   ← KIEL FJORD

Kiel

S C H L E S W I G

H O L S T E I N

Kiel Canal

Brunsbüttelkoog

Elbe River

Hamburg

WEST

GERMANY

N

| 0 | 10 | 20 | 30 | 40 MILES |

| 0 | 16 | 32 | 48 | 64 KILOMETERS |

The Kiel Canal and the Schlei Fjord

From the deck of the handsome, white *Olympia,* a 1,500-passenger luxury liner, we could dimly see the shore of northern Germany appear on the horizon in the soft morning light. We had boarded the ship the evening before, a Friday in early September, in Gothenburg, Sweden, just in time to find our cabin among the ship's 700, have a late dinner in one of her two restaurants, and take a turn around her enormous decks with their slot machines, duty-free liquor and gift shops, and lively bars.

While this overnight trip across the open waters of the Baltic on a high-seas speedster hardly qualified as inland waterway cruising, it added an interesting dimension to our otherwise leisurely crawl across Europe.

We were headed for Kiel, once Germany's most important naval port, birthplace of many of the world's largest ships (and the men who built them), home of the world-famous Kiel Week regattas, one of the great yachting capitals of the world, and the departure point for our next cruise. Since 1882 more than 600 vessels of all sorts —sail, motor, and muscle-driven—from all over the world have competed here each June for the legendary Kiel Week awards. It's the greatest yachting event in Continental Europe, and it provides the setting for social, diplomatic, and cultural exchanges often attended by the president of the Federal Republic and many of Europe's social elite.

Kiel is also the provincial capital of the land of Schleswig-Holstein, probably one of the less traveled regions of Europe. Located on the Jutland peninsula in northern Germany, between the Baltic Sea and the North Sea, it's as far north as Moscow or Labrador. A vast plain of marshes, islands, dikes, and poor, sandy soil, it is rugged and very quiet country.

Schleswig-Holstein was the home of the ancestors of Beowulf—perhaps of the ancestors of half the New World—and the starting point for countless Viking adventures. Here, in Germany's own fjord country, the Baltic has pushed its way far inland in several places, providing numerous waterway cruising possibilities.

Our journey for the next week would take us through two of Schleswig-Holstein's most interesting waterways. On the legend-dotted, history-silted Schlei Fjord, we would cruise from the Baltic inland to the fascinating city of Schleswig. Then we would cruise the 61 miles (98 km) of the Kiel Canal, the busiest waterway in the world—busier even than the Panama and Suez canals combined. Some 80,000 ships from 52 nations cruise this stretch of water every year—one every eight minutes, twenty-four hours a day.

While we sipped our morning coffee in the modern, glass-walled salon, the *Olympia* passed through the wide opening between Kiel's twin lighthouses and entered the broad Kiel Fjord, known familiarly as the Roadstead. On our left, in the suburban village of Laboe, rose the 280-foot tower of the German Naval War Memorial, shaped like the stern of a great ship. To our right stood the Olympic Center at Schilksee. Built for the 1972 Sailing Olympics, the Olympiahaven is an enormous, modern yachting complex that includes a saltwater swimming pool, sauna, gymnasiums, fine shops, a hotel, a café, and a 330-yard promenade that follows the fjord shore.

At 10 A.M. we disembarked and took a taxi up the waterfront to pick up our charter boat. Along the way we passed the College of Design, the art gallery (containing important works by North German expressionists), the zoological and ethnographic museums, the oldest botanic gardens in Germany (founded in 1665), yacht harbors, sandy beaches, handsome old beechwoods, and finally the Hindenburg Quay, the two-mile promenade along the Kiel Fjord, offering views of the harbor on one side and shaded parkland on the other.

The road climbed 140 feet over the Hochbrucke, the first of the high steel bridges that cross the Kiel Canal, and we gasped on our first view of the enormous chambers of the Holtenau Locks—as long as the Empire State Building is high!

We took the rest of the morning to explore the open, modern, and hospitable city and arrived at Charterboat Nord/Sud around noon. There we were greeted by the English-speaking owner and introduced to our Fram 25, a double-ended Norwegian motor cruiser that (it was claimed) slept four in its tiny forward cabin. We were about to learn some new twists in small-boat layouts.

The galley appeared to be located *under the helmsman's seat,* which folded forward to reveal a tiny, round sink with a hand pump and a compact two-burner alcohol stove (both quite satisfactory). What stumped us, however, was that there was no refrigerator—not even an ice chest; we hadn't brought one, and we didn't look forward to eating from cans for an entire week. There was an enclosed "head" in the cabin, and there was sufficient cupboard space for provisions. The afterdeck had a canvas rollaway cover, both for inclement weather and for nighttime privacy. We would carry 40 liters of fresh water and 160 liters of diesel fuel. Since both tanks were located on the starboard side, the boat listed decidedly to that side when the tanks were full.

With provisioning, setting up, and getting briefed, it was late afternoon before we were able to get under way.

Heading into Open Waters

The beautiful Kiel Fjord was glassy calm and pleasant as we worked our way slowly up the Roadstead past the villages of Heikendorf, Laboe, Schilksee, and Strande. It felt good to have the wheel in our own hands, good to be headed into open waters.

Turning west, we followed the coast past Eckernförde, a city with the oldest spa on the Baltic (established 1816), full of narrow streets, crooked houses, and a seventeenth-century church dedicated to St. Nicholas. Sunset found us approaching the shore of the town so uninspiringly named Damp, the home of one of the newest Baltic Sea resorts, Damp 2000. Covering 15 acres, it consists of a year-round holiday complex of apartment houses and bungalows with every sort of indoor and outdoor recreational facility imaginable.

The harbor was easy to spot, lit by a string of colored lights hung from stem to stern of the 120-foot derelict fishing boat embedded in the sand alongside the harbor entrance. We set out to explore the vast and amazing marina, with its adjacent high-rise luxury apartments, three heated pools, children's playgrounds, kindergarten, babysitter service, solarium, numerous restaurants, pubs, cinemas, well-tended gardens, and a huge "surfing pool" complete with simulated waves.

At 9:15 the next morning, having made our settlement with the harbor master, who was warmly hospitable and spoke excellent English, we cast off and headed north, up the coast toward Schleimünde, which the Vikings called Mynnaesby, or Mouthpoint Town—the mouthpoint of the Schlei Fjord.

We arrived at a sturdy-looking breakwater that seemed to match up with the Schleimünde indicated on our chart and, turning into the harbor, found ourselves in calm waters. A large navy ship, we noticed, was following about half a mile behind us.

We never saw the small sign that said VERBOTEN.

The One-Gun Salute

Counting a dozen transport and cargo ships, several submarines, and various tenders, we realized that we had entered a large navy base, yet we continued purposefully on our way, looking for the continuation of the Schlei. Only when we reached the end of the harbor and still had found no opening did it dawn on us that we might have committed a slight navigational error. Noticing that ours was the only nonmilitary craft in sight, Jarrett suggested that perhaps we weren't supposed to be there.

"If they didn't want us here, they would have turned us away at the breakwater. They'd have a guard or something. Anyway, we're leaving," Stan responded sagely.

He was interrupted by the loud report of a rifle. Jarrett was unable to muster anything more intelligent than a squeal. A green flare burned brightly only 20 feet in front of our little boat, which seemed to shy like a nervous horse. Had we wandered into the middle of target practice? And who was the target?

There ensued a scene of some confusion. Tower guards were bellowing at us, "You vill go to dock number seeex." A launch full of sailors came alongside to tell us to get lost. Finally, a businesslike tugboat came to retrieve us—forcibly if necessary. It turned out not to be necessary; we followed obediently to Dock Number Six.

A reception party of three awaited us. We could see the "brass" shimmering from 200 yards away.

"Oh no," Jarrett despaired. "They're going to put us away. No one will ever know what happened to us."

"Good grief, Jarrett. Put away the camera and tape recorder and be quiet."

The "brass" had been thoughtful enough to provide an interpreter, who politely asked for our passports. Having made quite complete notes on our identity, and having determined that we were probably *not* dangerous spies, the interpreter urged us to leave at once. The military police were on the way, he said, and if they arrived and found us, we'd have "big trouble."

No Fram 25 ever moved faster. As we pulled out past the control tower with its green flare guns and bullhorns, our little boat seemed to leap out of the water, straining to escape the military police, whose siren we imagined we could hear approaching.

A silly way to start our trip, we agreed as we sped through the breakwaters of Olpenitz Naval Harbor—a couple of *Dummkopfs* fleeing past the VERBOTEN sign.

The Gentle Schlei

At Schleimünde, not more than 500 yards beyond the naval base, two small peninsulas converge like gentle pincers, trying unsuccessfully to keep the sea from its inevitable course inland. Here stood the little fishing village of Maasholm, a jumble of red roofs over some pretty green houses in a mere street-and-a-half of civilization built around a fishing harbor. Herons could be seen standing in the shallows all along the Schlei, usually on one leg, blinking in bewilderment at the mid-morning sun.

Densely wooded banks soon closed in on the fjord, taming it, twisting it, and giving it a special green wildness. One lone sea gull followed us, leaving its seafaring companions behind in the Baltic. Rounding a deep, graceful bend to the south, we caught sight of Kappeln, the ancient capital of the old Anglia, home of the Angles. Kappeln was established at the first narrows where the Schlei could conveniently be crossed and defended.

The long curve of the town's waterfront held a dozen fishing cutters, some old schooners, a black barge up on the ways for repairs, and a couple of rusted tramp steamers. The town rose steeply in terraces, its winding main street and busy market-place a clutter of white stone, red tile, and oddly gabled rooflines. The big red-brick weighbridge poured a continual river of sweet-smelling grain down from its tall silos to the tramps and schooners below.

It was about noon as we slipped under the bridge at Kappeln, past the yacht haven, and anchored for a scenic open-air lunch of peppered salami, local cheeses, aromatic brown bread, and German wine. Across the Schlei stood a thatched farm-house surrounded by meandering sheep.

An hour later we weighed anchor and continued past the shipbuilding town of Arnis. Here the Schlei made another gentle curve to the southwest and opened to a straight, wide roadstead, giving us a clear view five miles ahead, past the villages of Winnemark and Karschau (with its thatched houses and reed-lined banks), Bienebek and Pagero facing each other further upstream, and Ketelsby and Sieseby beyond. The banks were lined with incredibly green fields and deep green forests, and we wondered why those lucky Angles had ever wanted to leave here.

At Missunde the channel twisted and doubled back southwestward again, disappearing around a peninsula, a slip of land dotted with summer cottages high on the cliffs and boats bobbing at moorings below. We made another kinky curve westward and then caught our first breathtaking glimpse of the city of Schleswig. It was still six miles in the distance, across the Grosse Breite and the Kleine Breite, two beautiful connected lakes; however, we could see the four spires of the Gothic Schleswig Cathedral dominating the skyline and the city spread helter-skelter in a wide circle around it.

We had company on our voyage into Schleswig: a flock of gulls trailed us, swooping and soaring above our wake, catching the elusive air currents from our passage through the strong wind. Their fine wings, aristocratic bodies, and narrow heads, along with their beautiful brown markings, distinguished them from ordinary sea gulls. They continued to soar and dip along behind us, peeling off occasionally to make a run alongside the boat, always staying close to us, until we entered Schleswig.

Passing through the narrow channel between the Grosse Breite and the Kleine Breite, we followed the buoys to Haddeby, site of the ruins of an early town, once

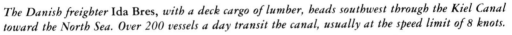

The Danish freighter **Ida Bres,** *with a deck cargo of lumber, heads southwest through the Kiel Canal toward the North Sea. Over 200 vessels a day transit the canal, usually at the speed limit of 8 knots.*

one of the greatest trading centers of the early medieval world. The main trading place of the Swedish Vikings in northern Europe, it was known as Haithabu, or Place on the Heath.

The Rise and Fall of Haithabu

Here, at the end of the Dark Ages, in the year 900, on the narrowest part of the Jutland peninsula, the Vikings established a much-traveled portage route for ships between the Baltic and the North Sea.

This route was one of the earliest known ways of avoiding the dangerous passage around the northern tip of the Jutland peninsula, known as Skagen, where the breakers of the North Sea and the Baltic converge with raw fury. This is the "hoary tip" that in modern times proved so dangerous that the Kiel Canal was finally built to bypass it. One can imagine that these earlier sailors would have found Skagen a formidable obstacle to their westward journey. The dangers become all too clear when one learns that, before the Kiel Canal was opened in 1895, ships were being lost in the passage around Skagen at the rate of 200 per year.

A causeway of smooth, rounded logs was laid across the narrow isthmus from Haithabu to Hollingstedt and the Treene, allowing ships to be rolled forward, pulled by a pair of hefty horses and steadied by men walking along either side. Every yard or two, men would lift the log that had come clear of the stern and drag it forward to place it before the bow. In this way ships moved overland the eight long miles to the Treene, in one of the most enterprising transport arrangements of the early medieval world.

Today only the great walls that once defended the town still stand, some 25–30 feet tall, for the visitor to see on the banks of the Haddeby Noor. And across the waters of the Schlei stands Schleswig, residence of the former bishops of Schleswig and the dukes of Schleswig-Holstein. The bishops built the striking St. Peter's Cathedral in the eleventh century and enlarged it throughout the Middle Ages; the dukes built their first residence here, Schloss Gottorf, in 1268. Today the two imposing landmarks, so beautifully situated on the banks of the Schlei, dominate the town.

As we drew close to Schleswig, we reached the Moeveninsel, or Isle of Gulls. Haunted with legends of medieval castles, magic cowslips that bloom once every hundred years, and strange nocturnal lights that glow from mysterious sources, the Moeveninsel was teeming with birds and looked to us like a perfectly ordinary wildlife preserve. But under the trampled grass covered with those oddly aristocratic-looking gulls lay the foundations of what is said to be the castle of the wicked Duke Abel. The gulls, we were told, are the restless spirits of the noblemen he employed to murder his brother, the good King Erik.

The island has been a bird sanctuary for more than a century, and for at least that long the city has appointed one man "king of the gulls" and assigned him to protect the birds who come here from the Baltic every spring to nest and breed. He collects the rare eggs, little olive-green things with black splotches, which are a gastronomic specialty of Schleswig and can be found in season in the local butcher and poultry shops.

So many legends are whispered about this magic place that it's hardly possible to recount them all; it remains an island of tantalizing mystery and lost riches beyond description. The birds that had followed us all the way from Weseby cried a mournful, gull-like adieu and peeled off from their course above our wake to land on the island, where they entered freely into the cacaphony of shrieks characteristic of the gull community in general.

Following the buoys, we gave the Moeveninsel a wide berth to avoid the silted shallows and rounded to the yacht haven in the shadow of the well-known Strandhall Hotel. Then, in the waning gray light of late afternoon, we walked the shady footpath toward Schleswig's highest spire, that of St. Peter's Cathedral.

St. Peter's contains one of the most famous of all art works in Germany, the Bordesholm Altar. The piece was carved by Hans Brüggemann in 1514–1521 for the Augustine monastery in Bordesholm and brought to Schleswig in 1666. A contemporary of Albrecht Dürer, Brüggemann carved this richly ornamented, massive oak altarpiece, depicting 392 figures with tender human features and rich traditional costumes, with a painstaking care that makes it worthy of the accolade "masterpiece."

Just a few steps beyond the church we found Holm, the old fishermen's quarter. Here the rose-bedecked houses were grouped snugly around the twelfth-century fishermen's burial ground below the 350-foot tower of the cathedral.

At dinner in the Strandhall Hotel overlooking the harbor, we were presented the wine list with a loud "thump," the waiter heaving onto the table a book of 244 wine labels, each lovingly placed on a separate page, representing the cellar of our hosts.

The third morning of our trip found us exploring the museums of Gottorf Castle, which number among their exhibits the world's oldest surviving seafaring vessel of considerable size: the Nydam Boat, a superb relic dating from the fourth century A.D. It's exactly the kind of craft that the Angles and the Saxons used to cross the North Sea to the British Isles in the fifth century, carrying as many as forty-five people, with their provisions and weapons.

Leaving Schleswig at noon, we returned as we had come, past the haunted and haunting little Isle of Gulls. Late that afternoon we were headed back into the Baltic, and by sunset we were well inside the welcoming arms of the entrance to Kiel Fjord and headed for the Strande yacht basin and the company of handsome 40-foot and 60-foot "goldplated" sail and motor yachts.

The next morning a heavy blanket of fog shrouded everything but the mournful bleating of the harbor foghorns. We worked our way from the Strande toward Kiel and the Holtenau Locks, which lead to the Nord-Ostsee Kanal, known to the world as the Kiel Canal.

The Busy Kiel Canal

Built between 1887 and 1895 at a cost of well over 500 million gold marks, the Kiel Canal replaced several earlier canals that bypassed the long and dangerous passage around the Jutland peninsula and its "hoary tip," Skagen.

We had already witnessed the relics of earler efforts to avoid Skagen by means of horse-drawn ships and roller-logs at the once prosperous port of Haithabu. Now we were about to embark on a 61-mile (98 km) frenzy of modernity on a scale sufficient to accommodate modern naval and cargo ships representing 52 nations, in their passage from one sea to another. The canal operates twenty-four hours a day and is illuminated at night to a startling brightness.

The Kiel Canal is one of the true wonders of man, a passage cut through the land with a single-mindedness of purpose of which only man is capable. There is no mistaking for a caprice of nature its blunt, straight, perfectly even banks, its four-story, concrete-sided locks and towering doors, its silent mechanization and wonderful efficiency—no more than it is possible to mistake the towering behemoths that travel

Yachts are usually waiting for the bridge to open at Kappeln near the entrance to the Schlei, a long arm of the Baltic Sea that reaches to Schleswig. During the summer months a ferry runs from Kappeln to Sønderborg, Denmark, carrying visitors between the two countries.

it for ballerinas. The Kiel Canal may not be a scenic wonderland, but it certainly is an education, the perfect antithesis and complement to most of the other canals and waterways we experienced on our journey through Europe.

By noon we were approaching the myriad light-towers, radio masts, and semaphores that transmit silent but eye-catching welcome or warning to the ships entering the four great chambers at Holtenau Locks. The two gates to the right, the Alte Schleusen, are older and smaller than the others, and we had been directed to head for these, since the newer and bigger chambers (1,082 feet long!) are reserved for large cargo ships.

It seemed unusually quiet as we approached the Alte Schleusen; there wasn't another ship in sight. We moved toward the great doors, humble and mute as Dorothy before the Wizard of Oz, waiting to be admitted to the chamber. Did they see us?

The red light clearly told us we were not yet welcome.

After ten minutes we were admitted to the great Holtenau Locks—and found we had the entire chamber to ourselves. Where were all those towering monster boats we were expecting? Where were all the Russian and Panamanian freighters? Where was the babble of foreign tongues, the excitement as bow met stern and topsides touched the heights of the great cavernous walls?

It seemed it just wasn't to be—no parade of proud and powerful vessels—at least not in this lock! We felt as though we had been invited to a great formal ball and then arrived to discover we were the only guests. We had been cheated of the spectacle. Well, we still had three more chances.

We moved to the front of the lock, the doors closed behind us with a resounding hollow thump of finality, and we found a place to tie up to the floating docks along the starboard wall. The floating docks are simply wooden rafts that float two inches high in the water; when we jumped onto them from our deck, they submerged under our weight, giving our shoes and the entire mossy surface a slick wetting down. Nevertheless they were a convenience, preventing us from having to climb steel ladders to the sky at the top of the lock chamber to find a bollard.

The chamber resounded with silence as slowly, without heraldry, the boat began to rise. It stopped rising as quietly as it had started, and the doors ahead opened ponderously and mysteriously, revealing a wide expanse of the heroically scaled yet completely deserted canal ahead.

After a long straightaway, we rounded a sweeping, freewaylike turn, which revealed a further expanse of empty waterway. A rusted gray steel cargo ship, the *Sambeek* from Amsterdam, was moored on the left bank—no other craft was in sight. Where were we, for heaven's sake—Death Valley?

Near the lovely old Lensau Bridge, a turn-of-the-century suspension bridge in brick and steel, a fisherman's shack occupied the right bank. Nets were hung out to dry, and a fishing skiff was moored on the canal bank. This broad stretch of canal, lined with pastures, fields, and dense woods, ended far ahead with a broad, majestic curve to the south. The little red-brick villages of Sehestedt and Ladestelle faced each other, throwing occasional thatched-roof glances across the canal and conversing via ferry.

In mid-afternoon we slid off the canal into the Obereidersee and headed for Rendsburg past enormous shipbuilding piers where we could see large freighters being born in clanking and banging heavy industry. A deep bay filled with sailing and power yachts dipped away to the south. This was the protected yacht basin called the Regatta Verein Rendsburg. We turned in toward the 88-year-old refuge (one of the few the Kiel Canal has to offer) and passed avenues of poplars and a beautiful public park with wide expanses of plush green lawn and children's bicycles.

A Haven at Rendsburg

A plump, elderly lady welcomed us in German as we pulled into the yacht haven, introduced herself as Frau Thomas, took our lines, and asked if we would like the baker to deliver fresh rolls or bread in the morning.

Rendsburg is an ancient town that occupies a strategic position at the crossroads of the main highway from Denmark and the Eider River, forming the original natural frontier between the duchies of Schleswig and Holstein. Founded to protect the Eider crossing, and having survived the many transfers between Danish and German rule (the last of which took place in 1862), Rendsburg is now a busy industrial center.

Rendsburg's old-fashioned railway bridge has become a curiosity because of its ingenious loop railway that takes speeding trains up, up, up, high above the height of the tallest ship's masts—a colossal 459 feet above the Kiel Canal. A transporter, slung by a complex cable system from the underside of the bridge, clatters along ten feet above the water, dodging ship traffic and carrying passengers and cars from Osterrönfeld on the opposite bank to shopping services and friends and relatives in Rendsburg.

Rendsburg contains some miraculously preserved sixteenth-century buildings. We walked into town to explore and found the old section tightly clustered around the sixteenth-century Town Hall, which arches over the wavy cobbled street of the main square. Magnificent half-timbered houses bore dates of 1555 and 1643; the romantic Hotel Landskneck, dating from 1541, was both half-timbered and elaborately painted with figures of jolly round men doing everything from reading important-looking books to exposing their ample behinds.

Back at the yacht basin, Frau Thomas was waiting to show us her Guest Book, full of globe-trotting private yachts and their crews, funny cartoons, photographs, and greetings in every language that knows the water. We were invited to add our own legacy to this vast and colorful canvas of yachtsmen, which we humbly did as Frau Thomas bent low over her kitchen table with us to watch each stroke of the pen.

Frau Thomas had recommended the Hotel Bahnhof for the "best meal in town," and there, amid the sparsely occupied tables in a brightly lit dining room, we enjoyed regional specialties, among them Gefüllte Schweinerippchen—pork chops stuffed with raisins, apples, and toast and laced with rum.

Wednesday morning, the fifth day of our cruise, we woke early and left Rendsburg before nine o'clock. The sun was beginning to warm the early-morning chill that had left a coating of frost on our deck and topsides as we gathered our fresh rolls from Frau Thomas and pushed off for the Kiel Canal. We had just 40 miles to travel to Brunsbüttelkoog, at the mouth of the River Elbe, where the canal meets the North Sea.

Stormy Weather on the Elbe

By mid-afternoon the weather had turned dark and threatening, and we were in the midst of a driving thunderstorm as we arrived at the Brunsbüttelkoog Locks. We joined three large cargo ships that had already tied up, and at last we were able to enjoy the steel skyline and the cacophony of languages that we had anticipated throughout the trip.

A fisherman mends his eelpot on the shore of Herring Cove at Schleswig on the Schlei. The low, double-ended skiffs on the beach are local craft, reminders in form of the old Nydam ship on view across Schleswig in Gottorp Castle. The Nydam ship, dating from the fourth century, is 23 meters long by 3 meters wide. It carried a crew of 36 oarsmen.

Leaving the locks, we entered the Elbe and bore right for about 100 yards to reach the shallow inlet that runs into the town of Brunsbüttelkoog. We found a berth along the right bank of the inlet, busy with children in prams and rowing skiffs, and went ashore to stretch our legs and learn more about Brunsbüttelkoog—which is mentioned in the guidebooks only as the terminus of the Kiel Canal.

Brunsbüttelkoog surprised and delighted us by being the German version of an English country town. Little canals shaded generously by willows ran through the winding streets, which were lined with gracious old timber-trimmed homes, crooked sidewalks meandering around front yards, and a great many flowers. Lace-curtained windows framed potted plants and violets; little alleyways led back to children's sandboxes; a tiny humpbacked bridge spanned the tiny canal, offering a languid scene framed by willows leaning over the water above a rustic old tar-painted punt. Sunlight and warmth streamed through the leaves and onto the little boat.

Thursday dawned ominous, cold, and windy—*very* windy, with great thunderheads moving swiftly across the gray sky. We were up and off by 7:30 A.M., our little engine straining as it pushed us into the 35-knot headwind coming up the inlet. As we moved through the opening into the junction of the Elbe and the North Sea, we were suddenly hit by ferocious seas, and we began nosediving down one wave and burying our bow in the next. We had only a hundred yards to travel to reach the Brunsbüttelkoog Locks, but it was apparently going to be a long hundred yards. And, as if to emphasize her disapproval of our little scheme, Mother Nature produced a downpour we could hardly see through.

We were making headway toward our destination, but as we neared the gates the seas began coming at us from every direction simultaneously. Red lights were flashing at the gates; we could see several ships inside the lock, but nothing seemed to be happening.

After twenty minutes of being aimlessly tossed around, with no action yet in the lock, we had had quite enough. We decided to try the other doors, those of the new locks, where we could see green lights flashing and several large ships maneuvering to enter. Although we had been told that the new locks were strictly for the "big boys," the open gates under the circumstances looked too inviting. After all, the worst they could do was to say *nein.*

We waited until three large cargo vessels, each about 250 feet long, had entered. Then, from behind us, steamed the awesome *Navalina* from Hamburg—all 500 feet of her. Her bow towered above us like a ten-story building, flared out like a cliff overhanging the sea. We respectfully awaited the monster's pleasure, not wanting to offend. She was pleased to enter, thank you, ahead of us, and by the time she had, a red 130-foot German barge, fully loaded, pushed inside the breakwater.

We looked at the barge, then at the space left in the lock. They just about matched. It didn't look as though there would be much room left over—and you don't argue with 130 feet of loaded barge. So we stood back, and in she went.

Now the coast was clear, and we followed the barge into the lock at a safe distance. She left us no room behind her, but we could see ample space between her bow and the *Navalina*'s stern, so we lithely slithered in toward the opening. A wave from behind us lifted our stern and gave us a firm push into the space as Jarrett, poised at the bow, prepared to jump onto the floating wooden dock. Stan saw her jump—and disappear!

As Stan bounded to the bow to see what had happened, Jarrett was just picking herself up from the slime-covered and waterlogged floating dock. It had all been one motion: the jump, the landing on both feet, and the second landing flat on her back in two inches of icy water. It was a soft landing, Jarrett said, for the floating docks presented little resistance, yet she looked a bit dazed. She was still clinging to the bow line, but the stern had gotten away. Sailors from the nearby red barge threw us a heavy line from lockside high above our heads, and Stan pulled the stern back in.

The sailors then began waving their arms urgently, signaling that the lockkeeper wanted us further forward, away from the *Navalina*'s enormous propeller. There was another space for us ahead of the *Navalina* and behind a Baltic freighter. We were thankful for the thoughtfulness; we didn't relish being converted into mincemeat when the *Navalina* began moving.

We threw the sailors their barge-size stern line, a soggy Jarrett climbed back aboard, ready to make her slimy jump again, and we worked our way alongside and past the *Navalina*—past mile upon mile of steel hull punctuated by rivets and rust stains—until we caught sight of an open dock space. This time our landing was more successful and less eventful.

Once secured, it dawned on us: we were in the new lock with the big boys, and no one had yet asked us to leave! We were in a steel Grand Canyon, neatly tucked into a tiny crevice, allowed to watch the monsters while they slept. And we were very quiet, careful not to wake them.

Stan climbed the steel ladder built into the concrete lock wall until he seemed just a tiny speck on the gray canvas sky. Then he disappeared, one shoe at a time, to talk with the lockkeeper and crews ashore. Jarrett contemplated the skyline from below, looking straight up at the underside of the *Navalina*'s great flared bow, feeling as though she knew her intimately—every rusty rivet, every barnacle on her waterline, and the several-ton anchor and chain hanging high overhead.

Stan descended the ladder just as a great bell began to toll, announcing the opening of the front gates. Following the Baltic freighter at a respectful distance, we noticed the time: 9:15 A.M. It had taken us nearly two hours to enter the canal.

Heavy Traffic in the Canal

One hour later we neared the first grand curve of the Kiel Canal, the wind coming from behind us in great blasts that picked up the tops of the waves, cast them into spindrift, and flung the spray clear across the canal. The wind made the trees gesticulate wildly and whipped up such a racket with our canvas awning that, standing next to each other, we had to shout to be heard. We had the distinct sensation that we were surfing (theoretically impossible in this kind of boat, whose speed is limited by the design of the hull to seven knots), having covered nine miles in the first hour.

The amount of traffic around us, as though attuned to the elements, had increased almost to the point of frenzy. The four giant cargo ships and the German barge with which we had shared the lock formed a grand procession ahead, and five large freighters and ships passed from the opposite direction. Altogether it was quite a majestic parade; where the canal had seemed a luxuriously overwide boulevard yesterday, it barely seemed big enough today.

Suddenly the little Burg ferry heroically and recklessly steamed out into the canal from the right bank, just in front of us and between two black freighters. Surely the ferry captain knew what he was doing, we thought, as we threw the engine into reverse, still moving at six knots before the wind. Soon the ferry emerged from between the freighters and passed no more than 20 feet ahead of us. With the waves, the spray, the low visibility, the gesticulating trees, the roar of ships' engines, and the

Hamburg lies up the Elbe River from the western terminal of the Kiel Canal at Brunsbüttel. Vessels from around the globe stop in for repairs at the shipyards or huge floating docks, and the fleet of tug boats that ply the harbor would be an impressive armada on any sea.

mad clatter in our wheelhouse, the scene was chaotic indeed.

And so it went, all day long, amid patches of blue sky, periods of rain, fog, and drizzle, and—always—the incessant and merciless wind, keeping the noise level at the top of the decible scale. As the wind increased, boats bound westward for Brunsbüt-telkoog had increasing difficulty making headway upwind. We began to see freighters towing small, underpowered sailboats; carelessly loaded freighters whose cargo-protecting tarps were flapping themselves to shreds; tugs helping small freighters whose bows were knee-deep in their own bow-waves as they struggled along; Russian ships, French ships, German ships. Today we could truly believe that this was the most heavily traveled canal on earth.

By mid-afternoon, as we approached the Holtenau Locks, the sun popped through the clouds to cast an eerie ray of light on some sodden grass before the very dark trees and almost black sky beyond. Fog hung moodily over the water; the wind lashed at us as hard as ever.

The *St. Nazaire,* a Liberian freighter, overtook us, while a Swedish coaster passed from the other direction. We followed the *St. Nazaire* toward the open doors of the big new lock at Holtenau, where a couple of freighters and some large motor-sailers were already waiting. The *St. Nazaire* was just settling in as we cleared the breakwater near the lock—but the flashing green light had changed to red. There's always room for one more 25-footer, we thought, so we pushed on toward the open door—until it began closing decisively in our faces. Not very polite, we remarked, as we quick-reversed.

That appeared to be the only operating lock chamber; the old locks all looked deserted, their lights not flashing, their doors closed, no one in sight. Bobbing around disconsolately, we heard the sound of a loudspeaker, in German, near the old locks. It didn't make sense: we could see no one, but we could hear that disembodied metallic voice firing away indecipherably. After about five minutes we turned around and found one of the lock doors open. No green light beckoned, there was no waving lockkeeper, and now even the metallic voice was silent. Nevertheless we poked our bow in the open doorway, and a tiny shadow inside the glass-walled control tower beckoned us to tie up on the starboard side. It was going to be a repeat of the "little boat in the big lock" trick. Sure enough, the enormous door closed silently behind us, and we were once again in "solitary."

Some minutes later, when we chugged toward the open door to the Kiel Fjord and the Baltic beyond, we gave the lockkeeper a good-natured wave of thanks, but he just waved us away, as if to say, "Ach, get out of my hair!"

Bouncing and rolling madly in the open water of the Kiel Fjord, we made for the nearby docks of Charterboat Nord/Sud and contemplated the full-sized bathtubs, full-sized beds, and man-sized meals that we intended to find for ourselves after this wet, windy, and adventurous day in the company of Liberians, French, Russians, Finns, Belgians, Swedes, Turks, Dutch, Indians, and of course our hosts, the Germans, on the busiest and most colorfully flagged waterway in the world.

Some Practical Information

The Vikings "discovered" Schleswig-Holstein, and today's traveler can do the same through a wide choice of cruising itineraries. There are two principal points of departure.

    1. *Kiel.* One can travel westward through the 61-mile (98 km) length of the Kiel Canal to Brunsbüttelkoog and, from there, continue southeast up the River Elbe to Hamburg. Or you might head north from Brunsbüttelkoog, along Germany's western shore on the North Sea. Alternatively, you might choose to remain in the Baltic waters north of Kiel, the favorite cruising grounds of many experienced sailors, with the Schlei Fjord and the wonderful offshore Danish islands as your destination.

    The established hire firm of *Charterboat Nord/Sud,* Falklandstrasse 1–3, Postfach 9045, 23 Kiel 17, with its base right on the Kiel Fjord (just north of the Kiel Canal entrance at Holtenau), offers a variety of self-drive power and sailboats for weekly hire. The boats range in size from small daysailers and outboard-powered skiffs to 36-foot cruising sailboats. The following are approximate rental rates:

		June-August	Other
25-foot (7.5 m) motorboat	4 berths	$450–550	$375–425
30-foot (9 m) sailboat	5 berths	$650–700	$550–625
36-foot (11 m) sailboat	6 berths	$900–1,100	$775–875

    2. *Schleswig,* situated at the head of the Schlei Fjord, just 29 miles (47 km) north of Kiel, is a bustling and exciting town. It provides the perfect starting point for numerous interesting and memorable side trips along both the Schlei and the Baltic coast. The Schlei Fjord itself, a peaceful fisherman's paradise, offers quiet, unhurried cruising grounds, wonderful secluded anchorages, and memorable fishing and waterside villages along its entire course.

    Sport-Renz, Stadweg 71, Postfach 1345, 238 Schleswig, charters self-drive boats, both power and sail, from their base at Port-Wiking, Schleswig. The following are approximate rental rates:

		June-August	Other
22-foot (6.5 m) sailboat	4 berths	$350–400	$250–325
26-foot (8 m) sailboat	5 berths	$450–500	$325–400
32-foot (10 m) motorboat	6 berths	$550–650	$425–525

Waterway charts can be obtained from:

Floating Through Europe, Inc.
501 Madison Avenue
New York, N.Y. 10022

Deutsches Seekarten
Stubbenhuk 10
Postfach 112045
2 Hamburg 11

Additional information on the region can be obtained from:

German National Tourist Office
630 Fifth Avenue
New York, N.Y. 10020

Office of Tourist Information
Schleswig-Holstein e.V.
Adelheidstrasse 10
23 Kiel

6
*Swedish
Smörgåsbord*

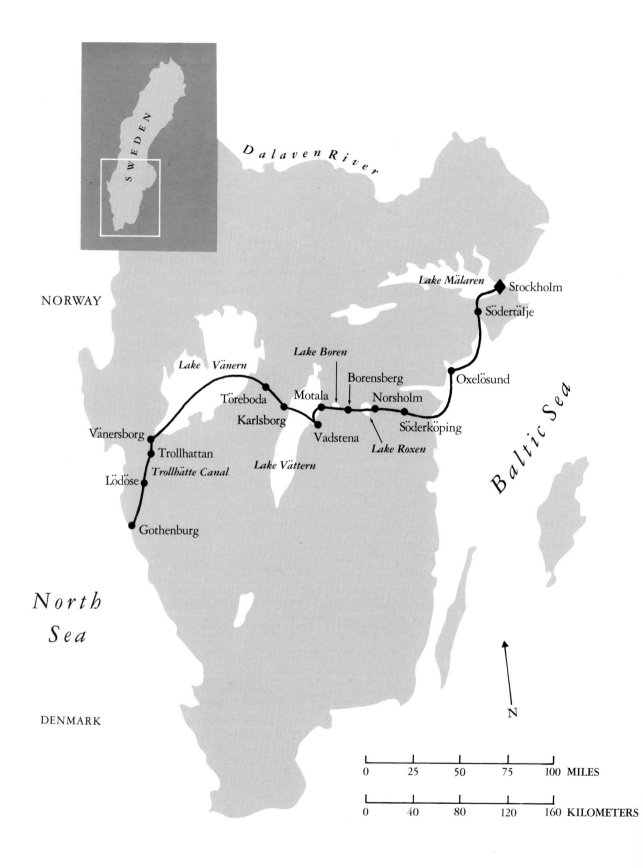

SWEDEN

NORWAY

Dalaven River

Lake Mälaren ◆ Stockholm
● Södertälje

Lake Boren
Borensberg
Lake Vänern   Motala ●   ○   Norsholm
Töreboda ●   ○   ● Oxelösund
Karlsborg   ○ Söderköping
Vänersborg ●   Vadstena
Trollhattan ●   *Lake Roxen*
Trollhätte Canal
Lödöse ●   *Lake Vättern*

● Gothenburg

Baltic Sea

*North
Sea*

DENMARK

N

| | | | | |
0   25   50   75   100 MILES

0   40   80   120   160 KILOMETERS

Cross-Country on the Göta Canal

Our trip on the Göta Canal began in the capital city of Stockholm on a Tuesday morning in early September. We would be spending the next three days and two nights floating down the canal between Stockholm and Gothenburg. Though the canal linking the two cities is commonly called the Göta Canal, in fact the Göta proper covers only 95 miles of the total 347 miles between the two cities. (In that 95 miles we would pass through 58 locks and 42 bridges.) The remaining 252 miles we would travel on the Södertälje and Trollhätte canals and natural lakes, two of them among the largest in Europe.

The M/S *Diana,* one of three short, high, pristine white vessels that take passengers across Sweden, was to be our home for the voyage. Built in 1931, she was powered by steam until the summer of 1968, when she received a diesel engine. By Rhine steamer standards the *Diana* is diminutive, measuring just 97 feet long, 22 feet wide, and 9 feet deep. A maximum 73 passengers fit into the tiny five-by-seven-foot cabins. We would be sharing the oak paneled dining room, beveled glass windows, and nineteenth-century charm of the steamer with our mostly American fellow passengers.

Linking the Lakes

When the news flashed across Europe in the fifteenth century that an Italian mechanic had invented the lock, a system for ships to "climb stairs" between different levels of water, the people of Sweden realized they had been endowed with 96,000 lakes, some of which were exactly suited for a lock system since they formed a perfect path across the country. Building such a waterway became more appealing after they calculated the money they paid in tolls to the Danes who owned Øresund, an essential passage for Swedish ships. Even more important was the fact that the locks offered an alternative to the long overland haulage routes required to transport iron, the primary national resource, from the inland mines to the coastal seaports.

However, it wasn't until early in the sixteenth century that a powerful churchman, financier, technician, and political sly fox, Bishop Hans Brask, put forward a far-reaching plan to connect several of the lakes and created a saying that swept Sweden: "Cut up Sweden between the seas and the lakes." This dream would occupy the Swedes for nearly three centuries before it was realized.

Despite the country's violent history, Sweden managed to push on with Brask's

133

plan, even after the bishop himself was forced to flee the country during the Reformation. King, tradesmen, churchmen, and peasants all agreed: Sweden needed a way to transport her iron ore, without paying tribute to the Danes, to the lucrative market-places of Europe. (And, in exchange for the metal, Sweden wanted wines, cloth, salt, spices, and many other items that could only be purchased abroad.)

Baltzar Bogislaus von Platen, born in 1766, deserves credit for the actual completion of the canal. Without Platen's lifelong stubbornness and persuasive power, no country as small and impoverished by violence as Sweden could have carried out such an ambitious project.

The cost was high—three times more expensive than the original estimate of 1810. In terms of manpower, it was staggering: some 60,000 conscripts, prisoners of war, infantrymen, and officers worked 23 years, twelve hours a day, to dig 65 locks and build 42 bridges, 35 lighthouses, 27 culverts, and three dry docks. Construction meant blasting through miles of solid granite and the building of portable shelters for thousands of workers, houses for administrative staff, hospitals, stores, cook-houses, bakeries, stables, barges, pumps, and cranes. It took more than 80 million man-hours to dig over 280 million cubic feet of earth, to blast seven million cubic feet of rock, and to lay nearly nine million cubic feet of masonry.

Platen didn't live to see his life's work finished—mercifully, perhaps, for in the end the canal was a financial disappointment as a commercial route. The Danish toll at Øresund had by then been lifted, the railways had dealt the deathblow to waterway cargo transport, and even the military and defense value of the canal had declined.

In the meantime, however, the route was discovered by travelers. In the nineteenth century it was used by pleasure seekers because of its speed and comfort, and today it is well traveled for its cultural and scenic beauty. Remaining basically unchanged for more than a century, the trip has become the classic tour through Sweden's heartland: old-fashioned excursion steamers cruise the blue ribbon of narrow canals, tamed rivers, and serene lakes that threads its way across the country through forests and lush landscapes teeming with history.

Since our cruise didn't leave until Wednesday, we spent Tuesday exploring Stockholm. A city built on islands, its unique ambiance is created by pines, silver birches, and rocky cliffs worn smooth by receding glaciers some 15,000 years ago.

We walked the twisty streets of the Old Town, passed the Royal Palace just as the guard was changing, saw the Ritterholm Church, and ambled by broad, green parks that aerate the city. Then we took a boat tour into the Stockholm Archipelago, which consists of more than 24,000 wind-blown, half-naked islands, islets, and skerries just off the mouth of Stockholm harbor and extending 80 miles northeast into the Baltic. Red-painted timber houses appeared on some of the islands, their porches adorned with gingerbread fantasies and lacelike wooden cutouts. The neat little houses exist side by side with ragged fishermen's shacks where fishing nets hang out to dry along the rugged waterfront.

Through Lake Mälaren

Early Wednesday morning we headed for the island of Riddarholmen (Island of Knights) to board the *Diana,* and at 9 A.M. we waved goodbye to the triple-crowned City Hall as the *Diana* began her short passage through the industrial outskirts of Stockholm.

We entered Lake Mälaren, which, like the archipelago to the east, was dotted with lichen-covered granite rocks and islands of birchwood and pine. Ospreys hid on their perches in dead trees or on isolated rocks, sometimes showing themselves high overhead. We would be winding through the lake for the next two hours, traveling the 23 miles to Södertälje Lock.

Mälaren is Sweden's third largest lake, 67 miles long, 29 miles at its widest spot, crowded with more than 1,200 rocky islands, skerries, and islets—all stacked behind one another like logs drying in a woodpile, forming narrow sounds, close bays, and quiet coves. The lake seemed like an ingenious network of narrow creeks and waterways set up to duplicate the famous maze at Hampton Court.

In the first century A.D. these shores were settled by the Svears, a tribe who gave their name to the country and who, along with the Goths, are accepted as the original ancestors of the Swedish people. They named the region Svealand, and by 98 A.D. Tacitus was writing in his history, *Germania,* that they were already well established as a kingdom and "mighty in ships and arms."

The lake was a vital commercial and political link for the kingdom of the Svears, as it has been for all those who have followed them. Its banks have housed all the major capital cities of Sweden's history: Helgö, Birka, Sigtuna, and today Stockholm. Majestic castles like Drottningholm and Gripsholm, Skokloster, Tynnelso, and Tido and many mansions surrounded by vast private parks and gardens also line the shores. The islands are dotted with summer homes, tiny gazebos adorn spits of land and rocks that jut out into the water, small sailboats are neatly moored in protected coves, and fishermen nod over their long poles in little lagoons barely visible through thickets of reeds.

Strange things have happened in this seemingly peaceful lake, and not only in the myth of ancient history. In the 1860s canal travelers could have wondered at the curious equipment and goings-on aboard a barge anchored in the middle of the lake. They might have been told it was only the laboratory of Alfred Bernhard Nobel, a struggling young Swedish inventor. What they probably would not have been told was that he was engaged in manufacturing, on a commercial scale, a delicate, newly invented chemical known as nitroglycerin. Nobel had become bargebound after his first factory exploded and the government refused him permission to build another one ashore.

Six miles southwest of Stockholm we came upon the small, steep, lump-of-rock island of Kungshatt. It was recognizable because of a strange memento left behind by a legendary king. To escape his pursuers, it is said, he plunged himself and his horse nearly 200 feet into the water from a rocky ridge on the island, leaving his hat behind. Today a tin hat hangs on a tall pole, marking his supposed point of departure. Whatever its origin, the cap's presence makes for good conversation and excellent navigation.

During Viking times Lake Mälaren was a well-protected fjord and a vital link with trade throughout Europe. From 800 to 1000 A.D. the island of Estbrote, across Fishermen's Bay from Kungshatt, was an important military "seal" on this industrious nerve center. Here defenders stretched heavy iron chains across the narrow sound, beneath the surface of the water. When enemy ships approached, the chains were suddenly raised, surprising the invaders and capsizing their vessels.

The next island was Ekerö, six miles long. Its ridge of hills was generously garnished with medieval towns, elegant castles, manor houses, and the burial ground of Viking chieftain Björn Järnside (Ironside, of course). Staring across the waters was Sturehof Castle, a simple but exceptional piece of eighteenth-century Swedish architecture.

Still abreast of Ekerö, we caught sight of Björko Island, whose green meadows and tall birch trees (for which it was named) cover the few remains of Birka, the first town of any importance in Sweden. It was here in 830 A.D. that Christianity was preached—for the first time in Sweden—by St. Angsar, the first apostle of Scandinavia.

In the ninth and tenth centuries Birka was the Svears' trading center and capital when the Vikings sold to the West the prizes they had stolen or traded in Russia and the East. The entire town was destroyed in the eleventh century, and today only a few crumbling walls and the ruins of the old citadel remain, along with an archaeological gold mine—2,000 Viking burial mounds.

Lillön, says the map; Helgö, say the historians. What is now the island of Lillön was famous as the trading center of Helgö even before Birka—as early as 400–700 A.D. Archaeological finds here have included coins from ancient Rome, bronze Buddhas from the East, and solid gold ornaments of unknown origin—indications of how far-ranging this trade must have been.

The Södertälje Canal to the Baltic

Having come nearly the full distance through Lake Mälaren, we entered the bay of Björkfjärden. There our ship turned in a wide, graceful arc to the south, and at about 11 A.M. we prepared to enter the 156-year-old Södertälje Canal. The canal itself is only two miles long, but it forms Lake Mälaren's all-important link with the Baltic Sea. It contains only one lock, but that lock—in the heart of the city of Södertälje—could have held eight *Dianas* in its 400-foot chamber.

Södertälje, situated deep inside the Hallsfjärden fjord, is one of Sweden's oldest cities. It bustled with trade during Viking times and in the Middle Ages rivaled

Stockholm as a port. Dominated by the tower of the twelfth-century St. Ragnild's Church, the town is centered around the lock and spreads out along the banks of the canal.

South of the town great steelworks, crane-covered docks, lumber mills, automobile factories, and many low, raw-looking factory buildings line the fjord. Out of all this rose the copper-clad tower of the church of Grödinge, and then, somehow, we were free of modern industry and traveling between windswept beaches.

A yawing sailboat, wings spread wide, sailed to us out of the sun, followed by steamers and tugs. The pretty village of Järna watched us from the right bank as we entered the Järnafjärden, the middle bay leading to the Baltic. A bit further downstream, on the island of Mörkö, was the eighteenth-century rococo castle of Hörningsholm. Perched high on a rocky outcrop above the northern shore, the castle is built upon the foundations of a medieval Viking fortress. The water shimmered silver as we headed toward the source of that cold northern light.

As we rounded Mörkö in the shadow of Hörningsholm, we entered the grand Himmerfjärden, the wide outer bay opening into the Baltic. Dime-sized, tree-covered islands dotted the bay, and gingerbread houses, half buried in tall pines, stood on the hills of both banks. It was a wild and beautiful place.

It was difficult to believe that this was the same Baltic Sea that washes the shores of Denmark, Finland, Estonia, Latvia, Lithuania, Poland, and Germany—160,000 square miles of water, of which the deepest are found here in Sweden, where in places it reaches down some 1,500 feet. Although the Baltic is known for sudden and frequent changes of wind and occasional violent storms, we were well protected here, surrounded by the chain of islands of the Trosa Archipelago.

Navigation in this veritable galaxy of islands was tricky; we had to duck in and out and wend our way through an entanglement of often unnamed and mostly uninhabited rocks and trees that dot the open sea.

We snaked down the ragged coastline, passing close to Studsvik, Sweden's nuclear research station, recognizable by its forest of masts and tall chimneys. Then we entered the Stendörren, or Stone Door, an extremely narrow passage among islands, skerries, and submerged rocks that demanded intricate navigations.

While the captain handled the tricky maneuvering, the crew attended to lunch. It was a wonderful smörgåsbord affair, with many small hot and cold dishes, served in the intimate dining salon.

By 4:30 P.M. we were floating by Oxelösund, a steelmaking town since 1913 and one of Sweden's most important ice-free ports. Smokestack after smokestack spewed its fumes over the city and the port, in distinct contrast to the pastoral peace of the coast both north and south of it. However, the city is justly proud of its new Town Church (1957), dedicated to the local St. Botvid. Designed by Rolf Bergh, its revolutionary architectural style attracted nationwide attention. Today its modern, stark white bell tower presides on a hilltop and serves as a navigational mark for sailors.

Land of the Eastern Goths

From Oxelösund we made a short passage across the open waters of Bråviken Fjord, one of the greatest bays in the Baltic, which cuts deep into the country and serves the major shipping city of Norrköping. In the middle of this open-water passage we left the land of the Svears and entered Östergötland, the land of the Eastern Goths. This is a rich, smiling region, well favored by nature. It was settled by a Germanic tribe that came from the south, following the receding glaciers northward, and made their home in the region of Lake Vättern some 5,000 years ago.

The land of the Eastern Goths lies between two coasts about as different as Nature could have made them. The eastern coast, on the Baltic Sea, is harsh and unyielding, beautiful in its boldness and ruggedness. The western coast is formed by Lake Vättern, a long, narrow inland sea around which nestle some of the nation's most treasured natural and historic sights. Between the two coasts stretch some of the most fertile farmlands and finest estates in all Sweden.

We picked our way through the Östergötland Archipelago, near the resort and port of Arkösund, with its popular beaches and large fleet of yachts. At 6 P.M. the first cloud of the day passed across the face of the sun, turning into a pink etching in the blue canvas sky and casting long pink shadows. We were nearing the mouth of the 18-mile Slätbaken Bay, which would take us inland again to begin our westward course to Gothenburg.

The great Bay of Slätbaken is protected by the island of Eknön and by one of Sweden's most impregnable medieval fortresses, the castle of Stegeborg (Fortress of Stakes), where the defenders would drive pilings into the narrow waters on either side of the fortress island so strategically placed in the middle of the narrowest part of the fjord.

The castle was more than the guardian of the fjord; it was the lock and key to all of Östergötland, and it was secure for centuries. It was only demolished by the Swedes themselves, in a period of austerity, when its stones were used to rebuild the city of Norrköping, which had been almost completely destroyed by the Russians in the eighteenth century. What we saw that September afternoon were the comparatively well-preserved ruins of the original fifteenth-century stronghold and its 85-foot round tower.

On the southern bank the charming little church of Skällvik sent its pointy spire and timber bell tower skyward. The uniquely Scandinavian timber bell towers are a national heritage dating from the seventeenth century, when nearly every church in the land had one. Of all the Scandinavian countries, Sweden produced by far the finest flowering of the art, the work of the local peasant-craftsmen constituting a special kind of folk art. The detached towers were built high so that their bells could ring out across the lakes and forests to the widely scattered congregation; they were supported by great crossed timber beams covered with tarred oak shingles, like the scales of some prehistoric reptile. Despite the ravages of time and fire and the many invasions of the Russians, Danes, and Norwegians, some 450 of these towers still stand today.

After dinner we entered at Mem the first lock of the Eastern Line of the Göta Canal and were raised eight feet to the level of the canal. This was the last lock to open officially—on September 26, 1832—and except for normal maintenance and repairs it is basically as it was then: hand operated and diminutive—just 98 feet long. In fact, all the locks from here to Sjötorp (at the western end of the Göta Canal) would be in the same near-original condition, offering a taste of the oldtime charm of the early nineteenth-century waterways.

Beyond the lock the meadows had signs warning BEWARE OF THE BULL! and the towpath was shared by children and wild foxes. It was a quiet region, the trees thoughtfully planted in curving lines across the plains and banks.

The last light had faded, for this was too late in the year for any "midnight sun." And still the *Diana* chugged on, as she would through both nights of the trip. We

Along the Göta Canal late summer is rainy season, and the Swedes in foul weather gear accept the gentle rain with fair weather spirit. Most of the canal forests are coniferous, but here just east of Lake Vänern are oak, ash, maple and elm. A five-horsepower outboard powers this fiberglass craft, sails furled, through the canal. Fenders are ready for the lock at Borensberg.

enjoyed the night; the glassy waters of the canal provided a perfect mirror for the dark bushes, reeds, and trees on the banks.

At Tegelbruket Lock, soon after Mem, the lockkeeper's family was grouped on the lawn in front of their white stucco house, drinking coffee. Their three-year-old daughter, allowed to stay up late to see the *Diana* pass through on her last voyage of the season, ran to the gate as soon as she spied us, her blond hair flying, eyes wide, face shining. Her strong, stocky lockkeeper father sauntered over and stood by the open gates, ready to receive the ship.

The huge, hand-operated gates were opened and closed with a heavy timber lever, which the lockkeeper pushed along a circular arc. The girl, tiny as she was, ran to help close the gates behind us. We watched her little, somewhat unsteady legs pushing and stumbling against the massive timber, receiving enthusiastic encouragement from her patient father. The job done, she stood at attention and waved at the captain and passengers, blowing kisses.

We glided out of the lock, waving to the family, and were no more than 200 yards beyond it when we came to a slow . . . sludging . . . shimmying . . . shaking halt in the mud near the left bank.

A Familiar Episode

Having gone aground numerous times on our own boats, we could appreciate the luxury of being aground with a crew of seven husky professionals. Let *them* worry about it; we would watch.

Soon there were four crewmen on the left bank, and the entire complement of passengers was standing at the port rail to watch. That in itself should have heeled the boat over far enough to get it off the soft mud, we thought—but no. The passengers stood at the rail and stared at the crew, and the crew stood on the bank and stared at the passengers, waiting for orders from the bridge. They began pacing up and down the bank, studying the predicament of the *Diana.*

Flashlights began glowing through the trees on the bank before us. By now our bow was nestling over near the grassy left bank and our stern was edging over to nibble the tender branches of overhanging trees on the right. The flashlights retreated again through the trees and appeared to be heading back toward the lock.

The ship's engines began running at an awesomely high speed, first forward, then reverse. The boat bounded enthusiastically up and down but made progress neither toward nor away from the lock. Nine helpers had by now assembled on the left bank, and a line was sent over to them from the stern. As soon as it had been secured ashore, the crew began winching the stern in toward the bank in order to coax the bow back out to the middle of the canal.

It worked. The stern moved to port just enough to dislodge the bow, and we were free. The port-rail superintendents were congratulating themselves when they saw the stern line being hooked up to a 1937 jalopy station wagon on the towpath.

The rumor flashed through the crowd that our propeller was fouled: we were going to back into the lock we had just left and empty the lock enough to reach the propeller and unfoul it.

The 1937 jalopy station wagon began straining at its heavy load, and the smell of burning rubber filled the air. Someone jumped up and down on the taut line behind the car to help get the boat moving, but the result of this strategy was to ground the stern near the left bank and nose the bow over into the trees on the right.

Lines were now being thrown from every angle, orders being shouted and carried out, and crew members working frantically on both banks. The activity spread the watching passengers out somewhat to both rails, thereby helping the ship's trim considerably.

Groups of curious townspeople had assembled, even children in their pajamas, routed out of bed to see the passenger boat *Diana,* bow and stern aground on opposite banks of the canal. There were bicycles, baby carriages, spotlights, and a good deal of muffled conversation. We had been backing and filling for an hour and were now some fifty minutes behind schedule.

Suddenly the captain threw the ship's engines into forward, full speed ahead. The *Diana* surprised everyone by fairly leaping out of the mud—accelerating so fast that the crewman holding the stern line was nearly pulled into the canal—and heading obediently for Söderköping.

The Night Watch and the Dawn

Söderköping is an idyllic, sleepy village of some 6,000 people, with old cobbled streets running between gabled white frame houses that lean wistfully toward the canal. Great beech and oak trees cast their watery reflections from the banks. Here the healing waters of St. Ragnhild's Spring, known to royalty since the Middle Ages, gave birth to a spa. Across the canal Ramunder Ridge (Raven's Mountain) loomed darkly over the ship, its history stretching back to the Bronze Age.

From here to Norsholm on Lake Roxen stretched 14 miles of canal punctuated by eleven locks and lined with moonlit fields, rolling hills, dark woods, and occasional manor houses. Wild and beautiful Lake Asplångan, a narrow piece of water some three miles long and closed in between rugged and rocky shores, followed the locks.

The air had turned chilly, and passengers began drifting off sleepily to their cabins, but we decided to stay up and watch the passing scene. In the early morning we reached Norsholm, gateway to Lake Roxen, a large, shallow lake whose low shores are protected by a flood lock at Norsholm.

Our moonlight journey across the lake covered 17 miles and took three hours; we passed shores dotted with manor houses and castle ruins. On the low south shore the steeple of the famous Linköping Cathedral soared in slim silhouette, marking the spot where the Swedish Church first affirmed its allegiance to Rome in 1152.

In the early-morning hours the *Diana* left Lake Roxen at Bergs to climb a staircase of fifteen locks that raised us 121 feet in a distance of less than two miles. The sun had just risen over our wake, and a few early risers were walking the decks as we approached the great technological sight of the Göta Canal's Eastern Line—the seven-lock staircase, followed by four pairs of coupled locks. Nearby stood a memorial honoring the 60,000 men who labored on the canal from 1810 to 1832.

We stepped ashore at the bottom lock and climbed to the top, walking a short way to Vreta Abbey. The sunrise was still very pink as we approached the 850-year-old remains of Sweden's first monastery. Only the convent's crumbling foundations and the monastery church survive, but they were surrounded, overhung, and filled with the sweet smells of flowers in the cool, crisp morning air.

Inside the church we found a twelfth-century Madonna, several early medieval tombs, a seventeenth-century pulpit carved locally, and a small octagonal chapel built by Field Marshall Count Robert Douglas, a tough young Scottish immigrant whose military honors brought him nobility in Sweden. The chapel was grand and rich, filled with copper coffins, marble urns, banners, medals, seals, and other panoply.

One by one we drifted into the courtyard formed by the convent walls, listening to the early-morning singing of bright birds and drinking in the colors and the fragrance of the flowers. No one broke the silence as we ambled back to rejoin our companions aboard ship.

Toward Lake Boren

Near the bridge of Ljung we looked down a long, shady avenue to the great white eighteenth-century house that had seen the birth and death of one of the most romantic adventurers in Sweden's history. Having taken part in the American Revolutionary War, Count Axel von Fersen the Younger became the king's secret agent at the French Court. During the French Revolution he became a close friend (and very likely a lover) of Queen Marie Antoinette and staged the royal family's unsuccessful escape attempt in 1791. He met his end in Sweden at the hands of an enraged mob that besieged him as the funeral procession of Crown Prince Carl August passed through the streets of Stockholm in 1810. (The people suspected him of having poisoned the young prince.) The good count now lies in the grounds of the nearby neoclassical church.

As the canal made a series of sweeping curves, the banks grew full of weeping birch, maples, oaks, and elms. A schoolboy stopped his bicycle, his schoolbag bobbing on his lanky shoulders, to give us a wave. Two women bent low over the wet grass, searching the shadows for mushrooms that might have popped up overnight. The trees were beginning to turn, and the early-morning light cast a golden spell on the leaves, hinting of the crisp fall to come. Lush, ripe fields took on a splendor in this golden light, their richness beckoning to be harvested. All was peace in the fertile plains.

Behind the silver birches lining the canal we could glimpse Norrby Lake and the Motala River, bending close and winding away again, following the curves of the hillsides.

At Borensberg our thirty-first lock lifted us into the eight-mile expanse of Lake Boren. Borensberg was a small place; the river crossing had begot an inn, and the inn begat the village. Today the old roadside inn still stands, wearing its coat of that rich, subtle red paint of the country farms and cottages that is so typically and exclusively Swedish.

This is Falu red, a natural, indigenous, protective paint that comes from the medieval copper mines of Falu in Dalarna Province. No better wood protection exists than this Swedish specialty. And it has other qualities. It has an economy and beauty of color—a deep, warm, ruddy ochre red that varies subtly from place to place and mellows with age. It harmonizes perfectly with the characteristic Swedish landscape of gray, lichen-clad granite and fir trees hovering over thick, fat, juicy bilberries. Thus the painted buildings offer vivid spots of color to brighten an otherwise subdued colorscape.

Boren, a remarkable lake, is full of the legends of Sweden's patron saint, Bridget (1303–1373), one of the most energetic and visionary women in the country's history.

Birgitta Birgersdotter was history's first internationally known Swede. Born on an Uppland farm, she was the daughter of the governor and county judge of Uppland, and her mother was related to the powerful Folkunga family who ruled at that time. At the age of fourteen she married young Ulf Gudmarrson and settled at Ulvåsa farm on the southern shore of Lake Boren, bearing and raising eight children over twenty years.

She had a series of religious visions and, when she was widowed, she recorded her experiences in a book, *Revelations.* One of her visions commanded her to found a new monastic order, a project that took her to Rome to seek the blessing of the pope. She never again saw her native land; from Rome she personally supervised the creation of Vadstena Monastery on Lake Vättern, an undertaking that turned an ordinary lakeside settlement into the most important religious center in the North.

Only a few miserable stones remain of her residence on the south shore. The beautiful white sixteenth-century manor house nearby, Ulvåsa, which rises proudly high above the water, has nothing in common with the original except the name and perhaps some of the land.

On the northern shore the famous church of Kristberg stands at a spot that has been church territory for more than 800 years. The truly remarkable thing about this church was something we were not able to see at a distance: the barrel-vaulted timber ceiling. It was built in the 1720s and covered with a type of folk art that is crude and naive yet vigorous, charming, and uniquely Swedish. Its origins go back to medieval times, when few people could read; in the gay times of the rococo period it developed into a joyful and delightful style characterized by brilliant coloring and no attempt at perspective. Cheerful decoration rather than realism was its aim. The queen of Sheba could appear in eighteenth-century Swedish dress, Jesus could preach under a sky of giant flowers, spotted horses could be green and John the Baptist's hair pale blue. A vigorous, truly vernacular art form, it went the way of so many folk crafts on the advent of industrialism. Now almost all examples of this style have been snatched up by museums and private collectors and can be acquired only at high prices —but the ceiling of Kristberg remains.

The canal boat Wilhelm Than *leaves Vadstena Castle en route from Gothenburg to Stockholm via the Göta Canal. The route is 322 nautical miles through 3 canals, 65 locks, 10 lakes and an inland sea. Yachts moor in the moat of the sixteenth-century castle whose thick walls are made of large fieldstones. The castle was once the home of Gustavus Vasa, founder of modern Sweden.*

The Climb to Motala

Approaching the western end of Lake Boren, we could see Motala spread out in terraces on the hills, its crown of red roofs piled haphazardly around the Five Locks of Memory, the dramatic flight of locks that leads from Lake Boren up into the town. A bitterly cold wind blew from that direction, and as we drew closer the locks resembled a giant's staircase, gushing water on all sides.

In the first lock the lofty front gates reached the height of the top of the *Diana,* and even before the paddles were opened water spurted up from the mossy bottom in gushing fountains. Five variously blond boys, all about twelve years old, ran down the path from town to see us lock up. Tall, tousled, and gangly, hands in their blue jeans pockets, they grinned with mischief like little truants (which they probably were, this being a Thursday) and operated on a system of dares.

One would venture out onto the lock gates to watch the water rush angrily into the lock, bubbling and frothing like some Frankenstein potion. Another would follow. One would sidle over to the gate on the far side of the lock, and the other would sidle along behind him. As the *Diana* rose swiftly to the second level, they would stay on the gate until the penultimate moment of its ponderous opening. They would watch from the moving gate until one boy jumped across; the other then had to move fast to clear the widening gap over the still-frothy waters whirling below, leaping sometimes frightening distances to the other, fast-retreating gate. And the *Diana*'s engines would already be revving up to move us into the next chamber. Then the water would tear into the chamber, sounding like continuous thunder, and the boys would start their climbing act all over again. We were beginning to suspect that children are the true canal people.

Away from the open water of the lake, the weather was milder: leaf-painted sunshine amove with the breeze. When we had reached the top chamber, we walked to the stern to catch the view, a Swedish flag flying in the foreground over a blue and green waterscape far below. We could see clear across Lake Boren to the pine forests on the hilly banks opposite. A few fluffy white clouds held counsel over the water, leaving the rest of the sky an uninterrupted blue.

The Motala River was now the canal's meandering companion. As we made our way through the city of Motala, the river appeared frequently between rows of trees. Then, beside the canal on the northern bank, we passed the last resting place of Platen, at a spot he himself chose. A huge, rough granite monolith bore the simple inscription PLATENS GRAV, and the small, flower-strewn piece of ground was encircled by a wrought-iron railing. The *Diana* paused in her silent travel to give two long blasts of the ship's horn, the traditional salute to the canal's creator.

Platen was also responsible for the growth of the town. The name Motala means Place of Sacrifice at the Meeting of the Roads—a pretty strong clue that a crossing over the Motala River has existed since the dim pagan past. But when the canal was begun in 1810, the town didn't amount to much: church, courthouse, inn, some small mills, a few scattered fishermen's huts near the river. Even when the canal opened in 1832 the town had only 88 inhabitants (and that number probably included a couple of cherished family pets).

This was one of four new towns Platen envisioned growing out of his canal project; having seen the need to manufacture products for the canal, he established the Motala Works in 1832 to produce lock gates, bridges, and vessels. Today there is no question that this burgeoning town of 30,000 is really Platen's creation; he even laid out the streets, which rise in concentric arcs up the hillside.

Lake Vättern and Vadstena

Just beyond Motala is Lake Vättern. This huge sheet of water, left behind by the receding sea following the Ice Age, is said to be one of the most beautiful of the 96,000 lakes of Sweden. A long, narrow inland sea, it is the country's second largest body of water, covering 738 square miles and extending nearly a hundred miles due north and south.

For all its beauty, the most whispered characteristic of the lake is its strange personality. Residents of the shores refer to the lake as "him" and regard it with awe because of its moody and unpredictable nature and somewhat mysterious habits. In addition to its swift changes of weather and the steep, dangerous seas that are known to come in three-wave spasms, the nontidal lake is said to "pulsate," rising and sinking eight times a day. In the quiet days of early spring, strange bubbling noises can be heard from the middle of the lake, perhaps caused by subterranean gases rising as the bedrock under the lake settles. Lake Vättern is actually a giant fissure—a cleft some 420 feet deep—in Sweden's central mountain ridge. Some say it is fed by subterranean springs; this would help to explain the extraordinary clarity of the water, which is still used for drinking.

The shores of the lake were inhabited at least 4,000 years ago by the Goths, one of whose Stone Age settlements has been discovered just east of Mount Omberg, the great and mysterious "sacred" mountain that rises a few miles south of Motala, beyond Vadstena.

Vadstena was to be our next stop on the cross-country tour. The name (pronounced "Vasstena") means Fortified Manor by the Water; the town dates from the fourteenth century. With only about 5,000 inhabitants, it draws annually some 40,000 tourists from all over the world.

St. Bridget received the blessing of the pope for her new order in 1370, but the building of the monastery at Vadstena wasn't completed until 1430, fifty-seven years after her death. It fell to her daughter Catherine to complete the building her mother had planned. For the most part the monastery was built around the existing buildings of a former royal estate, and the town grew up around the abbey.

Just after lunch we passed the small white timber lighthouse that stands guard at the end of a long breakwater. Across the small bay rose the elegant spire of the monastery church. But the central feature of the harbor was Gustav Vasa's great castle with its low, round bastions, soaring baroque spires, and encircling moat. This is the finest Renaissance castle left in Sweden, and it's ironic that Vasa, whose Reformation dealt the deathblow to Catholicism in Sweden, chose the sanctified ground of Vadstena for one of his great fortified castles. The result is a combination of sacred and secular architecture and ambiance that is nearly unmatched anywhere.

The castle languished in neglect—it was used as a granary from 1735 to 1930 —so there is little in the interior to educate the tourist. But the chapel, with its magnificent Gothic groined vaulting, was a splendid room where every sound reverberated, magnified itself, and echoed. The wedding hall, now empty except for its sixteenth-century wall paintings, received its name when Vasa, then fifty-eight, took his sixteen-year-old bride, Catherine Stenbock, here.

The monastery church was just a short walk away along a scenic waterfront promenade. Known as the blue church because of the color of the stone with which it was built, it is an architectural gem—with a bold, unornamented style that is impressive in its calm, spacious, and dignified simplicity. A fifteenth-century woodcarving of St. Bridget shows her with cute, pudgy cheeks and kindly eyes as she pores over her Bible, her little shoes pushing out from the many deep folds of her habit, which is draped carelessly over two old, tired, slightly bowed legs.

We continued walking through the town, past the fifteenth-century house of Marten Skinnare, a pious and wealthy fur, leather, and copper tradesman who was born in the town and made his fortune in Stockholm. Next we came to the tall fourteenth-century Red Tower, whose stepped brick gables are all that remains of the town's original parish church. The Bishop's House, one of the oldest surviving private houses in Sweden, was built for the bishop of Linkoping in 1473 as his residence on visits to the monastery.

In Vadstena, one writer records, "the winds from the lake and the fine spray from its waters remove all history's deep dust. Here, memories from 700 years in Sweden continue to live. They are worn shiny and have been washed clean."

The M/S *Diana* gave two genteel toots to call us back aboard, so we returned to the waterfront to continue our Swedish cross-cutting. As we sailed out into the lake, we could look back at Vadstena and see the great and mysterious wooded heights of Mount Omberg rising out of the water.

Omberg was an island surrounded by cold seas at the time the ice cap was melting. The blue-gray limestone that built the monastery church came from this mountain; a 4,000-year-old Stone Age settlement, Dagsmosse Bog, has been discovered just east of the mountain; and Scandinavia's most important rune stone, the Rök Stone, is just to the south. Omberg, so long ago the birthplace of Swedish civilization, is now a national park that offers interesting caves near the shores, rare flora and birdlife, and a magnificent view from its summit: "eight cities, 30 churches, and four provinces."

In the middle of Lake Vättern we crossed the imaginary line between the land of the Eastern Goths and the territory of their western cousins, which includes the city of Gothenburg. Soon we could see the incredibly massive Karlsborg Fortress crouching between low-slung bastions and surrounded by green forests. Nearly half a mile long, it's a remarkable pile of heavy stone and earth fortifications, squat round corner towers, and barracks buildings. Completed in 1909, it was outmoded by 1928 and closed down without ever having seen military action. Now it stares out across Vättern with empty eyes, and the whole pile seems enveloped in one large cobweb.

The Canal Summit

At 4:15 P.M. we were about to enter upon the most exciting part of the entire voyage, during which we would reach the summit level of the canal, 301 feet above sea level. The Western Line of the Göta Canal is an extremely difficult section to navigate. It is full of all the uncertainties that Nature can provide: the water is shallow, island follows island, and the narrow channel becomes cluttered with skerries. Man-made cuts, blasted into bedrock and just wide enough for one boat, twist tortuously through the wild and wooded countryside until the canal reaches Lake Vänern, some 40 tense miles away.

We noticed that the captain's wheelhouse door was closed—a signal to the passengers not to interrupt his concentration. This was unusual on the three-day trip, for the crew was cordial and informal, normally happy to entertain a question from a passenger on the lofty bridge.

As we passed through Rodesunds on the short canal that connects lakes Vättern and Botten, a small group of singers waited to serenade us in the lock. A woman handed a big bouquet of flowers up to the captain and blew him a kiss, to bless the end of the season for the canal. This would be the last little white steamer to pass until mid-May, after the long, cold Swedish winter.

We sailed through Botten Lake to Forsvik, where the most difficult navigation would begin. The little iron bascule bridge above the lock was made in England in 1813; it is kept there as a memento, having been described by a Swedish writer as being "as English as an iron bedstead."

Lily pads and reeds crowded the edges of the water, and there was no light prettier than the light that fell in the middle of the deep forest beyond—soft, dispersed, moving in little dots of brightness as the breeze stirred the branches.

Shortly thereafter we approached a seemingly impossible bend in the canal, where a crewman was waiting for us ashore to help with one of the trickiest maneuvers of the trip. A line from the bow shot out to him, and he neatly caught it and secured it on a bollard. Without this line for added control around the hairpin turn,

*A runestone stands near Lake Vän-
ern. There are about 2400 old runic
inscriptions in Sweden. Varied forms
of the letters carved along the right
side were used from the Black Sea to
the Baltic and Britain from about the
third century. There might be magic
in the inscription or a curse on the
bones of anyone who harms the stone.*

the *Diana* would have ended up in the mud amidst the weeping birches, reeds, lily pads, and ferns.

We then entered charming Lake Viken, 15 miles of narrow, twisting channels encircled by forest and dappled with islands. Platen had costly troubles in building the channel here, blasting away dangerous underwater rocks and having to rebuild the dam entirely. It was one of the most difficult periods in the entire canal-building process.

West of Forsvik we followed the Spetsnäs Canal, a short, narrow cut through Spetsnäset Island. Here we could almost reach out and pluck leaves from the overhanging trees as the *Diana* chugged softly by. Vika Forest loomed high above us on the left bank. Brosunden, with its ferry station, marked the end of the most difficult navigation, and we passed into the wider waters of the lake beyond.

The city of Tåtorp lay at the western end of the lake, and there began the longest pound of the canal—the summit pound known as Lanthojden. It runs from Tåtorp to Töreboda, cutting through primary rock in the mountainous ridge that separates Sweden's two largest lakes, Vättern and Vänern. The canal builders labored here for a full seven years, and when they finished, the result was a narrow, 24-foot winding ditch with exceedingly close and abrupt turns and occasional "wide spots" for two boats to pass. The entire section is renowned for its wild and beautiful primeval forest landscape. We glided through this remote region between pine carpets, with birch boughs brushing the *Diana*'s mast.

At Vassbacken, no more than a farm and a bridge to canal travelers, we emerged from the forest and ran through broad plains of high fields rich with barley and potatoes and filled with the sweet smell of wood fires. These were the Töreboda plains, where the canal, lined by grand linden trees, sometimes ran above the surrounding land.

As we lingered over dinner, the canal made an occasional elegant turn, but the mood had changed from the tortuous clawing through rock to a lazy and smiling saunter through rich and verdant farmland.

The Descent in Darkness

By 10:30 P.M. we were in the lock at the village of Töreboda, a busy canal station and industrial center. This lock was the first of nineteen in our long downward journey toward Gothenburg. Great clusters of stars hung suspended beyond the dark trees, the calm, silver waters were overlaid with mist, while the moon lent light to our journey. By the time we reached Hajstorp, with its two pair of coupled locks, most of the other passengers were sleeping, and we sat nearly alone, mesmerized by the stillness.

Going down those locks in the darkness was something like being in the front car of a speeding roller coaster. The boat seemed to come steaming up to the very brink of the lock, and we were always sure that it would plow through the gates and plummet down at its own wild pace. But always, at the last minute, the engines reversed, a line was slung over a bollard, and the boat stopped smoothly, short of the front of the lock by what seemed like inches.

Lockkeepers rode their bicycles from one floodlit lock to the next and received money wrapped in paper towels for their efforts. They wore black leather clogs, peaked hats, and increasingly sleepy expressions as the hours progressed. The air grew cold and crisp, and the stars grew incredibly bright against the pure black sky. The moon had set, and the stillness was shattered only by whistles signaling crewmen to empty the lock or to take the boat out.

The smoke from *Diana*'s stack made upward spirals in a path leading to the treetops, and the mist atop the water seemed to run along before our boat in the spotlight. Our bodies wanted to sleep, but our minds refused to give in. We were entranced by this dreamy voyage through the blackness full of slow-moving, silent figures.

Old Falu red timber warehouses in sleeping villages and farmhouses slipped by, and by 3:30 A.M. we had reached the final lock at Sjötorp, on the brink of Lake Vänern. The port leading into the lake was marked by the twinkling light of a tiny wooden lighthouse. We had finished with the Göta Canal proper, having conquered its 58 locks and 42 bridges. It was time to go to bed.

Lake Vänern

Until mid-morning we would be sailing across the open waters of Lake Vänern, the third largest lake in Europe, covering 2,156 square miles of water. The lake was quiet in the early-morning hours, but during the day it hums with ships that come directly from the world's oceans through the Trollhätte Canal to the industrial ports on its shores. Some of the local ships that ply these waters are the original broad-beamed Vänern sailing barges—shiny, black, and proud.

Early in the morning we peered out the cabin window to see in the south the wooded slopes of the Kinnekulle, one of the truly unique table mountains of this region, which rose out of the Arctic Sea during the last Ice Age. Climbing in terraces to the highest point, their steep rock faces frequently rise sheer from the ones below. Many strange stratified rock formations and grottoes are found among the fertile woods, and here and there stand old and interesting buildings. The Kinnekulle has been inhabited since the early Stone Age; many of its churches recall the earliest days of Christianity in the northern countries.

On the south shore, on the tip of the Kållandsö peninsula, lay famous Läckö Castle, a fine Renaissance building and a national treasure. This enormous palace is a magnificent work that typifies the splendor of Sweden in the seventeenth century. As we approached, we could see its gracious white walls and square towers mirrored perfectly in the still waters of the lake.

As the steamer skirted the peninsula and the rocky Ekens Archipelago, we entered the great western bay of Vänern. Over the last cup of morning coffee we saw along the shore the twin table mountains Halleberg and Hunneberg, each rising to a height of some 500 feet. Like Kinnekulle and Omberg, they contain great wilderness—Sweden's northernmost beechwoods, a herd of more than 150 elk, and the Royal Forests, a region rich in legend and ancient remains, including signs of prehistoric man and a number of Viking burial mounds.

We were approaching Vänersborg, an important shipping port between Lake Vänern and the Göta Älv, the canalized river that runs to Gothenburg. The town's beautiful lakeside park, laid out with that subtle sensivity to landscaping that is a Swedish specialty, offered a beautiful recreation area, and its trees protected the town from the great northerly winds that sweep down the 87 miles of open water. The city itself remained hidden behind the trees of the park until we neared the railroad bridge—the largest single bascule bridge in Europe, 130 feet high when opened.

The Vassbotten, a shallow bay south of Lake Vänern, is linked to the Göta Älv by the oldest Swedish artificial shipping lane, Karl's Trench. The two-mile cut, 104 feet wide, was excavated in 1607 by the son of Gustav Vasa and has been redug more than once to meet the increasing demands of modern shipping. Here, at Brinkerberg-skulle, we descended 17 feet in the first of the six magnificent locks of the Trollhätte Canal.

The Trollhätte Canal

Karl's Trench, the Vassbotten, and the Göta Älv are all part of the Trollhätte Canal, which embraces the entire navigable passage from Lake Vänern to the North Sea port of Gothenburg. This enormous work, which began taking shape in 1718 under King Charles XII, was completed in 1800; it was enlarged in 1844 and again in 1909–1916, when its locks were modernized and electrified.

As we passed beyond the lower gates of Brinkerbergskulle Lock, we could look back and see the old canal from 1844. A factory on the left bank spewed smoke over the vicinity, and above us power lines hummed their mighty song, for this was the electric power center of Sweden.

The great 206-foot falls at Trollhättan have been noted by travelers since early times; old engravings show the foaming cataract as a true natural wonder. Today it is hardly recognizable, for it has been put to work producing some 240,000 kilowatts of power—enough, it is said, to supply the daily needs of 3,200 townspeople every second.

During the two hours it took to lock down through the next two enormous locks, we were able to walk a winding path through the woods, moss, and wild berries and then along the Göta Älv to view some of the twenty-four older locks of various formats, dating from 1800, 1844, and 1916. The older locks represented an incredible technological feat, having been constructed without the aid of dynamite and hauling machines. The blasting was done with powder, and every boulder was rolled away on wheelbarrows by human hands. Joseph Acerbi wrote, in his *Travels Through Sweden,* "Should the age of darkness again envelop Scandinavia, and bring back the reign of ignorance and superstition, the works of Trollhättan, like those of the Romans, would doubtless be ascribed to giants, fairies or gods."

At the top of a wooded hill overlooking the Göta Älv, we followed the older locks to a fountain surrounded by a little park. Benches were well placed for contemplation in the midst of wild and beautiful forest, scattered granite boulders, and here and there the rusting hand-operated machinery of the original locks.

Within walking distance was the King's Grotto, a curious glacial cauldron seven feet wide, formed in the rock during the Ice Age. Inside, numerous kings and other personages have had their names inscribed during their visits to the fabulous falls.

All this walking through the cold, snappy air helped work up a fantastic appetite for that famous Swedish smörgåsbord—which was just being served when we returned to the *Diana.* She was still in the second lock, and she looked very small in her giant's surroundings.

The Göta Älv is the most built-up, most exploited industrial river in southern Sweden, but in spite of its bustling, clanking, smoking industry, there were places where the river seemed almost virginal, running between steep mountain ridges, sometimes cutting pockets into the banks where sand martins built their nests, some-

Two yachts cross an aqueduct of the Dalsland Canal at Håverud. The canal crosses a rushing stream, a railroad crosses the canal and over it all is a road bridge, a tiered construction that draws visitors to watch the action below.

times running through wide fertile meadows and fields. The sky had clouded over and the wind was picking up; an abundance of blankets was seen on deck, covering all but windblown heads and red cheeks.

At the market town of Lilla Edet on the eastern shore, we entered a short canal leading to a lock which would take us down finally to the level of Gothenburg. This was the Strömsholm Canal, named after the mansion of Ström on its banks.

South of Lilla Edet the countryside varied between flat, marshy banks astride a wide, lazy river and fast-running narrows where gray granite rocks made the going more intricate. Tall pines and occasional oaks lined the banks, embracing low, thick-growing wild berries beneath. Timber farmsteads and mills dotted the shores, wearing their brilliant coats of Falu red.

Then appeared the small dock and few shops of Lödöse, clustered beneath the tower of St. Peder's Church. In the Middle Ages Lödöse was a busy fortified market town and port, with ships sailing back and forth to England and Flanders. It functioned as Sweden's western seaport in the days when the province of Bohusland belonged to Norway and Holland was under Danish rule. In time, trade suffered from the heavy tolls extracted by the hostile commanders of Bohus Castle. Then, in the fourteenth and fifteenth centuries, it was completely leveled three times by invading Danes and Norwegians from across the river. Finally, in 1473, most of the inhabitants gave up and moved to a more comfortable spot at the river's mouth. The town they founded was Nya Lödöse, the forerunner of today's Gothenburg.

Soon, off the starboard side, we could see the Göta Älv splitting in two, the Nordre Älv shooting off westward while we followed the main branch southwest to Gothenburg. Behind the river's fork we could glimpse the 1,000-year-old riverside village of Kungälv, chosen by the three Scandinavian kings as their conference center in 1101, when it was called Kungahälla and guarded by the castle of Ragnhildsholm.

On the island of Fastingsholmen, sitting astride a rocky escarpment and commanding the confluence of both arms of the river, stood Bohus Fortress. This now-crumbling ruin was once the strongest fortress in Scandinavia, defiantly wearing its twin towers known as Father's Hat and Mother's Cap. Built in 1308 as a Norwegian border fort for defense against Sweden, the fort was besieged fourteen times but never carried by assault until the Swedes tried to defend it against 11,000 Norwegians and Danes in 1658. The Swedes had 900 men, who held out bravely for 49 days. But by that time the fort had endured 2,265 bombshells, 600 large grenades, thousands of ordinary cannon shots, petards, and stones. It was in a sorry state, and it never regained its architectural nobility. In the eighteenth century it was abandoned and fell into decay. It was used as a quarry until King Charles XIV happened to pass it on a river journey in 1838, and ordered it preserved as a national monument.

We watched Bohus clip by like a sleeping monster, swept by the cold winds and silhouetted against the darkened gray sky. The *Diana*'s kitchen crew had prepared hot tea with cakes and cookies in lieu of dinner, since we would be disembarking at 6 P.M.

Approach to Gothenburg

We were nearing the end of our three-day journey, and the pastoral scene gradually faded into the housing developments, shopping centers, and industrial activity of Gothenburg. As we slowly chugged our way into the city through its back door, we took the good advice of our Göta Canal guidebook and used the time to "pack your bags, settle the bill with the waitress, thank the crew for a pleasant trip, and relax."

By the time we had finished with all of that, we were passing under the railway bridge, where the inner port welcomed us with high-necked cranes bowing and waving over their cargoes. The harbor was bristling with activity as we pulled into the *Diana*'s berth near the bark *Viking* of Gothenburg, beautiful and graceful, her four tall masts bearing wide-flung yardarms and nautical nostalgia. With its hodge-podge of peoples—Dutchmen, Germans, Englishmen, Swedes, Scots—and its lively, cosmopolitan eye trained always seaward, the town promised adventure. We shouldered our duffels, waved goodbye to the *Diana,* descended the gangplank, and set out to find it.

Some Practical Information

Sweden offers what might aptly be called the Smörgåsbord of European Cruising. There one finds a thoroughly refreshing melange of inland and shoreline cruising and excursion possibilities that will delight the traveler for whatever time he devotes to this portion of his trip.

Both inland and coastal waters are ideally suited to cruising, with their vast natural and secluded areas, numerous sheltered and protected waterways, and the absence of tidal waters. A special treat for the midsummer traveler is the midnight sun, which lightens summer nights, bridging one day into the next with hardly any darkness to separate the two. (In Northern Sweden, near the Arctic Circle, there is no darkness at all from mid-May to mid-July.)

The waterway traveler has three main cruising areas from which to choose. They are attractively presented in the Swedish Tourist Board Pamphlet #11, "Holidays on Swedish Waters."

1. *The inland waterways,* most of them dating from the nineteenth century, offer the most interesting and unique way of exploring Sweden. Whether you travel the waterways on a self-drive charter boat, an excursion steamer, or your own vessel, you will discover scenic routes through secluded countryside and picturesque villages, sheltered safe harbors for overnight anchorage, modern locks leading to clear, deep lakes, and everywhere the warm hospitality of the Swedish people.

Perhaps the most noteworthy waterway is the Göta Canal, which together with the Trollhätte and Södertälje canals forms Sweden's famous Blue Ribbon linking the nation's two largest cities, Stockholm and Gothenburg. Of the 347-mile (558 km) distance between the cities, fully two-thirds consists of natural rivers and lakes, and along the remaining distance the canals' 65 locks raise vessels to a height of 301 feet (92 m) above sea level before lowering them again at the other end.

In addition to the three canals which comprise the greater Göta Canal, there are six others of particular interest: Dalsland Canal, Kinda Canal, Strömsholm Canal, Hjälmare Canal, Filipstads Canal, and Säffle Canal.

2. *The Swedish east coast* excursion area is limited to the Stockholm Archipelago, which extends from the capital thirty miles into the Baltic Sea and consists of some 25,000 islands and islets. Cruising options range from anchorages near wild rocky skerries to modern full-service yachting centers such as Sandham (world famous for its summer regattas), Saltsjöbaden, and Dalarö. There is a special bonus for

east-coast cruising: in the event of inclement weather, you'll be cruising in sheltered waters; the bad weather generally arrives from the west and southwest.

3. *The Swedish west coast* offers splendid cruising and touring opportunities on the nearly tideless waters of the Skagerrak and Kattegat, warmed by the Gulf Stream. Here there are countless deserted coves and islands, excellent fishing grounds, and extensive protected waters in the lee of islands and groups of skerries. In addition there are exceptional archaeological attractions—Viking ship remains, cairns and grave fields, Bronze Age rock carvings—and historic fortresses and quaint village churches.

There are a number of ways to enjoy the waters of Sweden:

BOOKING PASSAGE ABOARD A STEAMER OR EXCURSION BOAT. The possibilities are nearly endless. Can you spare only a few hours? Enjoy a two-hour canal trip of Stockholm or Gothenburg—or a half-day steamer tour of the archipelagos. A full day? Countless day excursions voyage alongshore and through Sweden's beautiful lakes and canals. Several days? Treat yourself to the fascinating three-day trans-Sweden cruise on the Göta Canal, the premier waterway trip in Sweden, operating from mid-May to the first week of September.

Some typical excursion boat fares are:

Day excursions
Stockholm 1-hour canal tour	$3.00
Stockholm 2-hour canal tour	$5.00
Stockholm Archipelago tour, 3 hours	$6.50
Stockholm summer evening boat tour	
(includes dinner at an eighteenth-century inn)	$18.00
Kinda Canal, 9-hour trip from Linköping to Hoorn	$14.00

Canal excursion
Göta Canal, 3-day trip from Stockholm to Gothenburg:
Berth in 3-berth cabin	$165
Berth in double cabin on bridge deck	$227
Berth in single cabin on bridge deck	$327

Göta Canal rates are per person for the three-day, two-night trip; they include all meals and service charges, and there are special rates for children.

Car transport from Stockholm to Gothenburg, or vice versa, is $130.
There are also special combination tours, Swedish State Railways plus Göta Canal Steamship Company, with one-way on the steamer and return by rail.

Booking information and brochures concerning canal excursions can be obtained from: Scanworld   Floating Through Europe, Inc.
         12444 Ventura Boulevard   501 Madison Avenue
         Studio City, Calif. 91604   New York, N.Y. 10022

Information and brochures may also be obtained from the individual canal companies: Göta Canal

Rederi AB Göta Kanal
Box 272
S-401, 24 Gothenburg

Trollhätte Canal

Trollhätte Kanalverk
S-461, 03 Trollhättan

Dalsland Canal

Dalslands Turistförening
Box 89
S-662, 00 Amal

Kinda Canal

Rederi AB Kind
Box 62
S-591, 01 Motala

Strömsholm Canal

Tourist Office
Storgatan 1
S-734, 00 Hallstahammar

Hjälmare Canal

Domanverket Informationssektionen
S-171, 93 Solna

Filipstads Bergslags Canal

Lockkeeper Tomas Hyybro
Filipstads Bergslags Kanal

Säffle Canal

Kanalkontoret Säffle Kanal
S-661, 00 Säffle

Södertälje Canal

Södertälje Kanalverk
Slussgaten
S-151, 36 Södertälje

SELF-DRIVE CHARTER BOATS are available throughout Sweden's many yachting centers. One can hire, by the week, sail or power boats accommodating from two to six persons; smaller boats are available on a daily basis. The Swedish Tourist Board's Pamphlet #9, "Boat Hire in Sweden," lists hire firms that are set up to deal with foreign charterers and provides detailed information concerning each firm's location, the number and types of boats for charter, and charter costs. In addition, the pamphlet provides general information concerning boat hire throughout Sweden.

Typical charter costs are:

Motorboat		May, Sept.	June-August
Albin 25	4–5 berths	$380	$400–500
Albin 30	6 berths	$550	$800–900
Sailboat			
Maxi 77	4 berths	$285	$325–460
Scampi	5 berths	$500	$580–700
Maxi 95	6 berths	$525	$600–850

CAPTAINED YACHTS are available in the major yachting centers such as Stockholm and Gothenburg. There are both motor-sailers and power boats, and they generally accommodate from four to seven persons. The owner of the yacht usually skippers it, his wife frequently participating as first mate and cook—often a delightful combination. The cost of the charter may or may not include food; this should be established during preliminary correspondence with the skipper or charter agent. Lists of captained yachts available for charter can be found in the Swedish Tourist Board's Pamphlet #9, "Boat Hire in Sweden."

Additional information concerning cruising in Sweden can be obtained from:

Swedish Tourist Board
Box 7306
S-103, 85 Stockholm

Svenska Kryssarklubben
(Swedish Cruising Association)
Gyllenstiernsgatan 15
S-115, 26 Stockholm

Swedish National Tourist Office
75 Rockefeller Plaza
New York, N.Y. 10019

Swedish National Tourist Office
3600 Wilshire Boulevard
Los Angeles, Calif. 90010

Marine charts can be obtained from:

Swedish Administration of Shipping and Navigation
Sjofartsverket
Fack
S-601, 01 Norrköping

*From
the
Alps
to
the
Orient*

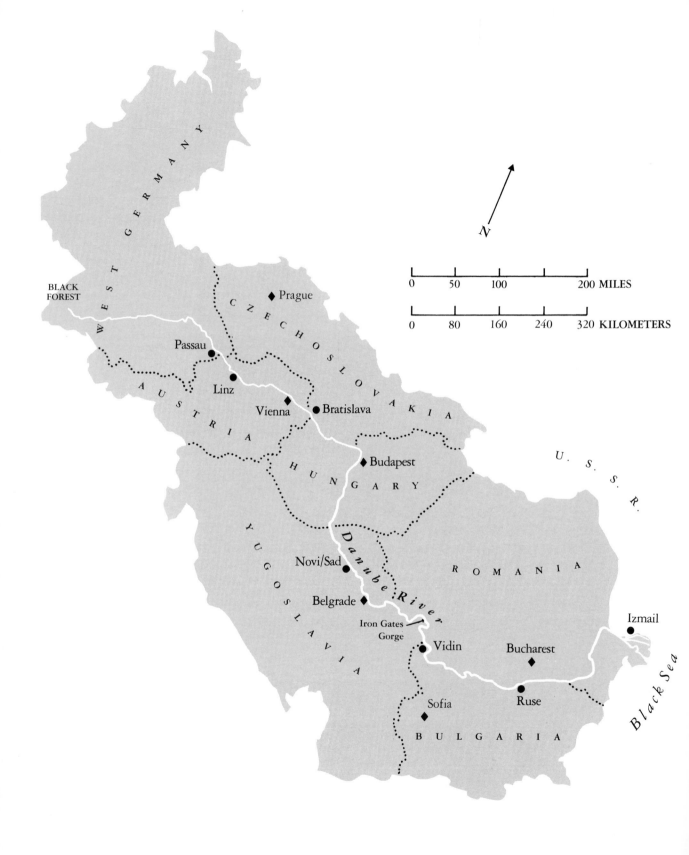

Cruising the Romantic Danube

The Greek historian Herodotus called it the Ister, "the greatest of rivers." It was the property of the savage Celts for 400 years before the advent of the Romans, the highway of conquest for Trajan and his legions; it was scourged by Attila and his terrible Huns, the meeting point of the Persian Darius and the Macedonian Alexander the Great, the pathway of Charlemagne, Napoleon, the Turks, and the Crusaders; it has been home to Teutons and Slavs, Franks, Burgundians, Avars, Magyars, and Bajuvars, the subject of Strauss waltzes and of much speculation about its color.

This is the Danube, the river that would be the pathway of our next cruise. We were to spend eight days traveling the waterway aboard a steamer from Passau to Yalta.

The Danube begins quietly, rising from subterranean sources 3,500 feet above sea level in the Black Forest of Germany, only about a hundred yards from the watershed of the powerful Rhine. But the waters of the nascent Danube, in contrast to those of the Rhine, refuse to head north, preferring instead the mystery of the Orient. The Danube is formed at the confluence of two streams, the Breg and the Brigach. This point, the Donauquelle, lies in the park of the magnificent Furstenburg Castle, where it is marked by a monumental nineteenth-century fountain.

The fountain provides an appropriate send-off for a growing river that will swell with the addition of sixty navigable and countless smaller streams as it crosses or skirts eight countries and five capital cities. On its course the Danube, the second longest river in Europe, links Germany with southeastern Europe until, having traveled 1,776 miles (2,850 km) and having drained an area more than three times the size of Great Britain, it flows into the Black Sea through several mouths on the east coast of Romania.

The Danube at Passau

When we stood on the riverbank in Passau, West Germany, on the Austrian border, the river's course was already one-quarter run. From its source in the rolling pine groves of the Black Forest it had flowed beneath the high limestone plateaus of the Swabian Juras, under the watchful eyes of somber castles and fortresses not unlike those of the middle Rhine. It had descended to the city of Ulm, where, among gabled houses, Albert Einstein was born in 1879. There it had absorbed the waters of the tributary Iller and then run along the northern edge of the rich Bavarian Forest until it reached Passau.

At Passau the Danube still has more than a thousand feet to descend before reaching sea level. Here the still young river joins the rivers Inn and Ilz to form a single, striated ribbon of brown, green, and black water that flows deep within the dark, wooded, rolling hills.

We had arrived in Passau the day before embarkation on our Danube voyage and had found a charming hotel in Schloss Ort. It was tucked back from the riverbank, through old cobbled alleyways, just at the point where the three rivers meet. Our room overlooked the fast and frisky Inn as it ran along the foot of the Schaiblingsturm, a turret built in 1481 as part of the town's defenses. We could also see on a wooded hill across the river the twin onion towers of Mariahilf Pilgrimage Church. And this was only a sampling of what the town had to offer.

Passau is a dramatically beautiful, historic city situated on a spit of land at the confluence of the three rivers. It rises in terraces from the river, beginning with the old houses of the waterfront—ancient settlement of the carriers, waggoners, fishermen, and bargees—and working up past the ancient walls, towers, and arches of the churches and patrician houses huddled in the shadow of the great dome of St. Stephen's Cathedral. Baron Friedrich von Humboldt (1769–1859), naturalist, writer, and statesman, called Passau one of the seven most beautiful cities in the world.

Passau has long competed with Xanten and Worms for the title Town of the Nibelungs, which each of these cities proudly bears. It is said that the great Teutonic epic was written by scribes within the walls of Passau in about the twelfth century. To remind the visitor of this, the great halls of the fourteenth-century Rathaus contain colossal murals depicting scenes from the saga, including Kriemhild's entry into Passau.

A walk before dinner took us along the promenade to the end of the peninsula, where the wild green waters of the Inn overpower both the wide and serene "blue" Danube and the calm and mysterious blackness of the River Ilz. Three hundred feet above us, on the towering Georgsberg Cliff, stood the sternly immovable Oberhaus Fortress, scene of the defeat of the Turkish army in 1715. Further along the Danube banks we found the Rathaus, whose painted facade, we knew, hid one of those wonderful Ratskellers. After having some delicious Danube sheatfish (giant catfish), we lingered over wine at a historic tavern steeped in atmosphere collected since 1358 and bearing the difficult name of Heilig-Geist-Stift-Schenke.

The following morning we explored the narrow, twisting alleyways of the old city, with their charming over-the-street archways connecting facing houses. We peeked around the scaffolding inside the cathedral, where artists were painstakingly restoring the eighteenth-century frescoes. Then we found the Residenzplatz, an elegant square bordered by the richly decorated facades of old patrician mansions and the "new" (1712) Bishop's Palace.

The midday bells tolled more than the hour for us: *The Russians were here!* Passau may have been able to shrug this off as a commonplace, but for us it approached the incredible. The Russians were to be our hosts for the eight-day downstream Danube trip, on board the M/S *Dnepr,* named for one of the loveliest rivers Russia can boast.

The *Dnepr,* 350 feet of white steel and glass, with luxurious accommodations for 170 passengers, was staffed by a crew of 85—a ratio of one crew member to every two passengers. No matter what your politics, Russian hospitality—superb and plentiful caviar, superb and plentiful vodka (in all its surprising variations), four exotic meals daily, and live music from a four-piece orchestra throughout the entire trip— can be utterly charming.

Our stateroom, like the other 81, was comfortable and tastefully decorated, with cabin-controlled air conditioning, a window writing table, signed lithographs, a roomy closet, plenty of shelves, and every possible amenity.

The ship offered restaurant, music room, and bar on the main deck; heated swimming pool on the inviting sundeck; the services of a hairdresser, a laundry and pressing service, dispensary and ship's doctor, and a film-developing laboratory. The facilities were spacious, comfortable, attractive—and we were duly impressed.

On the Threshold of Austria

Departure was scheduled for four o'clock, but we were under way by three. As the last passenger boarded, the sun emerged from the overcast early May sky, and the Russians lost no time in casting off. We left Passau behind and moved slowly, quietly through the darkly wooded hills and scenes that inspired painters of the sixteenth-century Danube School to create canvases quivering with hidden life, depicting the secret countrysides where roamed those legendary spirits inseparable from Germanic sensibilities. The mysterious, rocky slopes bordered a wide and imposing Danube as it meandered along its tortuous easterly route.

Less than two miles beyond Passau, Austria greeted us on the right bank— Austria, the country that convinced the world, for a while at least, that this milk-chocolate-colored waterway was actually *blue.*

Sweet Kasten sprinkled its houses over an immense rolling hillside. Then, in the half-light of late afternoon, with the sun peeking from behind the clouds, the beautiful rococo abbey of Engelhartszell appeared, with its two minareted churches. The valley began to squeeze in on us, rising now like a wall from the constricted, rushing river. Occasionally we could see the vague outlines of a fortified castle on the heights.

The Danube was working its way southeast in a procession of wide loops, sunk between the wooded gorges and reaches on either bank, winding around the valley of the Aschach. There were nesting swans, a mackerel sky, and on the romantic, rolling hillsides a fantastic mosaic of spring greens and soft, welcoming pine stands. From behind a hill the sun cast its warm light on the endlessly unfolding valley. The glasslike water was a lovely mirror for misty mauve and gold reflections and trees dressed in white flowers. Neuhaus Castle was struck by a patch of sunlight, like a spotlight focusing on history from above the dark valley.

While the *Dnepr* passed south of the Mühlviertel Mountains and north of the rich, undulating Inviertel farmlands, we found our way to our table—groaning with caviar and vodka—in the glass-walled dining room, where the orchestra was already playing a moody version of "China Moon." This was one of the most festive and alluringly luxurious moments we enjoyed on any waterway. And this extravaganza was only the first of eight such dinners, all of which included a rich selection of Russian and international dishes: Serbian pelmeni, Ukrainian borscht, chicken Kiev, shashlik, bliny, and Danube sturgeon. We were also invited to sample Armenian cognac, Russian champagne, and wines of obscure origin that proved to be delicious. It was no place to be on a diet, we thought, as we abandoned ourselves to an unbridled orgy of dining.

By the time we were served coffee, the orchestra had turned to the gaiety of Russian folk songs. The captain and his officers took a moment after dinner to welcome us all aboard and to wish us a good trip.

As we sat sipping the last of our coffee, we could see the Abbey of Wilhering, founded by the Cistercians in 1146. Soon the city of Linz, its lights reflecting silver and gold in the river, rose from quayside promenades to the point of the pilgrimage church on Postlingberg Hill. The capital of Upper Austria, Linz is the third largest city in the country, with a population of 200,000. Built on both banks of the Danube at a widening of the river, it owes a great deal of its current prosperity to the river; it handles more cargo than any other port on the Western European section of the Danube.

The Postlingberg Hill loomed high above us on the left bank as we drew abreast of St. Martin's Church. The church is one of the oldest in Austria, built by Charlemagne himself on the rubble of Roman foundations. The fifteenth-century Linz Castle, standing on its own hill on the south bank just beyond St. Martin's, was the residence of Emperor Friedrich III.

The Danube Park, with its swimming pools and vast recreational grounds, was ablaze with lights, and the sounds of music and laughter flowed over the water to greet us. Then, gradually, the lights disappeared astern and the banks receded into dark nothingness.

The valley opened out into a wide, fertile basin formed by the slit of the Danube and its tributaries, the Traun and the Enns. The ship's radar slowly revolved above the wheelhouse, and a spotlight scanned the irregular, unlit banks that from time to time jutted out toward our path.

At about 11:30 P.M. we approached Grein, a pretty country resort at the foot of a high wooded bluff that watched over the entrance to the Strudengau gorges. Rising from the bluff to guard the town was the romantic Grein Castle, its towers and turrets intact; below, the little town encircled its main square with turreted houses.

It seemed a pity to feel drowsy, to succumb to sleep. But this was an eight-day trip, and we would need to be rested throughout to enjoy it. So, as the boat made its way toward Krems, through a valley hollowed out of the granite hills of the

Waldviertel, and drove deep between the wooded cliffs of the lovely Strudengau, we returned to our cabin to sleep. The ship's engines were barely audible, and it was difficult to sense the motion of our steady, smooth progress.

As we dreamed, the *Dnepr* followed the river through the valley of the Nibelungen, where dashing Gunther and Hagen rode with their knights to visit Kriemhild at Attila's court; the valley of the Wachau, with its vineyards, orchards of plums, peaches, and apricots, fields of tobacco and corn—all flourishing in a sunny, mild climate; Durnstein Castle, where Richard the Lionhearted languished for a year until faithful Blondel came searching for him. (In those breezy gardens just hours earlier, aproned serving maids had been carrying trayfuls of superb Wachau wines.)

Vienna Love Affair

When we awoke and looked out the window, we discovered, in the sunshine of the early spring morning, Vienna. Not really the city of Vienna, for the city itself sits back a bit from the river; what we saw first was the famous silhouette of Vienna's giant wheel, a structure towering more than 200 feet over the Danube, the city, and the vast green park in which it stood. The park was the Prater, once the hunting reserve of the Habsburgs; it stretched from the river to the Danube Canal in the heart of the city.

The Prater was a fitting introduction to Vienna, for this was the very ground on which, in the early nineteenth century, the giddy and wonderful Viennese waltz was born. Then the Congress of Vienna—*"Elle danse, mais elle ne marche pas"* (It dances, but it never gets anything done)—furnished the opportunity for all kinds of exotic extravaganzas in the city's glittering ballrooms. Vienna at that time played host to a more impressive array of monarchs and their retinues than has probably been seen anywhere before or since; its Carnival season whirled with dazzling evening gowns, towering headdresses, feathered fans, perfume, champagne, hand kissing, flirtations, and several degrees of abandon.

It was, of course, Vienna's own Johann Strauss who set the wealthy, self-indulgent, and sensuous city swaying with his music. As the city's favorite conductor, he personally introduced the "Blue Danube," "Tales From the Vienna Woods," and other waltzes, and he soon became known the world over as King of the Waltz.

Over a breakfast of sausage, cheese, apple juice, and coffee with cognac, in the dining room of the *Dnepr,* we planned our day and evening in this inviting city.

Mid-morning we were standing in the first gallery of Vienna's great baroque Spanish Riding School, drinking in the pure whiteness of its splendid interior, bathed in light from the high windows, and marveling at the immensity of its *manège,* or indoor training ring. We were about to witness the *haute école* training of the gleaming white Lippizanner stallions, a tradition that goes back to pre-Roman times and has remained relatively unchanged since the fifteenth century, when the art of dressage, or balance and agility, was essential in combat.

The *manège* itself has seen even more incredible sights than horses performing the piaffe, the capriole, and the courbette. In its day it saw masked balls and great riding spectacles; it reverberated with Handel's music performed by seven hundred amateur musicians; as many as ten thousand guests at one time have shared its floor and galleries to watch lottery drawings and rope-walking displays; it has been a garden filled with palms and orange trees; it even hosted the Vienna Stock Exchange during the cholera epidemic of 1848. In 1808 the Swiss mechanic and aviator Jakob Degen tested his new flying device and succeeded, with 34 wing beats, in rising to within six feet of the pristine white, chandeliered 56-foot ceiling.

On the day of our visit the Spanish Riding School was all business. We were allowed to watch quietly from the gallery as, first, the new generation of young Lippizanner stallions, with their dark brown coats (which would turn white at four years of age), pranced in, their intense vitality and exuberance barely held in check by the skilled trainers on their backs. Then the older, more disciplined, and trained horses were put through their paces by riders in double-breasted brown frock coats,

At a turning of the Danube, 25 kilometers above Belgrade, Yugoslavia, the river cuts sharply into the sedimentary rock of the grassy plain. A road leads from the river, where an outboard-powered skiff rests on the beach, to a church where the apse shaded in the afternoon sun points, as is customary, toward the East.

two-cornered gold-braided hats, white leather riding breeches, and silver spurs. The gallery gave a collective gasp as one of the stallions performed the capriole, a great, high, perfect jump in place, in which the horse kicks his flanks back and tucks his forelegs neatly under him. In medieval times many a combatant was killed or injured by those high-kicking hindlegs when knights used this maneuver in trying to break away from the enemy. Now it is simply an act of near-perfect grace, a fusion into a single entity of horse and rider, both appearing to be suspended in air for a long, unimaginable moment.

In the elegant Josefplatz before the Austrian National Library, there was an appealing lineup of fiakers, those gleaming two-horse hansom cabs. A driver offered to show us old Vienna the old way, and on impulse we climbed in behind the two lovely white cousins of the Lippizanners whose performance we had just enjoyed.

The heart of Vienna is a mere square mile marking the site of the old Roman camp of Vindobona (Good Wine), the original Vienna. It began as an outpost of the Roman Empire and became a stronghold of Christianity that finally halted the westward march of the Turks. Our two handsome white horses clip-clopped us around sumptuous, copper-domed St. Peter's Church with its great bell, the Pummerin (Boomer), in a belfry that rose like a proud arrow 450 feet above the very heart of the old medieval city. We marveled at the magical clock in the Höher Market, its figures of famous Viennese characters parading at the stroke of noon to the music of Haydn, Mozart, Strauss, and Schubert. We paused briefly at the monument to the horror of the Black Plague of 1679. Then our carriage continued through tiny streets lined with bookstores and old print shops, through the medieval Jewish ghetto, and past the house where Mozart composed *The Marriage of Figaro.*

After a four-course luncheon on board the *Dnepr,* we set out again on foot to explore the Ringstrasse, that horseshoe-shaped belt of handsome, tree-shaded boulevards that encircles the inner heart of Vienna, where once the bastions of the old walls protected the town. Built in 1857 by Emperor Franz Josef, this vast project of public gardens, monuments, and baroque palaces has ever since lent its own special tone to the city.

Beginning at the Stadtpark, with its lovely artificial lake and a famous statue of Johann Strauss, we passed some of the great museums of Vienna, housed in enormous buildings that epitomize the baroque style for which the city is renowned—and then we came to Beethoven Square.

Beethoven loved Vienna more than any other city, and he lived here for the most productive thirty-five years of his life. In Vienna the rough and melancholy composer loved tragically and wrote the Moonlight Sonata for his "immortal beloved." Here he felt the first terrifying attacks of deafness, which filled him with utter despair; here he wrote the works that revolutionized musical expression; and near here, in Baden, where the great composer lay dying after a life full of disappointment, he said to his friend Hummel, "I had a certain talent, hadn't I?"

Further along the Ringstrasse we passed the Burggarten, with its statue of Mozart, who died a pauper's death here at the age of thirty-five.

We left the Ring for a drive to Schönbrunn Castle—named for the beautiful fountain *(schöner Brunnen)* discovered here by Emperor Matthias in the early seventeenth century—which contains 1,200 elegant baroque rooms behind its imposing ochre facade. Within the huge iron gates of the castle grounds, memories were manifold and vibrant in the maze of shaded walks, dove aviaries, vast formal flower beds, simulated "Roman" ruins, and zoological gardens. Here the child Marie Antoinette danced in shepherd pastorales in the court theater. In the concert room a young Mozart astonished Empress Maria Theresa and her courtiers with his amazing talent; an older Mozart sent his opera *Don Giovanni* to be performed at court. Joseph Haydn conducted in the family court theater. In 1805 and 1809 Napoleon set up his headquarters; and here, after his exile, he left his little son for protection. (The luckless boy, having led a short life of sad exile from France, died of tuberculosis at the age of twenty-one.)

At 4:30 P.M. we turned from our contemplation of the ghosts of Schönbrunn, seized suddenly with an undeniable compulsion. We found a taxi, whose driver nodded understandingly when we asked him to drive to the Hotel Sacher. It was time for Coffee.

Kaffee is a social institution in Austria—especially in Vienna, where the café originated in the seventeenth century. Abandoned among the baggage of the fleeing Turks in 1683 were large quantities of mysterious brown beans; an Austrian spy named Kolschitzky learned how to use them, was rewarded with the beans themselves, and opened Austria's first *Kaffeehaus.* Soon café life became an essential part of Vienna. From this city, coffee as a drink and the café as an institution made their way throughout the Western world.

The Hotel Sacher, opened in 1876 by Eduard Sacher, Prince Metternich's chef, is home to one of Vienna's best-known food specialties: Sachertorte, a rich chocolate cake covered with a layer of almost pure, candy-firm, chocolate icing and filled with apricot jam. (Created on orders from the Congress of Vienna, its recipe remains a closely guarded secret.) The pleasant sidewalk café was quite full, but we managed to find a table near the portrait of the redoubtable Frau Sacher, who looked down at us from above the bar. We ordered mocha coffee and Sachertorte. While we ogled and were ogled by the passersby, we lingered over our rich treat—and came to realize that we needed a way to work off some of the damage.

We found it a short distance down the shady Ringstrasse, in the Stadtpark, which enticed us with the strains of Strauss waltzes. Johann Strauss is still very much alive in this city; it is his music that gives Vienna its special smile. In the park, among peacocks, tulips in bloom, pansies, and lilacs, we joined the dancers—old and young, lovers and grandparents, tourists and students—in waltzing to the gay and infectious lilt of the music. Two hours had passed before we knew it.

After dinner aboard the *Dnepr* we hailed a taxi at the quay and headed for the

Vienna Woods to sample the new wine at one of the hundreds of heurigers, or private vintners' taverns, which dot the surrounding hills. The heuriger is another Viennese institution of considerable charm that hails from the enlightened era of Maria Theresa; today it is a favorite evening rendezvous of the Viennese.

When the vintner has drawn off the new wine, he hangs an evergreen branch or a garland of pine twigs and vine leaves over his door, inviting the public to try his beverage. Often arranged as an outdoor garden attached to the main house, heurigers are filled with plain wooden tables, long benches, and few decorations. Almost all offer some form of entertainment, ranging from aged zither players to groups of folk singers.

We shunned the better-known Grinzing heurigers, preferring to find less-frequented places in a little town called Heiligenstadt, where, in the little vine-covered, seventeenth-century house on the main square, Beethoven lived for some months in 1817. This same house had an evergreen hung outside the entrance to its lantern-lit patio, which was alive with chatter and the clatter of glasses. It seemed we had been invited to a heuriger!

By the time we returned to the boat and to bed, we were filled with warm memories of Vienna, a city so totally in love with itself and its great past—in love in such a charming way—that we had immediately been drawn into its spirit. Her people radiated a lighthearted wit, her music a pure, bubbling joy—contagious and very much alive.

Through the Iron Curtain

By the time we awoke in the morning (this was now our third day on the Danube), the *Dnepr* was already under way. She had departed Vienna at 5 A.M. and had since passed through Austria's March-Donauland, dubbed by many historians "the battlefield of Europe." We had also, quietly and unceremoniously, slipped through the Iron Curtain, where somber riverside watchtowers held the shadowy figures of armed guards. The left bank was now Czechoslovakia, culturally one of the richer of the Eastern European countries.

Slovakia, the area north of the Danube, abounds in folk culture, ancient folk traditions, and the most lavishly decorated costumes in the republic. Each region boasts its own indigenous musical instruments, from bagpipes to shepherds' pipes, and there are fine traditions of woodcarving, ceramics, embroidery, lacemaking, and hand weaving.

As we took our pre-breakfast stroll on the main deck, we were just passing Bratislava, capital of Slovakia, its thirteenth-century castle sitting 280 feet above the river on a granite ledge. St. Martin's Cathedral, the coronation church of the kings of Hungary from 1563, is situated nearby, bearing a cushion and a gilded crown atop its 180-foot tower.

The weather was perfect that morning: 63 degrees Fahrenheit at breakfast, with clear, sunny skies. The Danube was boiling swiftly down toward the Black Sea (it still had 540 feet to descend) and the channel markers, shaped like mini-missiles, resolutely faced upstream in a hopeless struggle against the fierce current. The Danube ran between low gravel banks, Czechoslovakia on the left and now Hungary on the right.

Most of what is Hungary today was the Roman province of Dacia/Pannonia. Home to the Magyars since the fifth century, this little country, no bigger than the state of Maine, has enriched the world with its splendid cuisine, first-rate wines, gypsy violins, Franz Liszt, and Béla Bartók.

At Bratislava we had entered the Danube Wildlife Preserve, which stretches all the way to Štúrovo, nearly a hundred miles, and constitutes one of the best natural habitats in Europe for waterfowl, pheasant, and small game. Our field glasses were as much a fixture as—and indeed were used more frequently than—the salt and pepper shakers on our luncheon table (which was laden today with sturgeon in jelly, salads, smoked foods, borscht and Georgian kharcho, roast beef, chicken in cream sauce, and wonderfully rich ice cream).

The ancient Roman settlement of Brigetio—now Szony—passed on the Hungarian side. Here large-scale excavations have unearthed important archaeological finds, among them murals in the style of Pompeii, a large treasure trove of gold coins, sarcophagi, marble and stone carvings, a primitive Christian cemetery, and the tomb of a bishop from about 330 A.D.

Nearby on the Czech bank was Iza, from the first to the fourth centuries A.D. the largest Roman camp to be found in Czechoslovakian territory. Its remains are well preserved; a square, fortified camp complete with gates and some twenty towers, its central heating and drainage systems are still in evidence.

A warm-weather haze had settled lightly over the Danube Valley as we wound through and around the old town, past farms and vineyards on the deep green, wooded, steeply rising hills of the left bank. These hills cradled the lush valley of Deep Sorrow.

The Enchanting Danube Bend

Passengers moved out onto the sundeck for basking and reading. There was even one hardy swimmer, but most bathers sought the less windy deck area just aft of the wheelhouse.

Having left the Czech border at Szob as the Danube flowed on into Hungary, we approached the famous stretch of river known as the Danube Bend, where the river breaks through the Börzsöny and Szentendre mountains and twists like a hairpin for an enchanting stretch of some 15 miles. The river's steady easterly flow, when it reaches the town of Vác, changes to an almost southerly course, and it moves then through a chain of riverside spas, bare volcanic mountains, and limestone hills. This area is the heartland of Hungarian history, the frontier district of the Roman Empire;

Soft light of the setting sun bathes the neo-Gothic Parliament Building of Budapest, a romantic, lacy stonework of dome, turrets, spires—and a newly added red star.

here kings set up their royal residences, ambassadors came and went, and great forces met and clashed.

In mid-afternoon we reached Esztergom, the official begining of the Danube Bend, where Marcus Aurelius, the philosopher-emperor, wrote the twelve books of his *Reflections*. During the early centuries of the Middle Ages the city became the capital of the Magyars; for a long time it was the residence of their kings as well as the seat of the archbishop of Esztergom, primate of the Hungarian Catholic Church. The great nineteenth-century basilica, patterned on St. Paul's in Rome, remains the largest church in Hungary, measuring nearly 400 feet long and 262 feet high. Below it lie the ruins of the thirteenth-century castle and fortifications.

At the southernmost point of the deep bend the stark, mist-shrouded Castle Hill of Visegrad appeared in the distance around the mountain. We were near Domos, with its ruins of a twelfth-century church where, according to local legend, King Béla I died in 1063 in the wreckage of his throne, which had collapsed under his own enormous weight.

The hills of the left bank, near Nagymaros, were covered with peach orchards and fields of grapes, black currants, and raspberries. We had reached Visegrad, which was for many centuries the seat of the kings of Hungary, and whose fourteenth-century palace was rediscovered in 1943, buried beneath the rubble of four centuries after the Turks had razed it. Six years before its destruction in 1542, the archbishop of Esztergom wrote that it contained 350 rooms and was surrounded with terraced gardens and fountains, vineyards and hothouses. We saw Visegrad's hexagonal 100-foot Solomon Tower and water bastion float dreamily by in the warmth of late afternoon.

The Danube suddenly emerged from the mountains that had been hindering its progress, entered the plain, spread out, and relaxed. Here, through the geological ages, the river bed has built up immense deposits of mud and pebbles, carried by the Danube from its source in the Black Forest. This was in fact the origin of the long, narrow, elbow-shaped island of Szentendre. The channel divides around it, and the *Dnepr* turned northeast to enter the main shipping channel, a passage dotted with tiny islands.

The ship followed the great curve of the river around to the east, passing Vác's large domed cathedral and maze of twisting alleyways. Only five miles further on, we were in the outskirts of Budapest, which claims 20 percent of the entire population of Hungary.

Budapest's Hungarian Rhapsodies

Budapest has one of the loveliest settings of any city in Europe, the grand Danube dividing the densely populated business center of Pest on the left bank from the residential districts of Buda, with their historic buildings, villages, and cottages hidden among the trees, on the right. Roses are grown in the city in such quantity that it has been called the Rose City. Unfortunately, there is very little distinguished architecture here, so much of it having disappeared in the countless battles, sieges, and civil wars of the centuries. Many houses remain pockmarked with bullet holes, and the city resounds with the constant chaos of building and rebuilding. Yet there are small details—unexpected corners, sudden delights—that reward travelers in this city of light and shadow, where moving beauty contrasts with ugliness and utilitarianism.

Margaret Island, a lovely park filled with plane trees, exotic plants, and flowers that covers nearly 400 acres, guards the northern entrance to the town. The river flowed grandly by the immense neo-Gothic parliament building of Pest, a structure that took twenty years to build and has probably witnessed more agitated and unparliamentary scenes than any similar building in Europe. Its central dome and fine pinnacles, arcades, and the windows of its large facade were all calmly mirrored in the Danube flowing at its feet.

We ducked under the lovely Chain Bridge, designed in 1839, destroyed in the last war, and faithfully rebuilt, to its original design, in 1949. The Korzo, or Danube Promenade, begins just beyond the bridge. This is a favorite strolling place for all Budapest, for it presents a wonderful panoramic view of beautiful Buda across the river. Cafés and terraces line the Korzo; as the *Dnepr* maneuvered alongside to tie up, the ship's orchestra launched into a popular song, and shoreside strollers waved in friendly welcome. The late-afternoon sun glistened on the moving water, greening the greens, darkening the shadows, talling the trees, paling the sky, and lifting the heat haze of day. Here, between the great Chain Bridge and the graceful Elizabeth Bridge, we docked in the heart of Pest, within easy walking distance of shopping, exploring, and entertainment.

After a dinner replete with bliny, red caviar, Languette and sturgeon, tiny mushrooms, and pâté, with gay music and the anticipation of an evening in Budapest, we cleared formalities and went ashore, walking three blocks to Vaci Utca, the city's fashionable shopping street.

We wandered and window-shopped awhile, then entered the Matyas Pince (Matthias' Cellar), a smart spot evoking the atmosphere of fifteenth-century King Matyas (Matthias the Just), Hungary's brilliant Renaissance monarch, the last of Magyar stock, who was elected by acclaim on the ice of the frozen Danube. As we descended, the sound of gay gypsy music, happy chatter, and the clink of glasses drifted up the stairs to greet us. The cellar was crowded; tourists and Hungarians filled the authentically decorated room with singing and laughter.

Escorted to a large booth, we ordered some Egri Pinot Noir and a bottle of the celebrated Tokay white that comes from the special volcanic soil of the rivers Bodrog and Hernad, both tributaries of the Danube. Tokay was already famous at the time of the Crusades, a golden aristocrat so proud it doesn't like to be compared to champagne and so fiercely sought after that the Tokay destined for the table of Catherine the Great was reputedly guarded by an entire troop of Cossacks.

We had journeyed from Strauss waltzes to Hungarian rhapsodies in just twenty-four hours; the mood had changed to the sultry, spirited, now lilting, now furious tempo of the gypsy, full of daring dissonances, barbaric and elemental visions, and the demonic imagination of the original ancient Eastern European folk music. And always it was charged with those complicated rhythms that made us want to get up and dance.

The tables around us were laden with a sophisticated and aromatic medley of Hungarian dishes, among them chicken paprikash and Halaszle, the Magyar version of bouillabaisse (which true patriots set far above the Marseilles variety). Once again we forgot our diets and ordered a "little something" to go with the wine.

Four musicians serenaded us, the leader planting himself at the end of our booth, his large, curved mustache topped by wonderful, twinkling eyes. The eyes opened wide, then half closed as he leaned back and sighed, then rolled in mock rapture as they launched into a Hungarian rhapsody.

The morning was crisp, but we were wilted. We hired a taxi to take us to the top of St. Gellert's Hill, the very oldest part of Budapest, first settled by the Illyrian tribes from the north during the Iron Age. From the summit, 770 feet high, the entire city spread out before us like a misty canvas. The panorama swept from the vast plain occupied by Pest on the opposite bank of the Danube, with its labyrinth of roofs, domes, cupolas, and spires, north to the lower tip of Szentendre Island, past Margaret Island's parks and gardens, and south to the huge iron and steel works of Csépel Island.

North of St. Gellert's Hill stood Castle Hill, named for the eighteenth-century baroque and neobaroque royal palace that stood on its crest. The siege of 1944–1945 reduced this district to a vast acreage of rubble, leaving only a few scarred pillars and fire-blackened statues poking out of the smoking devastation. Surprisingly, this incalculable loss was the source of a remarkable archaeological discovery. Beneath the ruins of the most recent foundations were the remains of earlier castles, including the medieval castles of the kings of the Arpad and Anjou dynasties, of the Holy Roman Emperor Sigismund, and of King Matthias.

Near the castle on this long, narrow plateau were streets full of miniature palaces, mansions of former church magnates, lesser nobility, and rich burghers, and a few medieval churches. The thirteenth-century Coronation, or Matthias, Church was almost completely destroyed several times and served as the principal Turkish mosque during the 150 years of occupation. It contains a miscellany of style as well as art works representative of much of Budapest's history. And on the same square we found the Romanesque Fishermen's Bastion, consisting of cloisters of white stone arches and columns and providing perfectly framed views of the city far below.

South to Serbia

The *Dnepr* pulled away from her berth near the Chain Bridge at noon, in the same festive atmosphere of music, waving, and cheering as when she arrived, and we left behind the second capital of our Danube cruise. Soon we saw the river embracing the northern tip of Csépel Island, more than 35 miles long, the largest Danube island that is Hungarian soil. Most of the industry of Budapest is concentrated there, along with homes for the nearly 100,000 people employed in the Csépel iron and steel works, oil refineries, tanneries, and felt and paper mills. Just south of the city, across the river from Csépel Island, were the great Budafok wine vaults, catacombs cut into the limestone and extending for several miles.

As we were served a leisurely lunch, we neared the end of Csépel Island and passed herds of dairy cattle in lush green pasture. This was the Mezofold (Meadowland) region, stretching along the right bank from just south of Budapest to the

Yugoslavian border. For centuries this was the region of the royal stud; now large, irrigated orchards occupy the rich lowlands near the Danube and the valleys that follow the watercourse.

The villages on the banks are favorite spots of Budapest fishermen and watersports enthusiasts. Here anglers' cottages are interspersed with orchards, cedar log cabins, and terraced backyard gardens on rolling hillsides, and budding vines promise more of those luscious Hungarian wines.

In mid-afternoon we were poised at the edge of the Great Hungarian Plains, or *puszta:* 20,000 square miles of vast flatlands prominent for cattle and horse breeding ranches. Once a seemingly endless stretch of shifting sand dunes covered with scrub, the plains were transformed in the nineteenth century by the effort and ingenuity of the people, who succeeded in binding and irrigating the sand, making it today a great Eden of green vineyards, orchards, and bright acacia trees. There still remain some of those vast prairies where herds of cattle, sheep, and horses range; the animals are tended by herdsmen who continue to wear the traditional wide, white linen trousers, blue shirts, and hats that weigh over two pounds—and they carry long whips that they use with unerring skill.

Poets and prose writers have praised the peculiar beauty of the Great Plains in romantic and fiery lines. Painters have tried to capture its special magic, and travelers have marveled at the mirage factor: a phenomenon of downward reflection caused by the uneven distribution of air density that sometimes results in what seem to be (in the words of writer Mor Jokai) "two studs grazing above each other." Here the Hungarian peasant has lived for centuries in a constant struggle with wind, weather, rapacious landlords, innumerable attacks, and foreign occupation. His struggle has left soft and stormy echoes in Magyar folksong.

At 4 P.M., under a hot sun and a warm, gentle breeze, we saw Dunaföldvár on the right bank, its squat, square tower standing since the fifteenth century on a hill over the Danube. It was a delicious afternoon, full of towns that had been river crossings since the time of the Romans, of fine old medieval and Renaissance buildings, large parks, riverside beaches, and fortified bridges.

After dinner, to pass the time through the unbroken plains, we were invited to take our chances in a raffle for items ranging from nesting dolls to hand-inlaid balalaikas from the ship's gift shop. At 10:30 P.M. we approached Mohács, the last Hungarian town before the Yugoslav border.

Yugoslavia has existed only for some fifty years, but the land itself was known to the ancient Greeks as Illyria, named for the tribes who settled there after coming south to the Adriatic coast and who, by the fourth century B.C., had built a powerful kingdom. Philip and Alexander the Great swept in and hindered their progress for about a century, but an even larger kingdom thrived by the third century B.C. The Romans finally succeeded in conquering them in 33 A.D., acquiring in the process some of their best soldiers and sailors and six Roman emperors-to-be.

The Pannonian Basin, the geographic area drained by the Danube and its tributaries, is the most fertile region of Yugoslavia. Politically, the Danube traverses Serbia, chief of the six republics that compose the Yugoslav federation. Reflecting its fertility, Serbia is mainly an agricultural region, devoted to cereals, industrial crops, and pastureland. Northeastern Serbia is known as the Vojvodine —a vast, intensively cultivated plain with immense, clay-daubed farms lost in the greenery of orchards and undulating plateaus and flecked with wells, coachhouses, and haylofts.

In the Vojvodine the peasants are said to eat well and to enjoy lives rich with living traditions and gay with the dances of their ancestors. Fish and stag are free for the hunting near the Danube. Only the hilly vineyards of the Fruska Gora, to the south near Belgrade, interrupt the great green and golden seas of waving grain that, during spring and early summer, extend endlessly toward the Hungarian and Romanian frontiers.

The rich Vojvodine passed us by while we slept; when we awoke, to our fifth day on board the *Dnepr,* we were treated to one of the great treasures of Serbia: Novi Sad. Once known as the Serbian Athens, the city contains splendid old Orthodox churches that abound in brilliant frescoes, superb icons, and richly decorated altars. Just across the river, set on a small hillside, is the huge castle and town of Petrovaradin, enclosed within a network of stern, unyielding walls. It was here that Prince Eugene of Savoy trounced the Turkish army in 1716 and captured the grand vizier's tent, a canvas so massive it took 500 men to pitch it.

At breakfast we watched Sremski Karlovci slip by on the right bank, one of the prettiest little towns in Serbia. Its tree-shaded squares are adorned with marble fountains, handsome baroque palaces, and cathedrals—treasures that endure from the seventeenth century, when Sremski Karlovci became Serbia's cultural and political center.

On the right bank were the lovely Fruska Gora (Mountain of Fruits) hills, dropping like razor cuts through the soft loess, their flat tops carpeted with fruit trees and meadowland.

Wandering the White Town

At 11 A.M. we were nearing Belgrade. We were early; the schedule called for a one o'clock arrival, but by 11:30 A.M. we had already pulled in past Kalemegdan Fortress. We came to a full stop in the middle of the harbor and then, suddenly, heard the rumble of massive chains emerging from the ship's belly, the *Dnepr's* hefty anchor being dropped from the bow. As we swung to face the current, we had a chance to study the activity in the harbor and the skyline of Belgrade—a city which perhaps no one has ever seriously called beautiful.

Maybe the most remarkable thing about the city is that it exists at all after having been devastated more than twenty times in its long history. The principal reason

At Estergom, once the capital of Hungary, most of the stucco homes along the shore of the Danube have red-tile roofs, T.V. antennas and gardens with fruit trees.

people continued to live here during the upheavals is its strategic position astride the two major rivers that form the crossroads between East and West.

Belgrade means "white town," probably a reference to the color of the limestone that was originally used for the walls and towers that ring the town. It has been inhabited since the Stone Age. The Greeks colonized the site, and in the third century B.C. the Celtic tribes built a small fortified town at the junction of the Sava and the Danube. The Romans built bridges and made it an important crossroads of land and river routes. In time the Huns, the Goths, and the Avars all possessed it, and the Slavs settled here. The Middle Ages brought the Crusaders and constant struggles with the Byzantines, Magyars, Serbs, Turks, and Austrians—yet, through it all, Belgrade never ceased to prosper.

Today there is little left in the capital to testify to its colorful past. What remained earlier in this century, when the city was still little more than a quiet and fairly small country town, was almost entirely wiped out in the violent bombardment of 1941. Much of its architecture could now be termed "postwar nondescript." But its people are delightful—vivacious and energetic, hospitable and fiercely independent—and this more than compensates for what has been unkindly referred to as "the drabbest of capitals."

As soon as we had tied up and were allowed to step ashore, we set out through the modern heart of the city, whose wide, tree-lined boulevards centered around Terazije Square. We strolled the old-fashioned outdoor market, bustling with women dressed in baggy trousers clasped at the ankles, small shawls, and embroidered blouses, who were buying live fish from enormous tanks.

A taxi took us to the only survivor of the original twenty Turkish mosques in Belgrade. The seventeenth-century Mosque of the Flag was used in Turkish times to fly a signal flag five times daily, announcing the moment when the other mosques were to call the faithful to prayer. This mosque and the Kalemegdan Fortress are virtually the only relics of Turkish occupation that remain in the city.

The small inner courtyard of the mosque furnished a quiet retreat in the noisy capital. Here we washed our feet in a fountain along one wall and exchanged our shoes for a pair of communal sandals from a nearby pen. Inside the mosque, the floor was layered with well-worn oriental rugs, and beads were scattered around the room.

Late in the afternoon we taxied toward Mount Avala just outside the city, climbing the Dedinje hill past elegant ambassadorial residences and the White Palace of Marshal Tito. Atop 1,700-foot Mount Avala stood the impressive dark polished marble and granite Monument to the Unknown Soldier, the work of Yugoslavia's eminent sculptor Ivan Mestrovic.

Soon we were motoring through renowned vineyards and orchards of apricots, cherries, apples, and pears, on our way to the suburban village of Grocka. A wizened old man trudged along the narrow road, carrying a heavy sack on his back; older peasant women were dressed in traditional black. Low houses huddled under square roofs, their decorated balconies overlooking gardens and orchards.

In Grocka, at the celebrated restaurant Vinogradi, Serbian specialties are elegantly served on a terrace overlooking vineyards and orchards, and far below them one can see a bend of the Danube as it wends its way toward the Iron Gates and Bucharest. It was a comfortably warm spring evening, and we shunned the firelit interior of the restaurant in favor of its second-floor terrace. There we were served a delicious four-course dinner: Serbian cheese and Dalmatian ham were offered with local plum brandy (slivovitz); young spring lamb, roasted on an open fire inside, was brought with Smederevscho Belo, made from the grapes we saw growing nearby; fresh vegetables, picked from the gardens below, were just at the right point for eating; Serbian pancakes, the specialty of the house, were accompanied by another bottle of that exquisite wine; and dessert showed a Turkish influence—honey cakes with nuts. Throughout the entire feast we were serenaded by an amorous cuckoo in a nearby tree.

The Spectacular Iron Gates

At 9 P.M. we managed to pick ourselves up and roll into a taxi to rejoin our ship —a contented, overfed, and joyously tired group. Two hours later the *Dnepr* quietly slipped her lines and departed. As the night progressed, we followed the river on its lazy meanderings around low-lying islands, passing vines that have been producing that wonderful smedervka wine for 2,000 years, the fortress of Smederevo (one of the most powerful Serbian strongholds of the Middle Ages), and a countryside almost entirely devoid of roads. We continued past the ruins of the fifteenth-century Turkish fortress of Ram, then moved gradually—over a distance of about 60 miles—into the foothills of the Carpathian Mountains.

We awoke on the sixth day of our trip to find ourselves moving along the southern border of Romania, a route that we would travel for 670 miles (1,080 km). This section of southwestern Romania, originally known as Dacia, presented an irresistible challenge to the Roman Empire: it was rich, distant, and enticing. In 106 A.D. the Roman emperor Trajan conquered the region, and the Romans subsequently ruled it for three centuries, leaving the ineradicable stamp of Roman civilization— including a romance language that, while generously flavored with contributions from Slavic and other sources, is still surprisingly close to the original Latin.

This Sunday morning was crystal clear and startlingly cold, and we hastened below to don woolen pants, sweaters, and jackets. On the previous day the sundeck had been crowded with swimmers and sunbathers; today we stood almost alone, gaping at the most rugged and fascinating scenery of the entire trip. We were approaching the Iron Gates Gorge, a superlative marvel of nature and one of the most utterly unforgettable places in all Europe.

This most spectacular part of the Danube, lavishly endowed by Nature, is now an international park. Yugoslavia (on the right bank) and Romania (on the left) have cooperated closely in preserving its natural beauty, along with the wealth of archaeological treasures from prehistoric, Roman, and Turkish civilizations, while harnessing the wild river for navigation and hydroelectric power.

The fortress of Golubac, one of the most majestic on the river, stands guard on the Yugoslav bank at the entrance to the Kazan (Cauldron), its ancient, legend-haunted turrets crowning the crest of a hill, a relic of Serbian noblemen and Turkish pashas.

Abruptly, a spur of the Carpathians reaches a long arm into the mile-wide river and forces the river to form a narrow channel between rock walls—and so begins the Djerdap, or Iron Gates. Here the Danube cuts savagely through the steep cliffs separating the Carpathians in the north from the Balkans in the south, forming a narrow gap—Europe's largest canyon—some 60 miles long. Soon after this boiling stretch of river began, we passed the rock of Baba Kaj, impressive in the midst of the raging water.

The river continued to narrow as we progressed toward Lepenski Vir. Here in 1965 a team of archaeologists from Belgrade made one of the most stunning finds of the century: the remains of one of the oldest and most complete neolithic settlements in the world, dating from 4500–5100 B.C. The archaeologists unearthed fifty-four curiously sculpted boulders, shaped with primitive stone tools by a community of Danube fishermen about 7,000 years ago. Some of the stones were carved into animal forms, while others were merely geometrical; but the majority were painstakingly chiseled into strange human faces.

At Donji Milanovac there was a brief break in the canyon walls, and then we entered the upper Kazan. Here, imprisoned by the sheer rock of the rugged Carpathian cliffs, the Danube is reduced to a raging, constricted torrent barely 500 feet wide. Yet so enormous is the volume of water that, at its narrowest point, the river bottom plunges to a depth of 230 feet.

On the right bank, submerged under 100 feet of floodwaters since the opening of the Iron Gates dam downstream, is the original Roman road linking Golubac with Orsova, constructed during the reign of Tiberius in 28 A.D. The immensity of this project still defies explanation. In effect, it was a road cut from the lower face of the mountain; in some sections it actually overhung the water. The side of the sheer rock was pierced with square holes, drilled into the cliffs by Trajan's legions. Wooden trestles were forced into them, and on the trestles were laid the huge wooden beams that comprised the road itself, which carried the thundering Roman chariots to victory over the Dacians.

Just at the point where the Danube convulsed northward, the remains of three Roman bastions stood silent guard over the Kazan. The cliffs towered nearly 2,000 feet on either side, and the sun barely penetrated the canyon below. The rock striations and tilting formations of the cliffs drew fantastic shapes from Nature's own imagination. The sinister yellow-brown waters swirled wildly, forming vast whirlpools whose murky depths hid the much sought after 500-pound giant sturgeon. When the captain sounded the ship's horn as we rounded a bend, the echo bounced from the towering rock walls for a full five seconds. In the silence afterward we could hear the pleading bleat of an unseen mountain goat far above on a clifftop.

Soon, on the Romanian side, we passed the Veterani Cave, in ancient times thought to have been the sanctuary of the Dacian god Zamolxis. Three miles further downstream on the Romanian bank stood the remains of a Roman sundial. Along the dusty road bumped an open horsedrawn wagon driven by gypsies in ragged but colorful clothing, towing some tired-looking oxen.

We entered the lake dividing the upper and lower Kazan. On the right bank, set into a sheer cliff at about eye level and graven in creamy smooth stone some 6 feet by 12 feet, was Trajan's Tablet. Rediscovered in 1855, this stone monument had been erected by order of the emperor Trajan in the year 102 A.D. to mark the completion of the road Tiberius had begun seventy-four years before and to commemorate Trajan's own victorious campaign against the Dacian tribes.

The *Dnepr* slowed, enabling us to read the inscription. In the silence inspired by its eloquent simplicity, we could almost hear the triumphant blare of the great Caesar's trumpets echoing through the thundering canyon: IMPERATOR CAESAR DIVI NERVAE FILIUS . . . (The Emperor Caesar, son of the divine Nerva, great pontiff, tribune for the fourth time, father of his country and consul for the fourth time, has conquered the mountain and the river and opened this road).

As suddenly as it had begun, just an hour earlier, the Kazan closed behind us; on the now-gentle green slopes of both banks grazed cows and goats. The mountains faded quickly into the misty blue background behind the fresh-looking panorama of bright spring green dotted with thatched houses.

We were approaching the massive Iron Gates hydroelectric dam, the result of the Yugoslavian-Romanian partnership and the largest scheme of its type in Europe. Its two 1,000-foot locks on either bank have quartered the time formerly needed to navigate this once dangerous and difficult passage—and increased fivefold the annual tonnage on the river.

We entered the locks on the left (Romanian) bank, beneath rugged hills with rocky outcrops. Lacy towers carried clusters of power lines up and over the mountaintop. Within the locks, the tall control tower was enclosed in glass and topped with radar, wind indicators, and other antennae. Armed guards in olive drab uniforms patroled the locksides while Serbian music blared from a shoreside radio. Two hours was required to negotiate the double locks; by 12:40 P.M. we were passing through the final gates.

At Kladovo, on the Yugoslavian bank, we could detect the traces of the first bridge built over the Danube. Constructed by the emperor Trajan in 101 A.D., it conveyed his legions more than half a mile over twenty graceful wooden arches to the conquest of Dacia. At each end of the original bridge there had stood a monumental gate topped with ornate trophies. Now, at Kladovo, we saw only the ruins of the approach to the bridge; across the river, at Turnu Severin, two of the original pilings remained.

We had a good view of Turnu Severin, with its ruins of the Castrum of Dobreta, a fortress built for Trajan to guard the northern end of the bridge. A town and Roman harbor grew up around the castrum and, although several times destroyed during the Great Migrations, this ancient place has survived.

At Turnu Severin the Danube left the Iron Gates behind, and we entered the rich plains whose inhabitants, the Vlachs, gave their name to the Romanian principality of Wallachia. These people speak a dialect abounding in words that are even closer to Latin than ordinary Romanian, and their costumes, songs, and dances are very different from those of their Serbian neighbors.

The river was broad and lazy, its banks low and green, wooded and rich. Broad vistas of farmland were scattered with tiny villages overlaid with a light blue mist and backed by low, rolling hills. Along the Romanian bank on the left, armed guards in tall black watchtowers followed us gravely with high-power binoculars. On the right bank, in Yugoslavia, things seemed more casual; watchtowers were few and far between.

At the Iron Gates, the Danube cuts through a narrow gorge in the mountain range called the Carpathians in Romania (to the right) and the Balkans in Yugoslavia (to the left). For ages invading armies have used this route. The river was once rocky and the current swift, but the current is now controlled by a great hydroelectric plant at Djerdap below the gorge.

Along the Romania-Bulgaria Border

Near Prahovo the river made an enticing bend to the right. Around the bend it would accept the waters of the River Timok, which separates Yugoslavia and Bulgaria. For the next 292 miles we would be following the border between Romania —by now our old friend—and Bulgaria. For nearly the entire length of this frontier, the low left bank runs back into the wide Romanian plain while the Bulgarian right bank rises in steep white cliffs above the river.

Astride these cliffs, among vineyards, orchards, and fields of corn and hemp, sit numerous villages and towns of Bulgaria. In this stretch of the Danube a hundred islands lie in the no-man's-land of the frontier, providing a home for herons, pelicans, cranes, and wild ducks, who feed on the many varieties of fish in these waters.

Bulgaria is the land of the original pre-Roman Thracian tribes, subdued by the Roman emperor Claudius shortly before the Romans conquered the Dacians to the north. After Rome fell, the country was overrun by the Bulgars; its history since then teems with conquests and defeats, intrigues and pacts, confused politics and disastrous reverses.

Bulgaria is renowned for its richly scented roses that supply almost all of the world's perfumes with a very essential ingredient: attar of roses. In May and June the Valley of Roses south of the Danube diffuses its damask-rose bouquet—sweet, full, honeylike—and the Bulgarian peasant women in their bright costumes come before dawn to pick the flowers still fresh with dew. Carts are loaded and then driven by men virtually buried in blossoms, the roses being taken to distilleries to produce the rose oil.

By late afternoon we were traveling past a sweet little unnamed village on the hills of the right bank, where each house had its own small field for fresh vegetables. The units made fantastic shapes—like the pieces of an intricate puzzle. A gray mist shrouded the air, pierced by the distant sound of a student practicing uncertain scales on a trombone. Beyond the town, near a well, an old woman in traditional costume carried a long hoe and led a donkey-drawn wagon and a dog along the high escarpment. On the riverbank below was a shepherd with his flock of sheep, and across the river, on the left bank, a hay wagon bounced slowly along behind an ox.

Vidin was the first Bulgarian town we saw. The chief town of Upper Moesia, it is the center of an important wine-producing area, with a large commercial port and expanding industry. It possesses the most impressive surviving medieval fortress of Bulgaria, thought to date from the end of the thirteenth century. Brooding over the Danube, the fortress of Baba Vida is built in a trapezoid shape entirely of stone. Flanked by four towers and massive gates with drawbridges, the citadel formed the central part of the town's defenses. In the circuit of walls there were several monumental gates facing the Danube. The cupolas of the old churches and mosques of the town furnished a backdrop for the lovely riverfront park with its profusion of roses and modern statuary.

While we studied the sights, the *Dnepr*'s crew was preparing the dining room for a festive evening of Russian cooking and vodka-tasting. There would be Russian folk songs, played by the orchestra and sung by young women of the crew, six kinds of Russian vodka, and a great deal of merriment throughout the ship.

Meanwhile we continued downstream, working our way toward Giurgiu and Bucharest, passing the pre-Christian Celtic settlements of Archar and Lom, passing the immense riverside monument to the Bulgarian revolutionary poet and national hero Christo Botev, whose name is spelled out in red, white, and green flowers (the Bulgarian national colors) in a great garden that extends over the hillside of Kozloduy.

Twenty-five miles further along, near the Bulgarian village of Gigen, were the remains of the Roman Oescus, a fortified town founded in the first century A.D. Excavations here have exposed handsome streets paved with large stone slabs and laid out like a checkerboard, the ancient water supply system, a network of drains, the forum, and the foundations of a large temple and a great palace. In 1948 a superb Roman mosaic was discovered within the palace foundations, representing a scene from Menander's comedy of the fourth century B.C., *The Achaeans.* It is one of the most outstanding archaeological discoveries made in Bulgaria.

On the same bank, perched above steep cliffs, stood the ruins of the fortress of Nikopol, once an imposing stronghold with twenty-six towers.

Beautiful Svishtov, encircled by hills on the right bank, is one of the most attractively situated towns on the river; it marks the southernmost reaches of the Danube—the latitude is about the same as that of Portland, Maine.

We awoke on Monday, the seventh day of our trip, to see the Bulgarian port city of Ruse climbing in three grand terraces from the river. Bulgaria's busiest port on the Danube, it once held the principal Roman Danube fleet and was defended by the proud fortress of Sexanta Prista (Sixty Ships). It bustled this morning with barges and ships headed to and from Russia, Romania, and Danube ports far upstream.

Across the river, just over a mile downstream on the Romanian bank, was our morning's destination: Giurgiu, another important river port, which handles more than one-quarter of all the cargo on the Romanian bank of the Danube. It lies at the river end of the vital oil pipeline leading from the oilfields at Ploesti; its basins are always crammed with barges filling their bellies with the precious cargo.

Busy Capital in a Pastoral Setting

More interesting to us was the location of Giurgiu, some 40 miles south of Bucharest, the fourth capital we would visit on our cruise. Transportation and the services of a Romanian guide had been arranged for us, and soon we found ourselves in a large bus, bouncing along a modern, tree-lined road, climbing from the Danube Valley to the higher ground of the commune of Crucea de Piatra.

Our bus was unique, outnumbered by horsedrawn wagons and carts of every type and tractors—all rumbling along the road at about the same speed. Oxen grazed at the roadside, near some of the richest-looking fields we had ever seen, full of babushka'd women working the earth with their hands. This was Wallachia, the granary of Romania.

Progress was slow as we wound our way through the series of rickety carts and past women feeding geese from buckets. Scattered between the huge collective farms were charming peasant houses, all with their own unique carved birds and ceramic vines bordering the principal window frames, and all surrounded by tiny plots of ground, every inch of which was thoroughly tilled, planted, and carefully cultivated.

A bridge took us over the River Arges, about 12 miles outside Bucharest; six miles further on, we entered the outskirts of the city through streets shaded by old lime and horse chestnut trees. Bucharest enjoys a delightful natural setting in the midst of a plain enveloped in woods, forests, and lakes and dotted with parks.

The city's character, that of a modern metropolis full of broad, tree-lined boulevards, spacious courtyards, and bright flower beds in green parks and gardens, is due in part to its violent history—in particular, a fire in 1848 which destroyed most of its old buildings. The people of Bucharest retain a reputation for their cheerful and open temperament, warm hospitality, an agreeable Latin penchant for café life (they dine almost as late as the Spaniards do), for music and dancing, theater, opera, and ballet.

We stopped at the Park of Liberty, laid out on a slope formerly occupied by vineyards and dominated by its new Monument to the Heroes of the Struggle for the Liberty of the People and the Motherland, and for Socialism—perhaps the most unwieldy title for a monument we had ever heard.

Just five minutes away, on the crown of a gentle hill, stood the Church of the Patriarchate. Many events in Bucharest's history—including assassinations and protests by the people against aristocratic oppression—took place here. The church was also the scene of the first outbreak of the revolution in Wallachia in 1848 (the great church bell was rung as a signal). At the top of the hill, near the spot where a monastery stood in medieval times, there was a fine view through the trees of Bucharest below.

The interior of the seventeenth-century church was resplendent in rich Byzantine colors, great chandeliers, ornate decoration in gold and silver, and priests in silver and white vestments. Nearby stood the Palace of the Patriarchate and the imposing building of the National Assembly, guarded by young soldiers bearing machine guns.

Soon we were motoring down a wide boulevard that led to Herastrau Park, an immense green space covering some 450 acres, with grass and flower beds and little paths lined with slender poplars and stately chestnuts. The park holds one of Bucharest's principal attractions: the Village Museum, the "village of villages."

This unique open-air ethnographic museum contains more than two hundred examples of peasant and rural architecture assembled from the hamlets and villages of all the regions of the country. We spent hours wandering among the dwellings, stables, barns and storehouses, summer kitchens, granaries, gates, churches, iron founders' and potters' workshops, windmills standing among fruit trees, and lawns and gardens full of flowers. Within each of the buildings are original furniture, textiles, household objects, tools, ceramics, and costumes, illustrating essential aspects of the various peasant cultures from the seventeenth to the twentieth centuries. A small distance across the waters of Herastrau Lake was the Island of Roses, a charming place connected to the shore by gently curving bridges. Its flagstone paths were lined with dozens of varieties of roses, in full fragrant bloom this sunny May afternoon.

Leaving the museum, we wandered over to the garden terrace behind the hotel-restaurant Lido, where we sampled tzuica, Romanian black plum brandy similar to the slivovitz of Yugoslavia. From our table under a canopy of vines and flowers we looked out over a spacious courtyard enclosing a handsome pool with statuary and gardens. We were about to experience traditional Romanian cooking.

We were neither rushed nor kept waiting as the bustling waiters presented us with plates of dainty hors d'oeuvres: mushroom caps, ground beef with green peppers, and cream-cheesey things, accompanied by more tzuica. Next came the pirjoala, corn meal batter rolled very thin into a light crepe and filled with highly spiced minced meat. A crisp green salad followed. The main course was slices of tender spring lamb, which we washed down with some exceptional Riesling wine, fruity and fresh, labeled Podgoria Iassi. (The Romanians, with their Latin exuberance and love of wine, produced good wine centuries before the Romans arrived. Here the fruit is slightly sweeter than the same grapes grown in France or Germany.) Tiny tarts made from local oranges followed, and the lavish and relaxed meal was rounded off with strong Turkish coffee.

By 3:30 P.M. we were back on the road, headed toward Giurgiu and the *Dnepr,* passing dozens of one-horse wagons driven by men and carrying as many as six or seven women (the predominant field workers) home after their day's work.

On to Russia

No sooner had we reboarded the ship than she slipped her lines and headed downriver again, passing under the two-level steel Friendship Bridge, which claims to be Europe's largest. Twenty miles later we were admiring the lovely Bulgarian town of Tutrakan, rising on the slopes over the riverbanks opposite the River Ardzes. Tutrakan is now the largest center of freshwater fisheries in Bulgaria, farming sturgeon, carp, pike, and sterlet.

After a wonderful dinner of shashlik, that favorite Russian dish of mutton and vegetables, we left Bulgaria behind. Romania now commanded both shores, and we had begun the northward leg of our journey—toward the Russian border.

By the time we were stirring on Tuesday morning, our eighth day, we were able to look over to the left bank and see the Soviet Union, that incredible land which stretches from the Baltic almost to the coast of Alaska, embraces eleven time zones, and is home to 250 million people in fifteen individual national republics. Its history is peppered with names that conjure up romance, violence, and mystery: Rurik, Oleg, the Golden Horde, Ivan the Terrible, the Cossacks, Boris Gudonov, the Romanovs, Dostoevsky, Chekhov, Tolstoy, Gogol, Pushkin, Rasputin, Anastasia, the Bolsheviks, Lenin, Trotsky, Stalin. . . . Its vast plains, plateaus, mountain ranges, tundras, swamps, snowfields, and great rivers abound with polar bears, foxes, sable, antelope, camels, flamingoes, sturgeon, and salmon. Any further attempt to characterize here this amazingly complex and little understood land would be presumptuous.

We were in the midst of the great Danube delta, where the river deposits some 70 million tons of alluvia a year, a monumental landfill that has created the newest part of Romanian territory. The Danube delta, its landscape continually changing through erosion and deposit, is an enormous natural laboratory for wildlife exploration, with its luxuriant vegetation, floating islands of reeds, and lagoons gay with white and yellow water lilies.

Not far from the banks of the river stand the Macin Mountains, the most ancient range in the country. Rising gently in rolling, wooded abundance to a height of 1,500 feet, they were cloaked in dark mystery and magic.

Northeast of Tulcea the Danube begins to spread out into a fan shape. We followed the northern arm, the Chilia, an estuary which accounts for 70 percent of the total volume of muddy brown water that rushes toward the Black Sea.

At Isaccea, 103 miles from the Black Sea, there was great shipping activity—ocean freighters, cranes, and heavy, smoking industry. Further on, from Ceatalchiui to Pardina, we could see the center of the Romanian reed-gathering industry, which provides the raw material for cellulose, paper, and artificial fibers. Pardina Island promised nests of wild geese and colonies of pelicans and spoonbills; the field glasses were in constant demand.

Izmail: Gateway to the Black Sea

Precisely at noon, under sunny skies scattered with friendly, puffball clouds, the band struck up "On the Sunny Side of the Street" and we slipped up to the modern, glass-walled terminal of the largest Soviet port on the Danube. Izmail's brightly colored aqua, blue, red, and green loading cranes contrasted vividly with the thatched roofs of the Romanian peasant village across the river. Had these little country houses witnessed all of the tumultuous history of thousand-year-old Izmail? If they had, they gave no hint of what they knew.

The actual date of the founding of this great Russian port is unknown, but the Scythians visited even before the Greeks founded their colony here. In the fourth century A.D. the Romans ventured to this outpost, but the Slavs soon drove them out. From the second half of the eighteenth century until 1944, the town was the object of bloodshed, heroism, and diplomacy between the Turks, the Romanians, and the Russians. To this day, Russian and Turkish cannon adorn the public buildings of the town, commemorating the long and bloody fighting over this vital gateway to the Black Sea.

Today Izmail, 70,000 people strong, has become not only the largest but the most modern seaport on the Danube, with shipbuilding yards that rank among the largest on the river, modern fish-processing plants and wine cellars, and new homes, schools, hospitals, and libraries.

At Izmail we said good-bye to the river ship *Dnepr* and transferred to the 331-foot oceangoing *Ocetiva* for our overnight cruise to Yalta in the Crimea. Though clearly beyond her prime at the venerable age of forty, this elderly matron of the Black Sea still retained her old-world charm with lace curtains, an antique Russian piano, geranium pots, decorative frosted-glass doors, mahogany walls, and facilities "down the hall."

When the ship pulled out of Izmail at two o'clock, the skies had turned cloudy. The captain, wearing gold braid and impeccable white gloves, appeared at the helm, and as the crew cast off, the *Ocetiva* gave three sharp blasts on her deep-throated horn. The now-deserted *Dnepr* wailed mournfully in reply. We stood at the bridge to watch our own sendoff as the ship pulled out to begin the 90-mile run to the sea. On the right bank, young horses kicked up their heels at the sight of us and followed us downstream along flooded banks.

The Russian town of Kilia was situated 40 miles further on, facing Romanian Chilia Veche, site of the Greek city of Achilea founded in the fifth century B.C. Along the Romanian bank stood Letea Forest, a richly overgrown tongue of land containing the Garden of Omar, famous for great oak trees surrounded by a thick blanket of shrubs and giant climbing plants, the lianas. The area is frequented by migrating sea fish like sturgeon, source of the coveted caviar. Millions of migrating birds halt here each spring and autumn—more than three hundred species, including pelicans, egrets, spoonbills, swans, and cormorants. Roaming the banks are wild boar, wolves, foxes, mink, and otters.

The final Danube port before the deluge poured into the vast Black Sea was the small Soviet town of Vilkovo, a fishing center with rich, productive orchards. Then we were on the high seas, sailing the nontidal, nearly currentless calm waters of the Black Sea.

Journey to Yalta

During our passage to Yalta that evening, the band made merry music for dancing, the bar was very busy, and an atmosphere of festivity pervaded the ship on this last night of our cruise. The sun set over a calm sea as gulls swooped and dipped behind the stern promenade, where we stood protected from the cool breeze yet open to the stars and the moon. It was to be an incredibly romantic crossing, with dancing and laughing and standing high on the tiny observation deck as the ship plowed purposefully through the dark, shimmering waters under a nearly full moon.

In the morning we awoke as we skirted the wide arc of the Crimean peninsula, passing the softly sloping sandy beaches and the long string of picturesque vacation resorts along the southern Crimean shore. Yalta, at the southern tip of the peninsula, lay snuggled in a valley deep within the horseshoe formed by spurs of the oak- and beech-covered Yaila Mountains. Behind Yalta rose Mount Lopata, which along with others in the chain forms a vast amphitheater that shelters the town from the hot breath of the steppes and the cold winds in winter and makes it famous for its health resorts. Cheerful little snow-white houses lay in the midst of gardens. Roses often bloom in the open here at Christmas, and the promenades of the town are rich in acacia, laurel, magnolia, and palm trees. The region is also famous for vineyards and orchards of pear, almond, peach, apple, and apricot trees.

The history of Yalta dates from the time when the Greeks established trading relations with a people known as the Cimmercians, who inhabited the peninsula then known as Cheronesus Taurica. The Russians annexed the Crimea in 1783. Since the advent of the Soviet regime, Yalta has become one of the largest and finest seaside resorts of the USSR—indeed, of the world.

Yalta has known many famous men. Chekhov, Tolstoy, and Gorky lived here; Tchaikovsky spent time here; Chaliapin and Rachmaninoff gave recitals here; Mark Twain visited the town; and, in February 1945, it hosted Roosevelt, Stalin, and Churchill for one of the most important and controversial political and military conferences of modern times.

The actual setting of the Yalta Conference was a former imperial palace at Livadia, a picturesque village two miles outside Yalta. In the nineteenth century the czars built their imperial residences here, and the Russian aristocracy soon followed, establishing their villas throughout the neighboring orchards and vineyards.

Disembarking in Yalta, we were met at the pier by a young Intourist guide and a driver, who were to take us to Simferopol Airport. Since we were some hours early for our flight to Leningrad, we arranged for a tour of Livadia, where we visited the scene of the conference, including the ground-floor study where Franklin D. Roosevelt stayed and the great round table where the actual discussions took place.

En route to the airport, we motored along the 2,400-foot summit pass through the Yaila Mountains, the Chater Dag rising over 4,500 feet on our left. We turned for a last look, over a vast and gloriously rugged panorama, at the Black Sea and Yalta.

We were both aware, in that instant, that we were looking back at more than an impressive natural scene. We were, each in our own way, reflecting on the eight eventful days and nights we had just experienced. We spoke about the Bavarian couple, fellow passengers aboard the *Dnepr,* who were making their seventh Danube trip—with all the excitement and anticipation of first-time travelers.

As we quietly contemplated our feelings, we both realized that, of all the waterways we have traveled during these several years, the Danube alone could inspire such devotion. Its banks could summon us back time and time again.

Some Practical Information

Europe's second longest river (after the Volga), the Danube traverses eight countries as it spills helter-skelter from the Alps to the Black Sea, carrying cargo and passengers up and down the length of its 1,776 miles (2,850 km). Fortunate travelers who cruise the river are treated to an exciting mélange of countries and cultures, sights and sounds.

At present the Danube can only be traveled by scheduled steamers and excursion boats, as red tape and travel restrictions make it virtually impossible to cruise any distance in a private yacht. However, the waterway traveler can choose from a broad range of steamship excursions, from one-day trips to a ten-day cruise of the entire length of the river and across the Black Sea to Yalta. The latter trip is unique—floating you through eight countries and five capital cities.

There are five lines that have scheduled services in the waters of the Danube:

The Soviet Danube Steamship Line (SDGP), Suworow-Prospekt 2, Izmail, USSR, offers two modern 350-foot (107 m) ships, the *Dnepr* and the *Volga,* which cruise the river between Passau and Izmail. At Izmail one can transfer to another ship to cross the Black Sea to Yalta or travel to ports of the Mediterranean. The cruisers' 212 passengers are attended by a staff of 85, and service is both hospitable and efficient. The comfortable, air-conditioned two- and three-berth cabins are well laid out and offer private facilities and showers, an intraship telephone, and ample drawer and wardrobe space. Other amenities on board include an outdoor heated swimming pool, sun lounge and promenade deck, a fine dining room, hairdressing salon, souvenir kiosk, and an attending doctor and dispensary.

Approximate fares per person are:

	Cabins	Suites
Passau to Izmail (7/8 days)	$367–509	$650
Vienna to Yalta (7/8 days)	$378–558	$750
Passau to Yalta (10 days)	$452–658	$850

The First Danube Steamship Company (DDSG), Mexicoplatz 8, A-200 Vienna, Austria, with a fleet of five steamships, offers complete Danube cruises between Vienna and the Black Sea, as well as daily excursion service between Passau and Vienna.

Approximate rates per person are:

Vienna to Black Sea to Vienna	13 days	$810–950
Passau to Budapest to Passau	7 days	$400–500
Vienna to Budapest to Vienna	4 days	$175–250
Passau to Vienna*	2 days	$35

| Linz to Vienna | 10 hours | $20 |
| Vienna Water Tour | 1 hour | $3.00 |

*Bed not included; available at extra charge.

The Czechoslovakian Danube Shipping Company (CPSD), Ulica Cervenej Armady 39, Bratislava, Czechoslovakia, operates hydrofoil service between Vienna and Bratislava. The round-trip fare is $11.00.

The Hungarian Danube Shipping Company (MAHART) runs hydrofoil service between Vienna and Budapest, operating from May through early September. The trip takes six hours; the one-way fare is $18.00, which includes refreshments on board.

The Danube Shipping Company (Wurm KG), D-8441, Irlbach bei Straubing, West Germany, offers passenger service between Deggendorf and Engelhartszell. The trip takes five hours; the round-trip fare is $18.00.

Danube cruises can be booked either through a local travel agent experienced in Eastern European travel or through the following firms:

March Shipping Corporation
One World Trade Center
New York, N.Y. 10048

Floating Through Europe, Inc.
501 Madison Avenue
New York, N.Y. 10022

Transtours
49 Avenue de l'Opera
Paris 75002

Kuoni Travel Ltd.
Neugasse 231
Zurich

One word of advice: book as early as possible, for there is frequently a long waiting list for cabins during summer months.

TRAVEL RESTRICTIONS. You will be traveling through Eastern European Socialist countries, where travel regulations are more stringent than in the United States or Western Europe. Probably the best approach to any uncertain situation is to ask permission in advance. During our Danube cruise we asked permission frequently: May we photograph this? May we rent a car and tour independently? May we travel out of the city? We found that by asking in advance we eliminated potential problems and misunderstandings, and we were generally permitted to do all the things we requested.

TRAVEL DOCUMENTS. Besides a valid passport, the only documents we needed during our entire Danube trip were Russian and Hungarian visas. As requirements may change, it would be advisable to check with your booking agent when you make your reservations.

CURRENCY. United States currency and travelers' checks are accepted throughout Eastern Europe, and you'll have an opportunity to purchase local currency along the route. Retain the currency exchange slips which you receive with each exchange transaction until the trip has ended and you have returned home, as you may be asked to produce these slips at border checkpoints. Major United States credit cards are frequently accepted for dining and shopping.

SIGHTSEEING AND TOURING. On the longer Danube cruises, from Passau or Vienna to the Black Sea, the ship will stop at places of interest where passengers can take guided tours. On the Soviet Danube cruise tours are offered at Vienna, Budapest, Belgrade, Bucharest, and Yalta. Before booking a tour, make certain that the guide will be speaking English, as very few of your fellow passengers are likely to be English-speaking. (We staggered through one half-day bus tour given in Russian and German.) You can arrange for a private car and guide if a bus tour doesn't suit you, but remember to book this with the purser or ship's interpreter one day in advance.

AFTER THE DANUBE CRUISE. If you book the downstream Danube cruise, you'll embark at either Passau or Vienna and travel southeast to the Black Sea. There you'll have several intriguing options: you can cross the Black Sea on a steamship of the Soviet Danube Line to Yalta, where you can travel through Russia on your return home; you can book passage to other Black Sea ports or to ports in the Mediterranean; or you may continue on to the Near East. Whatever your choice, you should schedule and book your entire trip when you make your original booking for the Danube cruise.

Additional useful information may be found in an excellent Danube pamphlet, "The Danube—One River, Eight Countries," published by the Danube Area Tourist Promotion Working Committee, Vienna, Austria. You can obtain this pamphlet from your travel agent or from Floating Through Europe, Inc., 501 Madison Avenue, New York, N.Y. 10022.

Information concerning the individual countries can be obtained from:

Austrian National Tourist Office
545 Fifth Avenue
New York, N.Y. 10017

Bulgarian Tourist Office
50 East 42 Street
New York, N.Y. 10017

Cedok-Czechoslovakian Travel Bureau
10 East 40 Street
New York, N.Y. 10016

German National Tourist Office
630 Fifth Avenue
New York, N.Y. 10020

MALEV (Hungarian Information)
630 Fifth Avenue
New York, N.Y. 10020

Rumanian National Tourist Office
500 Fifth Avenue
New York, N.Y. 10036

Yugoslav State Tourist Office
509 Madison Avenue
New York, N.Y. 10022

8

The Royal Highway

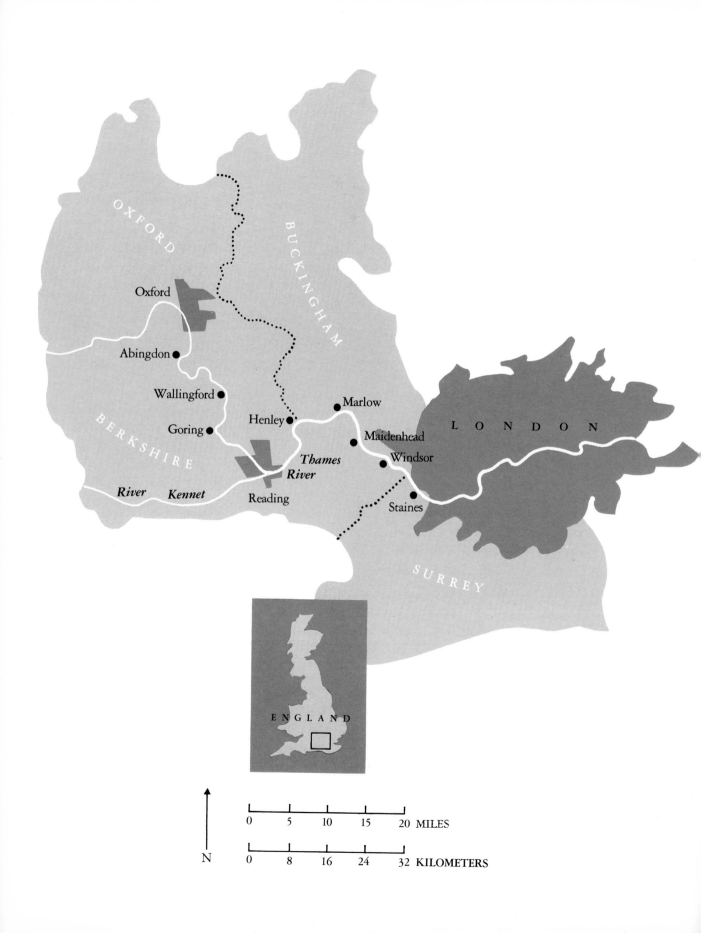

Upstream, Downstream on the Thames

There are two things scarce matched in the universe:
The sun in the heaven and the Thames on earth

SIR WALTER RALEIGH

The River Thames extends almost entirely across southern England, rising in a buttercup-spangled meadow in the dreaming Cotswold Hills of Gloucestershire and flowing east through Oxfordshire, Berkshire, and Buckinghamshire before its search for the sea ends east of London. The river twists and curves through cow-filled emerald green countryside and past picturesque villages.

Because of its long association with England's royalty, the canalized river is known as "the Queen's Highway . . . most noble of rivers." The Thames is as redolent of poetry as it is of nobility. "Sweet Thames run softly, till I end my song," Edmund Spenser wrote in his *Prothalamion.* The river provides a panorama of English life through the beauty and tranquility of the country's meadows and woods, the grandeur of its great houses and noble estates, the dignity of its ancient churches and colleges, the simple charm of its riverside inns, cottages, and gardens, and even in the sterner faces of its factories, warehouses, power stations, and docks near London.

The Thames reflects the traditional English fondness for subtleties. At its official source, Thames Head, the great river emerges from under a big ash tree as a stone spring, never more than a few inches deep and often seemingly dry. With a fall that is the gentlest of all England's rivers, the scenery is neither wild nor dramatic. The allure of the Thames lies in this very peacefulness; the low-key, subtle beauty of the river, mirrored over and over in the towns along the bank, distinguishes the Thames holiday from other adventures and is especially pleasing to those of us not accustomed in our everyday life to such simple pleasures.

The gardens are the river's chief glory; they line it with curried lawns, judiciously planted cedars and chestnuts, topiary and flower beds with herbaceous borders. These artificial creations of successive generations of gardeners are so well established they seem like part of the natural landscape. Elegantly dressed ladies and gentlemen can often be found in the gardens, sitting on white wicker chairs beneath willows, perhaps resting from croquet. Small boats rock quietly at their moorings nearby or may be seen peeking from shingled boathouses.

Thames lock gardens are themselves an institution that developed at the turn of the century. Lockkeepers had been gardening for years when, in 1898, the Thames

Conservancy (which governs all aspects of the river) began to reward these efforts by giving prizes to the finest. Enthusiasm, pride, and green thumbs account for most of the competition and rivalry, which builds throughout the spring and leads to the judging that takes place in early July.

"Father Thames," Robert Burns said, "is liquid history." And indeed, this 100-mile stretch of river between Oxford and Teddington reflects two thousand years of English history. (The theory has been advanced more than once that the river was once a tributary of the Rhine and that together they flowed into a great plain that is now the North Sea.) While the Thames has served primarily as a means of transportation and communication since early Roman times, pleasure boating began on the river as early as 1846.

It was an instant success. Forty years later, crowds were flocking to the river to board hundreds of steam launches; there were endless processions of every kind of floating craft, from light canoes, dinghies, and outriggers to the lordly, much-decorated houseboats that lined the river. Its banks were thronged by joyous, gaily dressed holidaymakers, merry and loving couples leisurely towing boats, horses drawing skiffs and houseboats, and innumerable spectators—especially at the locks.

During the idyllic Victorian days some of the Thames locks were resorts of high fashion that were often visited by royalty. Beruffled ladies went afloat hatted, gloved, and shielded by gay parasols. Their beaux, in straw boaters and blazers, struggled gallantly with oar and sail.

Today the Thames above London is the ideal boating river: its commercial traffic is light, its current gentle (except after floods), and its varied scenery unsurpassed for quiet, typically English beauty. After the Norfolk Broads, the Thames is the most popular waterway in Britain and easily the best-maintained river in a nation proud and conscious of its waterway ecology—its locks and riverbanks elegant and spruce, its waters clean and inviting.

The Royal Valley Begins

We arrived at Staines, a London suburb and the beginning of the Thames Valley, on the first Friday in June, the day before we would begin our trip upstream to Oxford and back. We checked into the Pack Horse Inn, a comfortable old inn on the north bank of the river, for the one night. In the riverside restaurant we dined lavishly on two English favorites, roast beef and Yorkshire pudding and steak and kidney pie. The gracious and intimate atmosphere was of course 100 percent English, and it put us in the mood for our week on the Thames.

We walked through Staines that evening, and the following afternoon we picked up our 27-foot motor cruiser, *Quadrille Lady.*

Ten minutes after leaving the dock in Staines, we arrived at the attractive Runnymede Bridge, which spans the river just above tiny Holm Island and frames the view of pretty Bell Weir Lock. The banks were lined with graceful willows and small gardens perfect with roses and early summer flowers.

Soon the great and glorious expanse of Runnymede Meadow came into view, Cooper's Hill rising in the background. As we rounded a deep double curve skirting the parkland, which was alive with picnickers, lovers, children playing games, dogs, and baby strollers, we approached the memorials inspired by the signing of the Magna Charta, that "great charter" of English liberties forced from King John by the English barons and sealed June 15, 1215. On that day the barons encamped by the rushes lining the Thames, and great barges carried the king and the barons from Runnymede to the island near the north bank of the river, known thereafter as Magna Charta Island. Here the earliest of constitutional documents in modern history was signed, "for the preservation of peace, and every individual perpetually secured in the free enjoyment of his life and property."

From Picnic Point at Runnymede to Old Windsor Lock was a delightful mile and a half lined with formal gardens and broad green lawns edged with willows. Lifejacketed children set out on the river in their little skiffs, accompanied by mallards and moorhens with their redheaded chicks. A shady road dotted with dainty cottages ran up the bank to the Bells of Ouzeley, a picturesque inn whose "bells" were cast into the river during the reign of Henry VIII.

Old Windsor, bordered on three sides by the Great Windsor Forest, dates from Saxon times, when it was the seat of the Saxon kings. Then the Great Forest of Windsor offered the finest hunting grounds, and ever since royalty has been attracted to this richly endowed part of England. The Saxons made Old Windsor a royal manor; the Great Councils of England met there as early as the eleventh century. Here was the palace of Edward the Confessor, where Earl Godwin, suspected of having disposed of the king's brother, protested his innocence and declared his hope that the piece of bread he was about to eat might choke him if he lied. Whether he lied or not is not recorded, but he choked nevertheless.

The old Saxon palace is long since gone, and the official royal residence was moved four miles downstream to New Windsor in the twelfth century.

At Old Windsor Lock we passed the fringes of Windsor Great Park, the royal grounds where tall poplars marched in perfect rows along the bank. Suddenly, between the poplars, we caught our first breathtaking view of Windsor Castle high on a chalk cliff above the Thames. It was a fairytale picture—incredible, magical, indelible—the largest and grandest castle in England (more than a mile in circumference) and the biggest inhabited castle on earth. It was everything we had ever imagined England would be: the delightful green of the park, the rich grass, the fragrant flower beds, and—high on that cliff in the distance—the frowning gray turrets of the castle begun by Henry II in 1169.

Approaching the castle, we passed along the weir stream which branched off the main river at Romney Lock and led to the playing fields of Eton College, perhaps the most widely known of all English schools, founded in 1440 by Henry VI. The college's stately courtyards were full of mellow brick buildings and young scholars dressed in broad white collars and dusty tail coats. Thomas Gray used to walk through Eton; his favorite path is still named Poet's Walk.

Coming into Windsor, we craned our necks upward to see the massive Norman castle but saw instead the town's narrow cobblestone streets perched high on the hill. Having visited Windsor before, we slid on silently under Windsor Bridge and along the Windsor Promenade, whose banks were crowded with tourists. We floated past beautiful 80-foot lacquered mahogany excursion boats with classic clipper bows, low-slung sheers, and names like *Windsor Belle.*

From here to Maidenhead stretched a pleasant and quiet six miles of river, where pheasants and partridges occasionally burst into flight from the deep grass, bright metallic blue and green damselflies rested on reeds and rushes, and their larger cousins, the dragonflies, hovered over the calm waters. It was after seven o'clock, yet the sun was still shining warm and bright, casting long shadows as Maidenhead came into sight.

Maidenhead can honestly claim to have always been a pleasure center. Even in Edwardian days it played host to champagne and punting parties, especially during Ascot week or when the court was at Windsor. During the 1920s it was renowned for its drinking clubs.

We moored near Boulter's Lock for our first night on the river. Boulter's, one of the busiest locks on the Thames, has been famous since Edwardian days, when on any fine weekend it would be crammed with steam launches, punts, and skiffs full of men and women dressed in the height of river fashion. Tonight all was peaceful on the river near the lock, and we enjoyed a quiet dinner on board the *Quadrille Lady.*

Sunday on the Fashionable Middle Thames

At 9 A.M. Sunday we locked through to enter one of the most beautiful and highly traveled portions of the Thames, Cliveden Reach. The 263 acres of superb National Trust property contains famous Cliveden House and the glorious tree-studded slopes of Cliveden Woods. Chestnut, holly, beech, oak, and elm trees, ivy, and rhododendron covered the grounds right to the banks of the Thames, and the scent of yellow azaleas and sweet chestnuts filled the air.

The British consider this section of the Thames their most spectacular stretch of riverway, and we lingered beneath the rolling, tree-covered hills that seemed to rise and fall in one long harmony of shades of spring greens. One of the chief delights along the river was the old cottage at My Lady Ferry, a station which operated until 1957. The ferryman's cottage looked as though it had been transplanted from a tinted etching. We could picture the ferryman answering a hail from the towpath and bringing across one of his two splendid boats to pick up the parasol-bearing ladies and straw-hatted gents wishing to cross the river.

Cliveden Reach came to an end as the river entered Cookham Lock Cut. Hedsor Parish spread out around a little side stream. The town's lovely little flintstone church and priory sat perched on the hill above, the very embodiment of an English village church. The hillside was covered with a profusion of wildflowers, scenting the air and delighting our widened eyes.

We moored at the foot of the square tower of the church at Bisham, amidst the weathered and flaking tombstones. Inside the church, we explored the famous and elaborate sixteenth- and seventeenth-century monuments and tombs. Bisham Abbey stood nearby in an attractive woodland. Dating from the reign of Stephen (1135–1154), it is said to be haunted. The charming village of Bisham was set back from the river, with little houses whose doors were just under five feet high, whose roofs slanted down steeply and very low, and whose walls leaned crazily this way and that behind tiny, neat gardens. It seemed to have been built for a race of "little people."

In Temple Lock children bathed in the river in the company of great crested grebes, those gentle, curious-looking river birds that return to the same nest year after year. There were Canada geese as well, first introduced in England as ornamen-

Upstream from Runnymede, above Magna Charta Island, the Thames makes a loop around the royal grounds; then the trees along the bank open for the first view of Windsor Castle, chief residence of English sovereigns. Even in the soft light of a drizzling morning, the castle is impressive, with its striking main turret and the flag flying briskly above.

tal birds for private ponds and gardens and now become wild, flourishing in the middle reaches of the river.

Under way again, we came upon Hurley Lock situated beneath well-wooded chalk cliffs. Here wandered a delightful little side stream dotted with tiny islands where profusions of Loddon lilies grew and where the swans played hide-and-seek with weekend boaters and swimmers. The eighteenth-century Harleyford Manor, purported to be the Toad Hall of Kenneth Grahame's immortal novel *The Wind in the Willows,* stood in the quiet backwater. The superb grounds, by the famous landscape artist Capability Brown, swept grandly down to the weir stream behind Harleyford Marina, where *Wild Fury* was moored alongside *Tenderly.*

Not far upstream stood Medmenham Abbey, an ivy-covered riverside gem and one of the most romantic sights along the entire river. Founded in 1212 by austere Cistercian monks from France, it had fallen into decay when Sir Francis Dashwood brought in Italian workmen to reconstruct the buildings in 1745. Then, in a spirit of licentiousness in tune with his times, he founded the Monks of Medmenham, an order of "Franciscans" better known as the Hell-Fire Club. To this secret society has been attributed all the orgiastic excesses of the age—in particular the carrying off to Medmenham, with or without their consent, a large number of "wenches." How true all this may be, and to what extent it may have been carried on, is a matter of conjecture, for understandably no records exist. In his *Dictionary of the Thames, 1897,* Dickens wrote:

The audacious motto of the club may perhaps have had something to do with the holy horror which it excited. "Fay ce que voudras" was not a good motto at a time when doing as you pleased was about the last thing that good old-fashioned Toryism was likely to tolerate.

By mid-afternoon we were approaching Henley, the most popular river resort in England, a classic Thameside town, and one of the oldest towns in Oxfordshire. Nestled under the Chiltern Woods, and with the straight mile of the world-famous regatta course extending into its heart, the town still manages to be both popular and elegant.

Temple Island, just downstream of Henley, owes its name to the picturesque little building—nothing more than a pretty ornament—created as a vista for Fawley Court upstream. Here the river abruptly stops its winding and for just over a mile upstream to Henley Bridge is almost dead straight. This is the famous Henley Reach, home of the world's premier rowing regatta.

Henley, during Henley Royal Regatta week in early July, is one of the highspots of the social summer; it attracts tens of thousands of visitors to watch the races from shoreside stands and boats of all types and sizes moored along the banks. In Victorian days the regatta became (and has remained) an excuse for a glorious river picnic, where people went to see and to be seen, on one of the finest reaches of the Thames at the height of the English summer.

Everyone, from society leader to the ubiquitous London cockney, was attracted by the annual event. The scene was a potpourri of Victorian sights and sounds: jolly young weekend watermen in white flannels, straw hat, canvas shoes, and umbrella (there was a saying that it always rained at Henley); singers, burnt-cork minstrels, conjurers, and fortune-tellers; the brilliant liveries of the rowing clubs; pretty girls in bright dresses with skintight bodices, feathered and flowered gay hats, and parasols; houseboats overflowing with glorious flowers and flags; steam launches, electric launches, punts, and skiffs.

The races themselves were often lost in the parade; the magazine *Punch* was wont to remind its readers, "It is desirable to bear in mind that, pleasant as riparian life may be, Henley is, after all, a regatta, and that consequently some sort of attention should be paid to the racing."

Later in July Henley sees another colorful occasion: Swan Upping is the traditional name for the gentle annual ceremony of branding mute swans on the river to show ownership. All swans on the Thames belong to the queen, with the exception of those which, by royal charter, are the property of the ancient livery companies of Vintners and Dyers. Once a year a procession of six skiffs moves up the river, led by the Royal Swan Warden resplendent in scarlet, who has with him the Vinter's Keeper in green and the Dyer's Keeper in blue. Their oarsmen are dressed in red, blue, and white jerseys. The full ritual lasts for several days; by the end of it some one thousand birds have been examined for ownership.

After tying up in Henley, we strolled along elegant Hart Street, from Henley Bridge to the Victorian Town Hall, past the fifteenth-century White Hart Inn. We stopped at a local teahouse, which proved one of the pleasantest memories of our trip. We found ourselves in a small, sundrenched dining room adorned with white tablecloths and freshly cut flowers. An elaborate assortment of dainty tea sandwiches, crumpets, scones, jams, and cup after cup of tea awaited us. Not surprisingly, tea became a daily event that we eagerly anticipated.

As we made our way upstream, Henley diminished behind us—a palette of primary-color parks filled to overflowing this Sunday afternoon with babies in umbrella'd carriages, soccer players shooting across broad green lawns, stationary meditators planted under poplars, and lovers gracing fantasmagorical cushioned swings. A chain of tiny islands dotted the main channel of the river, and their presence transformed the majestic atmosphere of this broad and lazy river to that of a sweet, intimate stream full of gliding swans and mallards all going about their private business—pecking, searching, bottom-upping, tending their young.

In the 20-mile stretch between Henley and Goring, we would pass through the designated Chilterns Area of Outstanding Natural Beauty, comprising 309 square miles of the most beautiful scenery of southern England.

Nine miles beyond Henley, the sun was sending long shadows over the river as we approached the bustling commercial city of Reading on the southern bank of the Thames. Reading has long been famous; it was a royal borough in the year 871, in the dim days of King Ethelred, when the Danes anchored their warships in the town.

The town grew up around the great abbey founded by Henry I in 1121 to shelter two hundred monks. Here the earliest of all Old English songs, and the first known piece of music for several voices, "Sumer is icumen in," was written by a monk in about 1240.

The city of Reading actually straddles the River Kennet, a tributary of the Thames. It is possible to slip up the Kennet, from its junction with the Thames, to High Bridge, the heart of the city, where shopping and sights are all at hand. From here it is an easy walk to many of the wonderful Victorian buildings and a museum with one of the most interesting archaeological collections in the country. We stood before the fragmentary ruins of the old abbey at the edge of Forbury Park, paid a visit to the flinty tomb of Henry I, saw the gatehouse once occupied by the abbey school (whose pupils included Jane Austen), and studied the off-balance Maiwand Lion outside the abbey, a memorial to the men of Berkshire killed in the Afghan wars. We visited the old Reading Gaol nearby, where Oscar Wilde wrote *De Profundis* in 1897, and strolled through the marketplace in the old center of town.

Reading does the Thames a favor by confining its industrial heart to the River Kennet, for the frontage along the Thames' banks was green, open, and well landscaped. King's Meadow and Christchurch playing fields surrounded ponderous Reading Bridge with tennis courts, a lake for model sailboats, and a large cricket pitch where a very earnest group, dressed all in white, dashed about. There were good moorings along the playing fields, and families were flying kites from the towpath or lounging on the lush grass that lined the riverbank.

Reading's counterpart on the northern bank of the Thames is the city of Caversham. Just beyond Caversham Bridge stood the Caversham Bridge Hotel, flanked by pleasant riverside gardens and a promenade and looking out over a stretch of the river much prized as a rowing reach. We had passed enough moorings for one day and, with sunset approaching, we decided to tie up for the night in front of the hotel. We dined deliciously in a room overlooking the river, gazing out at the tree-lined bank where our little cruiser bobbed gently in the current.

The Goring Gap

The third day of our journey was one of stark contrasts in the moods of the river. At nine o'clock we set out for the Goring Gap under bright skies, with sunlight flashing from dancing wavelets, shining on the gray-green beeches, glinting through the dark, cool woodland paths, throwing kisses to the lilies, and brightening every tiny town. Then a bank of gray clouds moved in, and the river soon grew solemn and misty; the woods, dark and silent, became shrouded in mists of vapor, standing like ghosts on the silent banks and sending a chill through the air. The sun and the clouds would continue this *pas de deux* throughout the day.

Before reaching the gap we came upon historic Mapledurham House, a huge Elizabethan mansion built by Sir Michael Blount and famed for centuries as the residence of that esteemed family. Alexander Pope, poet and satirist, was a frequent visitor here; he kept up a correspondence amounting almost to a love affair with Martha Blount. The house faces the park, away from the river, and is approached by a magnificent avenue of ancient elms. A great old-fashioned iron gateway leads from the house to the churchyard of St. Margaret. Television followers usually recognize this house nestled amid the trees in its quiet parklands, for it was used as backdrop for the final episodes of *The Forsyte Saga.*

Mapledurham's much-painted sixteenth-century mill inspired some of Ernest H. Shepard's drawings for *The Wind in the Willows.* With a cluster of period houses and cottages surrounding it in the water meadows, it reminded one of many an early nineteenth-century landscape painting.

This part of the Thames Valley is delightfully wooded, with spacious houses, greenhouses, flower beds, and clean, broad lawns that stretch to the water's edge. The little islands in Mapledurham Reach are clearly popular with nature-loving campers. Great crested grebes pushed along the right bank, and herds of beef cattle helped themselves to the free water along the banks and grazed in adjacent fields full of buttercups. A scholarly heron stood stock-still and patient, stretching his long neck skyward, waiting for lunch to swim downstream. As we passed Goring Heath and a beautiful row of sinewy, gnarled willows, Lady Luck offered us our first glimpse of the spectacular (and tourist-shy) kingfisher. Gaudy in his iridescent turquoise suit with scarlet bib, he darted over the water with whirring wings and went into a sudden vertical dive to snatch some unsuspecting fish.

Many millions of years ago the chalky Chiltern Hills and Berkshire Downs formed a continuous ridge, the Thames flowing northward toward the sea while the River Kennet to the south meandered on a southerly course. Then, during the Ice Age, a wall of glacial ice barred the Thames from its natural course, forming behind the hills a vast lake that began eating slowly through them and, with constant scouring, flood, sun, drought, and frost, created the lovely narrow gorge known as the Goring Gap.

At few places on the river was the combination of almost every variety of Thames scenery so striking and pleasant as at Goring and Streatley. This was the most beautiful part of the valley, with gently rising hills clothed in junipers and wheatfields and emerald meadows receding reluctantly from the river.

Wallingford and Beyond

As we moved on, the valley began to open up again, becoming broader and flatter, with long expanses of flat meadows teeming with wildlife and literally blanketed with cottony willow blossoms that settled in a film over the river, covered the boat, and nestled in our hair.

Just before Wallingford we became acquainted with our first classic Thames boat, a slipper launch, or "slipper stern." This type of boat is long, low, and sleek; its varnish gleams in the sun.

Wallingford was one of many river crossings that have seen use by invaders since time immemorial. The Britons, the Roman legions, the Saxons, the Danes, and the Normans all left their footprints in the banks here, and all contributed to the building of the town.

We passed under Wallingford's delightful medieval bridge, its seventeen arches reaching 900 feet across the Thames, and we were fascinated by the open-work spire of St. Peter's Church, rising above the town. Mooring our boat just below the bridge, we set out to explore—and to enjoy a shoreside lunch at the Fleur de Lys, a small teahouse offering a hearty and delicious three-course luncheon for the equivalent of $1.50.

After lunch we walked the tiny, twisting streets lined with fine Georgian and Tudor buildings and found the old marketplace, a square dominated by its seventeenth-century Guildhall. Wallingford struck us as a sweet, sleepy village, its military significance all but forgotten, now left with its quiet memories and its place on the Thames.

We pointed the *Quadrille Lady* north, continuing along the Thames past the ruins of a castle and the lovely Howbery Park, an old mansion set in well-tended grounds. The river wound through Benson and Shillingford and then swept gently to the left past Little Wittenham Wood. Just opposite, the delightful little River Thame entered the Thames. Above the Thame the Thames is known poetically as the Isis, as in

> Beauteous Isis and her husband Thame
> With mingled waves for ever flow the same.

The great abbey church of Dorchester rose on the right bank, a grandly proportioned, remarkable example of Norman workmanship. Its most important feature is the Jesse Window, a stained-glass window representing the genealogy of Christ.

Would-be visitors to Dorchester should be warned that they must leave their cruisers either here at the mouth of the Thame or upriver at Day's Lock and take the footpath across fields full of tiny white flowers and the fragrant tang of sweet woodruff.

After seeing Dorchester we sailed on toward Abingdon, one of the truly ancient towns of the Thames Valley, going back to a Saxon abbey established here in 675 A.D. The abbey spires and towers rose high above the grassy meadows, while the Thames meandered, twisting and turning, alongside the city streets. The sun was low in the sky when we tied up to a willow on the left bank, in front of the large Abbey Meadow, a park surrounding what remains of the original abbey. The meadow was busy and gay, perfect for children and adults alike, with swimming and wading pools, tennis courts, café, putting greens, and lots of short-cropped grass and shade trees.

We took a walk along the towpath to Abingdon Lock, whose history goes back some six hundred years.

After dinner we walked the narrow streets of this little Berkshire town, where delicate spires rose over graceful bridges, a stately Guildhall, and a stern nineteenth-century gaol. We treated ourselves to a pint of ale at the local pub and good conversation with the publican. Dr. Samuel Johnson once said, "there is nothing which has yet been contributed by man, by which so much happiness is produced as by a good tavern or inn"—and we heartily agree. The Thames is lined with interesting pubs that provide an excellent way of getting to know England's heritage. A Thames "pub crawl" has been the highlight of many a trip to England.

It was a moonlit night and wonderfully romantic returning to the *Quadrille Lady,* moored to "our" willow in front of the abbey ruins. Our ever-present friends the swans came begging for bread, music emanated from somewhere near the town, and

Sonning Lock has carefully tended grounds, a fine display of flowers and a gracious lockkeeper. It seems appropriate, as early evening shadows lengthen, to see a stemmed crystal glass pass from the yacht to the lockkeeper. His hand lifts in the traditional gesture of a toast.

we shared the funny parts of Jerome K. Jerome's *Three Men in a Boat,* occasionally falling into laughing fits.

The Romantic Upper Thames

Tuesday morning we awoke to another beautiful, sun-warmed day filled with gentle breezes and ever-so-slight wisps of clouds moving slowly across the pale blue sky. We had to dig ourselves out from under the "snow" that had fallen through the night from the willow tree, but that was quickly accomplished, and then we were off —to a nearby inn for a traditional English breakfast. The English savor their breakfasts —no "juice and coffee" in this country!—and we feasted on juice, cereal, eggs, bacon, kippers, toast with fresh butter, and the most wonderful strawberry jam we had ever tasted. What a way to start the day!

Above Abingdon on the left bank all was farmland—pastures, wheatfields, and hayfields. Just before the lock at Sandford, near the backwater known as Sandford Pool, a proud white stallion and its barefoot lady rider were bathing tentatively in the river. It was one of those quiet morning scenes straight out of England's past.

We were now on our way to Oxford, passing through a curious mixture of woodland, suburbia, and light industry. Near where Hinskey Stream pours its waters into the Thames, we caught our first glimpse of the spires of Oxford some two miles away. With the sun shining on its towers, turrets, and pinnacles, each different, all beautiful, "that sweet City with her dreaming spires" looked like a setting from a medieval fairy tale. Ah, Oxford—home of scholarship, erudition, and Oxford English!

Iffley Lock, a quarter mile above the bridge, was a pretty lock; after tying up we walked to Iffley by a bridge over the weir, passing through a gate at the site of the old mill. Iffley promised treasures from the past: thatched medieval ruins, a famous Norman parish church, and a yew tree nearby that probably furnished longbows for the French wars of Edward III.

Just above Donnington Road Bridge the Thames was joined by a branch of the Cherwell, a famous bit of punting water lined with old Oxford barges in various states of disrepair and much frequented by students. Its many branches lead through leafy tunnels, past colorful gardens and the grounds of many well-known Oxford colleges.

Young men and women were lolling about the banks, swimming, walking dogs, bicycling, and, as we came into Oxford itself, punting. In Victorian days the punt was "the gondola of the Thames," often a vehicle for elegant ladies reclining on soft cushions. Punting, or "shoving," is an art; Dickens gives a detailed description of the fine points in his *Dictionary of the Thames,* 1897. There is certainly more to it than pushing a pole, and the beginner is advised to find a secluded spot for his initial attempts. (Such efforts were a favorite subject for Victorian river humor, which usually pictured the helpless shover hanging onto a disembodied punt pole while his boat floated hopelessly out of reach.)

Here the river was also full of earnest young oarsmen, working "entirely too hard," their trainers following them along the banks on bicycles and bellowing good-natured abuse through bullhorns.

When we disembarked at Folly Bridge (the "folly" was a tower demolished in 1799), we walked up to the octagonal cupola of Wren's Sheldonian Theatre and—looking out over the maze of towers, gates, domes, and chapels and reveling in the circuit of Saxon, Tudor, Perpendicular, Renaissance, Norman, and Victorian architecture that surrounded us below—discovered the glory of Oxford.

There are thirty-four colleges in Oxford, each one a marvel of period architecture. This vast concourse of noble institutions provides for the education of comparatively few students—just under 11,000—the objective being not mass education but the training of individuals.

The chief pride of Oxford is its High Street. Winding like a stream through the town and lined with the most beautiful colleges, it is one of the most impressive streets in the world.

Knowing the folly of trying to see the entire town in one afternoon, and having been advised that "English universities are hopeless in big doses," we limited our touring to Christ Church, the High, and Magdalen College, where we lingered in the 100-acre park and strolled among its deer, followed the water walks along paths overhung by trees, and enjoyed cool vistas of water and lawn with ancient graceful stone in the background.

Downstream Is Different

Returned to the *Quadrille Lady,* we turned ourselves around to head back toward Staines. Cruising in the opposite direction on the same river was a surprisingly different experience. Vistas were altogether new, and familiar towns took on a different character. We passed Radley, with its well-known boy's public school founded in 1847 by Dr. Sewell, who believed that even small schoolboys could be influenced by their surroundings and consequently filled his Queen Anne mansion with lovely gardens, linen paneling from the House of Lords, ancient woodwork and, outside the chapel, classical columns from Italy.

There was something soft and sensual about the Thames here, something that brought mothers to it with their babies and found couples unabashedly romancing on its banks, amid the aromatic fields, the soft greens, the breeze, and the lushness of it all.

We moored for the night across the river from Nuneham Park, a stately eighteenth-century mansion standing immense and magnificent on one of the low hills, surrounded by a 1,200-acre parkland. If you're quiet, they say, you may spot one of the deer that roam the grounds—and we did. We were also rewarded with the loveliest birdsong we'd ever heard, which the rude mocking-bird—who cares for nothing—picked up and ridiculed, giggling off madly at the end.

After an early start the next morning, already day five of our week's trip, we traveled down the Culham Reach. Daisies bloomed along the narrow Culham Cut, which took us under the seventeenth-century Culham Manor and grounds and into Culham Lock near the village green. Beyond Culham Lock we turned into a side stream, floated under the three-arched Sutton Bridge, and meandered into Sutton Pools, the most beautiful backwaters of the Thames. The wide, colorful pools were bordered on one side by meadows and on the other by well-tended gardens; sandy islands and peninsulas were doted over by weeping willows.

We moored before two small houses and climbed a fence near a row of half-timbered cottages to explore the village of Sutton Courtenay. We followed the footpath, then the road, past curious and picturesque cottages and farmhouses from the Elizabethan period and beautiful white-brick half-timbered houses with leaded glass windows—all covered with climbing roses. Further along we passed the weathered wooden gate leading to the vicarage and continued on to the shady village green. Here we visited the churchyard, one of whose tombstones belonged to George Orwell (Eric Blair), then stopped in at the twelfth-century square-towered Gothic church. A little country lane took us past Norman Hall, the manor house of Sutton Courtenay, an amazingly original twelfth-century building.

Country ladies in tweeds picked us out as strangers and relished showing us the highpoints of the village. We bought provisions from the grocer, then returned to our boat.

Clifton Hampden, with its small twelfth-century church and its old-fashioned thatched cottages dainty with flowers, was situated at the foot of a little cliff downstream. The famous Barley Mow Inn is reputed to have been built in 1350; Jerome K. Jerome called it "the quaintest, most old-world inn up the river."

Shillingford's exquisite Tudor mansion, surrounded by terraced gardens, sculptured shrubs and trees, and lawn furniture, stood on the left bank as we approached the village. Near the three-arched bridge was the Shillingford Bridge Hotel, its lawns covered with large numbers of Canada geese. A sharp elbow turn took us around a pasture that gave off the most wonderful flowery aroma; it was a popular mooring spot, crowded with families sunning and swimming.

This was another hot—very hot—day. We found a likely-looking spot to moor and flung ourselves into the Thames. It was delightful, the water cool and refreshing, kept scrupulously clean by the Thames Conservancy. (Nothing whatever may be dumped into the river—not even waste sinkwater.)

At Benson Lock we left the boat and journeyed two miles up into the hills rising from the watercress beds near the banks, to explore the brick and flint village of

Ewelme, a place of pilgrimage for lovers of Jerome K. Jerome (who lies buried in the churchyard), Chaucer (his son Thomas is entombed in the church), and beautiful Chiltern villages. Ewelme is the most beautiful of all the Chiltern towns, a remarkable fifteenth-century survival lying in a cozy hollow.

The banks at Pangbourne were lined with delightful, half-timbered, rambling gingerbread homes and white stone and thatched cottages—all squeezed between a chalk cliff and the riverbank. Just across the river was Whitchurch, a peaceful, pretty little residential annex to Pangbourne. The tiny black and white house at Whitchurch Lock, with its pointed Gothic windows, looked much as it did a century or more ago when it appeared in river prints and pictures. A wide sweep of water cascaded gently over the little dam, to languish in the great depths of the pools below, just beyond the lacy white iron Victorian bridge.

Shiplake Lock is in the Henley section of the Thames River where the Royal Rowing Regatta is held. Ten craft, five to a side, lock through under the eyes of a large and attentive audience. Often where the lock is accessible by foot, an appreciative audience is part of the locking-through experience.

The bells of Sonning announced evensong as we approached. Sonning Lock is considered one of the prettiest locks on the river and is famous for its display of flowers throughout the season. The village is also renowned for its excellent inns and eating places; two of them (the White Hart and the French Horn) receive three stars from the Michelin Red Guide.

We moored for the night in front of the White Hart, a beautiful, rambling, white frame inn, some parts of which date from the sixteenth century. It is perfectly situated behind wide lawns and rose gardens, all of which provide a wonderful setting for a relaxing drink.

Since the banks were thick with willows, it required a few minutes' walk inland to discover that Sonning is perhaps the most fairy-tale nook on the entire river—with its Georgian-fronted houses, its cottages smothered in roses, and its ancient mill and church looking as though they had stood unaltered for centuries. A path through the peaceful churchyard, walled in soft brick, led to the Bull Hotel, a veritable picture of an English country inn. Here in the hotel's square green courtyard the old men of the village group on seats beneath the trees, drink their ale, and gossip about village politics. Inside, the inn was a maze of low, quaint rooms with latticed windows, awkward stairs, and winding passages.

A Lazy Day

We took our time getting started on Thursday, lingering in Sonning until mid-morning. The river below Sonning wound in and out among pretty wooded islands along Sonning Reach, a placid, hushed, lonely oasis of peace with views of pleasant fields and gentle hills.

Shiplake is a lovely village precariously situated on the side of a steep chalk hill that overhangs the river. Alfred Lord Tennyson was married to Emily Sellwood in the church here in 1850, after a courtship that lasted fourteen years. And another literary figure is associated with this area: at the tail of the weir stream near Shiplake Lock, the River Loddon, Alexander Pope's "Lodona," joins the main river.

Further downstream we came upon the town of Wargrave, whose church was burned to the ground in 1914 by angry suffragettes frustrated by the stubborn vicar who refused to take the word "obey" out of the marriage ceremony.

In mid-afternoon, about ten miles beyond Wargrave, we were approaching Marlow, one of the prettiest river centers on the Thames. Though not a large town, Marlow was a bustling Georgian community where the poet Shelley lived when he composed "The Revolt of Islam" (while floating on the Thames in his little boat). Mrs. Shelley (Mary Wollstonecraft) busied herself writing that romantic horror classic *Frankenstein* during their stay. Byron and T. S. Eliot both visited here.

Marlow boasts one of the most beautiful bridges on the river, the Marlow suspension bridge, built in 1835 by W. Tierney Clark (who later built a similarly designed bridge in Budapest). As we approached the bridge the elegant spire of Marlow Church rose above the town on the left bank, beyond the riverside park.

We moored in the park, just two minutes' walk from the center of town, and wandered into Marlow through its wide High Street—so bright and airy, yet still retaining its Georgian flavor. We walked past a great Georgian mansion that is now the post office; past the old Town Hall, reputed to be the work of Christopher Wren; down West Street, a gem of fifteenth-century architecture, where Shelley and his wife lived and worked; back toward the bridge—and into Burgers Continental Confectioners, which had set our noses atwitching from afar. We completely lost control of ourselves in the presence of the vast assortment of homemade chocolates and rich pastries, and we lingered over exotic Indian teas.

Enchanted with Marlow—and quite unable to move after our sweets orgy—we spent the night in the peaceful riverside park.

The Royal Benediction

Early in the morning of our final day we headed into Marlow Lock, set beside a millstream and traditional mill buildings, with the famous Compleat Angler Inn nearby. Beyond the lock the river completed a sweeping bend to the east, and we skirted the great Quarry Woods, 25,000 acres of superb beeches laced with narrow climbing paths and winding glades, a great orchestra of slender brown buds and oval sun-spotted leaves whispering of cool breezes and sunny summer days.

The Bourne End Reach was alive with sailing races, and we had to do some fancy maneuvering to avoid a few of the little one-designs as they raced for the mark. Rolling, gentle Winter Hill dominated the river on the south bank, partly hiding the village of Cookham Dean. Here Kenneth Grahame wrote stories for his small son that were afterward collected to form *The Wind in the Willows,* one of the loveliest of English books.

Cookham, the riverside counterpart of Cookham Dean, is famous as the home of Stanley Spencer, whose great canvases caused such a stir in the first half of this century. His painting was done in and around Cookham, and many of the characters he depicted were drawn from among the local people. We entered Cookham Lock —which, in the opinion of many travelers, has the best natural setting of any lock on the Thames, nestled deep in the valley at the foot of Cliveden and Hedsor Woods.

Dominating the scene from the heights of Cliveden Woods was Cliveden House, former home of the Astors, an imposing nineteenth-century mansion. Its history, filled with drama, scandal, and triumph, includes post-Cromwellian indiscretions, duels, disguises, salons, and masques. The anthem "Rule Britannia" was first introduced in the little amphitheater in the glade here in 1739, and the political intrigues and scandals ending with the Profumo case took place here in the 1960s. It was, we decided, a pleasant spot for a picnic lunch—under the willows in the quiet peace of the river.

A narrow boat under a bridge in the upper of two flights of locks that connect the Staffordshire & Worcestershire Canal to the Severn River at Stourport. Two marks of this canal are the oval black signs with gold letters identifying bridges and the wild flowers along the banks. The width of the locks is just over two meters, hence the narrow canal and narrow boats.

Some hours later we motored downstream to the village of Bray, commonly identified with the notorious vicar of Bray, the man who bent like a reed to the ever-changing winds of religious politics during the reign of the four Tudor monarchs. Incredibly, he changed his creed three times.

> "And this is the law, I will maintain
> Until my dying day, Sir
> That whatsoever King may reign,
> I'll still be Vicar of Bray, Sir."

In his defense, Charles Dickens says, "It is not surprising that the ancient vicar, so celebrated in song, should have persistently determined to live and die vicar of Bray. For a secluded and quietly beautiful place of residence few more agreeable spots can be found." The fine old church with its vicarage stood close to the river, near Bray's Waterside Inn (which rates four stars from Michelin).

Bray Lock, just downstream from the town, is famous for its supremely colorful gardens and is considered one of the prettiest locks on the river.

Nearing Windsor, we slid into the shadow of the great castle, then wound past the once-royal residence of Frogmore House and the Royal Farm and Gardens in the Home Park. Fortunately, these beautiful places near the riverbank can be seen by Thames travelers—in fact, short of owning a home on the opposite bank, the Thames is the *only* vantage point for these lovely private places.

On the left bank, across from the Home Park, were the stately homes of Datchet, behind expansive lawns and manicured gardens. Datchet Mead is best known to the world for certain disagreeable experiences of the immortal Sir John Falstaff. It was here that Shakespeare's merry wives of Windsor played their scurvy trick, inflicting the well-deserved punishment upon the too-fat, too-amorous, too-confident, too-villainous, and too-agreeable Falstaff. They threw him "hissing hot" into the cool Thames from a laundry basket, where he had been hiding from a jealous husband, coiled up amid dirty linen "like a piece of butcher's offal in a barrow."

Within an hour of Staines, where we had started out one week before, this wonderfully crusty bit of Shakespeare's comedy seemed a fitting benediction to our thoroughly enjoyable trip on the lighthearted, learned, lovely Thames.

Some Practical Information

The inland waterways of England, a network of some 2,200 miles (3,540 km) of navigable rivers, lakes, and canals—all modest in size—boast some of the most interesting and varied cruising possibilities. You can choose broad, flowing rivers bordered by royal castles, world famous universities, and spectacular natural bankside scenery with some of the finest and best-kept gardens in the world—or you can travel the quiet, peaceful lakes and fens, surrounded by bird and animal sanctuaries.

Much of the credit for the well-maintained and highly utilized waterway network belongs to the British Waterways Board and to the dedicated and persuasive body of inland waterway enthusiasts throughout England who campaign vigorously for the retention, restoration, and development of their waterways. Both the Inland Waterways Association, a national voluntary group of some 12,000 members with seven regional branches, and the innumerable local waterway preservation societies throughout the country are instrumental to the continued existence and improvement of the waterway system.

In addition to the narrow canals (discussed in the following chapter), prospective travelers find three types of waterways on which to cruise.

1. *The Rivers* that are most accessible to travelers are the Thames, the Avon, and the Severn.

The Thames. England's historic royal river is navigable and nontidal for 125 miles (200 km) from Teddington Lock (near London) to Lechlade in Gloucestershire. You can float past Runnymede, site of the Magna Charta signing, Windsor Castle, Hampton Court, Cliveden Reach, and such memorable old towns as Maidenhead, Marlow, Henley, and Oxford.

The Avon. Navigation having recently been extended to Stratford-on-Avon, the river now forms a quiet and lovely link with the adjacent narrow canals and can therefore offer a number of outstanding circular cruises. One such excursion, the 109-mile (175 km) "Avon Ring," provides a serene two-week journey through the heart of Shakespeare country.

The Severn. At 215 miles (346 km), this is England's longest river. Navigable from Stourport to Gloucester, it carries the traveler through such famous and exciting towns as Worcester, with its historic cathedral (portions of which date from 1084) and the Royal Worcester porcelain factory; Upton, with its unique half-timbered architecture; and Gloucester, site of important Norman architecture and an ancient town center.

2. *The Broads,* including the Norfolk and Suffolk Broads, contains the highest concentration of hire-boats in England. Comprised of three principal rivers, the Bure, the Yare, and the Waveney, several smaller rivers, and numerous lakes, the entire area of the broads measures a compact 20 by 25 miles. The small waterways are almost totally interconnected, without the aid of locks, and they offer excellent sailing (a sport not possible on most other English waterways). Also in abundance are fishing areas, wildlife preserves, and fine shoreside hotels and pubs, all within three hours by train from London.

3. *The Fens,* located just west of the Norfolk Broads, is a 150-mile (240 km) river system that travels through five counties yet remains the quietest and least commercialized of England's waterways—and therefore it is ideally suited for the novice boatperson. With only fifteen locks, half of them attended, the Fens' quiet rivers flow through sleepy villages and market towns as well as through Cambridge, with its historic university and rivers, and Ely, the center of the Fenland river system and home of a famous Norman castle.

There are a number of ways to cruise these intriguing waterways:

SELF-DRIVE BOATS, from 18 to 50 feet and accommodating two to twelve persons, are available on all the waterways mentioned above. It is easy and convenient to obtain information about them and to book a self-drive boat holiday through any of the central booking agencies listed below. Representing dozens of diverse fleets, these central booking firms publish excellent brochures (there may be a modest charge) that are both informative and educational.

Floating Through Europe, Inc.
501 Madison Avenue
New York, N.Y. 10022

Bargain Boating
Morgantown Travel Service
127 High Street
Morgantown, W.V. 26505

Skipper Travel
210 California Avenue
Palo Alto, Calif. 94306

Hoseasons Holidays Ltd.
Sunway House
Lowestoft, Suffolk NR32 3LT

Blake's International Holidays Afloat
Wroxam, Norwich NR12 8DH

Boat Enquiries Ltd.
7 Walton Well Road
Oxford OX2 6ED

Typical weekly charter costs are:

		June-August	Other
24-foot (7.5 m)	2–3 berths	$250–300	$200–250
27-foot (8 m)	4 berths	$300–350	$250–300
35-foot (10.5 m)	6 berths	$375–450	$325–375
40-foot (12 m)	8 berths	$450–525	$400–450

HOTEL BOATS in many instances were originally workboats and barges that have now been skillfully converted to accommodate from seven to eighteen guests. They usually have a crew of from three to six and offer all meals from wake-up tea to a three-course dinner—all of which has an enormous appeal for many travelers. Hotel boats, ranging in size from 60 to 100 feet and powered by modern diesel engines, are sometimes accompanied by their own shoreside minibuses (chauffered by crewmembers), which are used to transport passengers on touring and shopping excursions. Cruises usually last three to six days, and there is generally a high degree of enthusiasm and hospitality on the floating hotels throughout.

Three major operations offer hotel barge service:

Floating Through Europe, Inc., 501 Madison Avenue, New York, N.Y. 10022, operates two hotel boats on the English rivers and has a third boat scheduled for operation in 1980.

The Bonjour, 72 feet long, accommodating seven passengers with a crew of three, cruises the Thames between Windsor and Oxford from May through mid-October. Approximate weekly rates, per person, including six nights on board, all meals and table wines, and the use of the boat's minibus for excursions, are:

	June-Sept.	May, Oct.
Double cabin	$450	$410
Twin cabin	$400	$360
Single cabin	$500	$460
Entire boat	$2,900	$2,700

The Beverly K. and *The Jean K.,* a pair of hotel boats 65 feet long and 12 feet wide, cruise the delightful waters of Shakespeare country between Stratford and Tewkesbury, along the rivers Avon and Severn. Each carries twelve passengers with a crew of four, and all cabins have private facilities. Approximate weekly rates, per person, including six nights on board, all meals and table wines, a performance at the Shakespeare Memorial Theater, and the use of the chauffered minibus for excursions, are:

	June-Sept.	May, Oct.
Double cabin	$450	$420
Twin cabin	$410	$380
Single cabin	$500	$470
Entire boat	$5,000	$4,700
(12 persons)		

The Queen of the Thames, 112 feet long, carrying twenty passengers and a crew of seven, is scheduled for service in May 1980. A modern-day interpretation of the large and luxurious Thames houseboats of the Victorian era, the *Queen* will provide the comforts and amenities of a modern cruise liner.

River Barge Holidays Limited, Mill Green, Caversham, Reading, Berkshire RG4 8EX, England, operates the hotel barge *Guidance* for three-day and six-day cruises of the Thames. Approximate fare for a three-day cruise, including all meals and table wines and transport for excursions, is $240 per person.

Actief Barge Cruising Holidays, Lillie Towers, 241 Lillie Road, London SW6 7LN, England, operates the hotel barge *Actief* for three-day and six-day cruises of the Thames. Approximate prices for the cruises, per person, including all meals, are:

	Six days	Three days
Double or twin cabin	$350–385	$195–210
Single cabin	$420	$230

DAY-EXCURSION BOATS offer delightful trips, from an hour or two to an entire day, on all the rivers, with tickets available at dockside. Salter Brothers Limited, Folly Bridge, Oxford, has, for more than a hundred years, been operating daily passenger services on the Thames. For information concerning other day-excursion boats, write to the English Tourist Board, 4 Grosvenor Gardens, London SW1 ODU. Approximate costs of Thames excursions are:

Windsor to Runnymede	(1¼ hours)	$2.00
Windsor to Staines	(2 hours)	$2.40
Windsor to Marlowe	(3¼ hours)	$2.80

Books, maps, and guides to the waterway system are available from Floating Through Europe, Inc., 501 Madison Avenue, New York, N.Y. 10022, which maintains an extensive inventory of these publications.

9

*The
Narrow
Canals*

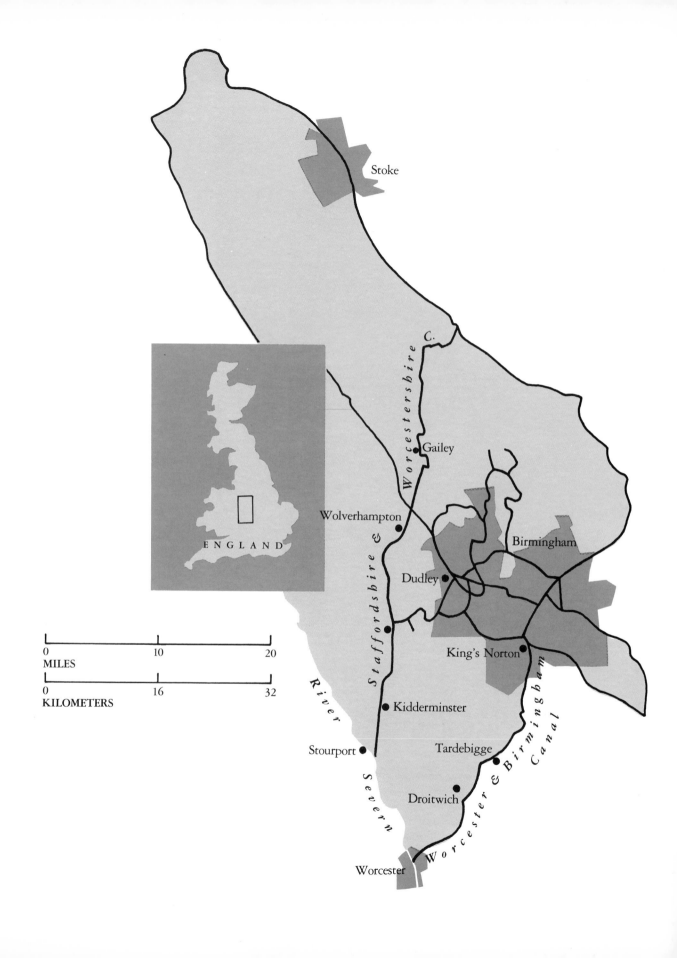

Stoke

Worcestershire C.

Gailey

Wolverhampton

Birmingham

Dudley

King's Norton

Kidderminster

Tardebigge

Stourport

Droitwich

Worcester

River Severn

Staffordshire &

Worcester & Birmingham Canal

ENGLAND

0   10   20
MILES

0   16   32
KILOMETERS

A Circular Tour Through the Heart of England

On a Saturday afternoon in mid-June we arrived at Gailey Lock on the Staffordshire & Worcestershire Canal in the English Midlands. We were embarking on a circular tour of the heart of England that would take us south from Gailey to Stourport-on-Severn, down the River Severn to the cathedral city of Worcester, northeast to Birmingham, and west through the Black Country to Gailey again.

This classic English canals trip was to provide a stark contrast to our previous week's trip on the Thames. As the Thames is a royal river, so the canals of England, for generations after the coming of railroads, were like illegitimate children. Considered a blight on the landscape, they became community dumping grounds and were generally—because they were hidden away in quiet countryside—neglected and abused. Some well-meaning and industrious communities actually went so far as to fill in their canals just to be rid of the eyesores they had created.

While the royal river has been protected by the Thames Conservancy or its equivalent since 1866, no one paid the slightest attention to the dismal state of the canals until about two decades ago. In the early 1950s a small group of waterway enthusiasts banded together, lobbied, organized, and literally dug out abandoned dry cuts with their own hands, to make them once again navigable—for a purpose the original canal builders had never contemplated: pleasure boating.

Today the several hundred miles of Midlands canals are woven together, winding through villages and towns and remote countryside, providing surprisingly quiet grounds for the appreciation of natural history and industrial archaeology.

Birth of the Midlands Canals

In the field of industrial archaeology these canals are truly unique. Great Britain's impressive economic development during the late eighteenth century, which we have come to call the Industrial Revolution, could not have taken place without the development of her canals.

In the mid-eighteenth century Britain lacked an economical way to transport coal and other bulk goods. In general products were carried from their source to markets by trains of pack horses, each of which could carry just 200–350 pounds. The high cost of transportation made it economically impractical to ship coal beyond a radius of twelve miles from the mines. However, on the existing navigable rivers a single horse could pull a barge carrying 30–40 tons of cargo. Waterway transport thus fired the imagination of England's leaders.

In 1761 the Duke of Bridgewater, who owned a mining estate in Lancashire, ten miles from Manchester, turned to a civil engineer named James Brindley to construct a canal that was to shake England's economy and bring her right into the heart of the Industrial Revolution. With the opening of the Bridgewater Canal, the price of coal immediately dropped by half—and England went on a canal binge. Eight years later, James Watt patented his steam engine, which utilized coal as fuel. The engine was to revolutionize the country's important textile industry and make Britain the world's technological and economic leader.

Brindley was commissioned to lace the countryside with waterways. Construction schemes, promoted by companies promising gigantic returns, attracted everyone with a shilling to spare. Out of these small, independent schemes Britain's canal system developed. Most canals were dug out by navvies, or "navigators"—laborers with shovels and wheelbarrows—and were designed to the very tightest of budgets.

The result was an extensive network of narrow canals, some no more than 20 feet across, whose locks were only seven feet wide. The traditional English narrowboat, specially designed for these canals, is about 70 feet long, just under seven feet wide, and has a freight capacity of little more than 30 tons—a load that a single horse can pull. By the mid-nineteenth century the narrowboats plied a network of nearly 4,500 miles of navigable canals and canalized rivers, and the "canal people," the barge families, had developed their own society, law, art, architecture, songs, and slang.

Without this network and its society of canal people, exports from the textile factories, the ironworks, the potteries, and the mines of the industrial Midlands and the north could never have reached the country's great estuaries quickly and economically. As a result of the canals, the wharves of the great rivers groaned beneath the weight of goods to be shipped throughout the world—and England prospered as never before.

The irony of it all was that the canals made the coal available to power the steam engine, and the steam engine operating on railway tracks in turn sounded the death knell for the canals. Throughout the world the invention of the steam locomotive, with its speed and power, signaled the end of the canal age.

On the Cut

Our week-long adventure began at the hire base of Gailey Marine, where we were shown to our craft, a 45-foot steel narrowboat. More like a tiny railroad car than a boat in its interior layout, it had four single berths. Our party of two would clearly have plenty of space despite the boat's diminutive beam, and that's just the way we like it.

By five o'clock we had finished our provisioning, unpacking, and orienting, and we cast off, turning south into the late-afternoon sun, to begin our trip on the Staffordshire & Worcestershire Canal.

Gailey, as it turned out, was the perfect starting point for neophyte narrowboaters, for we had a long stretch of canal before a lock would come into sight. That gave us plenty of time to get accustomed to the intimate dimensions of our surroundings.

The canal followed a twisting course to maintain a level position as it worked its way through rural farmland and back-country village alleyways. The canal banks were liberally sprinkled with yellow iris and buttercups and, behind them, birch trees and farm fields. White wildflowers stood out like stars among the reeds lining the canal.

The Staffs & Worcs Canal, opened in 1772, was one of the first Midlands canals to be completed. Designed by James Brindley as part of a Grand Cross system linking the rivers Thames, Trent, Severn, and Mersey, it provided the basis for the intricate network of Midlands canals that followed.

Few other waterways convey so well the spirit of Britain's early canals. It has its own distinctive character as it twists and turns through the gentle valleys of the rivers Sow, Penk, Smestow, and Stour to reach the Severn. Meandering through remote wooded countryside, it is one of the prettiest and quietest of England's canals. Some say that it is the country's finest cut, outclassing even the more famous Llangollen and Macclesfield canals in its scenery and charm.

Our destination for dinner was just a few miles down the canal at Coven. There, at the Anchor Pub and Steak Bar, we moored near a tabled terrace full of ale drinkers and canal admirers (known to the canal people as "gongoozlers"). The pub, decorated in startling red velvet, offered generous portions of hearty food to hungry boating customers.

The Canal Pubs

One of the wonderful things about England's waterways is the convenient scattering of canalside pubs, which allows the waterway traveler to mingle frequently with other boatmen and with shore people. The canalside pubs, or "public houses," grew up for the refreshment of the commercial boat people and the stabling of their horses at points where working boats tied up for the night.

Waterway inns and pubs were among the few places where the canal people had brief contact with life "on the land." Since narrowboat families had little time or inclination for town entertainment (and usually regarded places even a short distance from the cut with suspicion), the canalside pub was an important facet of their social life—a place to moor for the night, to drink with friends, to play simple games in the bar, and to enjoy their own form of music and dancing. In these pubs everyone spoke the language of the cut; there were no eyebrows raised at the widespread illiteracy of the boat people or their ignorance of landward matters.

Publicans ran an unofficial news exchange for the boat people, reading their messages if they were unable to do so themselves and acting as post office of the cut. Often the publican would find himself the unwitting conductor of a youthful court-ship, writing a letter dictated by the son of one boating family to the daughter of another and putting it in his window until the girl's boat passed and she claimed it. Having then read its contents to her, the publican would write a reply at her dictation —and the process would continue. The only other occasions on which the lovers could exchange sentiments might be a few moments during a passage at some lock or as their respective boats passed each other (and then having to converse at the tops of their voices).

More important, publicans functioned as a kind of employment agency, telling the captain of a short-handed boat that a lad several miles down the canal was available for work. They also served as an important commercial center, for skippers knew that here they could find a local tradesman who wanted a load of timber or mixed goods carried. Through the grapevine (which still exists today) it was a simple matter to pass on information to a carrier looking for a load.

Today, though commercial trade has dwindled to nearly nothing, the old wharves and lock heads still have their mooring rings, and enterprising brewers and publicans are developing canalside pubs in a new way that takes full advantage of their situation for the cruising trade. Former boatmen who have taken to keeping locks and maintaining the canals can still be found in some of these pubs, quietly drinking their pints. If encouraged, they will talk about the condition of water, weed, and bank on their sections of the cut. Occasionally they can even be persuaded to tell stories (many of them unprintable yet highly entertaining) of canal life in the days of the working boats and the characters who manned them.

Roses & Castles

After dinner we pulled away from this popular spot and moored for the night just beyond Cross Green Bridge, near a field of mauve bellflowers and pink forget-me-nots. The natural beauty continued to delight us the next morning as we entered a stretch of canal so narrow and overhung with trees and shrubbery growing from the high red-rock banks that our boat scraped against them. The little humpbacked stone bridge ahead was almost entirely obscured by greenery; it was a dreamlike scene, the sun shining through the trees and reflecting in spots on the murky water.

We reached the outskirts of Wolverhampton at Autherley Junction. At Aldersley Junction, a short distance further south, the Birmingham Canal Navigations emerged from a flight of twenty-one locks leading down from the city of Wolverhampton to the west. We took note of this quiet spot, for we would be descending those locks to complete our circuit at the end of the week.

A fleet of red-white-and-blue narrowboats lay moored on the right bank, their painted hulls ablaze with roses, hearts, castles, scrollwork, and geometric designs. This highly stylized English folk art, known as Roses & Castles, has become the symbol of English canals. It originated on the old working narrowboats, where it traditionally covers every available inch of space, sharing the limelight with gleaming brass fittings and elaborately decorative ropework.

In addition to the exterior paintwork, every household utensil and possession of the narrowboat families—including water cans, dippers, stools, and items of cabin furniture—was treated with some kind of floral decoration. The horses that towed the barges wore brass ornaments and brightly colored harness beads, were fed from flower-painted bowls, and on special occasions could be seen wearing lace caps over their ears. The result was a gaudy feast for the eye, and for us there is nothing on the world's waterways quite so pretty or charming as one of these pencil-slim old boats done up in its full glory.

At Compton Lock we began our 294-foot descent to the River Severn, a descent that involves thirty-one locks and is considered one of the loveliest stretches of canal in England.

Working the Staffs & Worcs

The original lock and canal architecture, hardly ever used for commerce now, has remained relatively unchanged over the centuries. Cruising boatmen come into contact with a wealth of unique, locally designed gates, paddles, walkways, side weirs, footbridges, cast-iron name and number plates, period lock cottages, picturesquely worn bollards and battered balance-beam caps, and scores of other relics of a day when architecture and craftsmanship were based on ingenuity, taste, and durability.

At Compton Lock we were introduced to the creaky lock machinery with its greased levers and gears and leaky oak doors. There was no lockkeeper to instruct us on timing or procedure, but we soon accustomed ourselves to the logical progression of events. We carried our own windlass, or handle, to operate the sluices, known in England as "paddles." The windlass had been given to us by the hire company with a warning not to drop it into the canal, for this was our "key" to progress through the locks.

Weeds grew out of cracks in the cavernous chamber walls, and as we descended in the long, narrow chamber, water streamed through the cracks onto our decks and through open windows, requiring a quick mopping up. When fully lowered in the lock, all we could see was the sky above our heads.

Once through the lock, we found ourselves in a hilly, horse-country landscape that gave no clue we were skirting the city of Wolverhampton, capital of the industrial Black Country. The canal, meandering about the quiet countryside, provided access to one of the few pieces of wild and untouched nature left in the Midlands.

In the afternoon the slate towers of Bilston waterworks appeared in the distance. We were nearing the celebrated Bratch, a curious flight of three locks descending 30 feet, each lock a separate entity, with only a four-foot-long pound separating one from the next. This flight is said to be the predecessor of the now typical lock staircase—

so closely related, in fact, that a two-lock descent just two miles further on is built to the staircase design.

Looking down from the top of the Bratch, its locks surrounded with whitewashed bridges, parapets, and a delightful black and white eighteenth-century octagonal tollhouse, we had a fine view of the countryside.

The afternoon was unsurpassed for quaint, superbly English names: Bumble Hole Lock, Mops Farm Bridge, Himley Hall, Hockley Lock (with its Devil's Den, a lockside cave said to have been occupied since the Iron Age). Stewponey Lock's charming name was painted on the balance beam of the lock and surrounded by a spray of flowers. But the best one of all was Giggety Bridge, a name that just rolls out of the mouth. Such pleasure! How do the English do it?

At Dunsley we entered the historic and scenic area of Kinver Edge, a 300-acre ridge of heath and woodland laced with footpaths and designated a site of special scientific interest. Situated on a long wooded cliff, it provides excellent views over Staffordshire to the Lickey Hills beyond. Here, where prehistoric man made his home, an Iron Age fort survives, along with bright orange sandstone cave dwellings, among them Holy Austin's Rock and Nanny's Rock (add those to our list of names!).

Dusk had come in Kinver Edge, surrounded by history and natural beauty, and we moored there for the night.

Monday, our third day on the canal, we got an early-morning start, ducked through the short Dunsley Tunnel, and slipped into Hyde Bridge Lock, where we stepped ashore and strolled over to the cream and dark green frame cottage that offered a delicious menu of home-cooked delicacies "for boaters only"—and sold fresh produce and souvenirs as well.

Arriving in the village of Kinver just as the shops were beginning to open, we unloaded the bicycles we had on board and pedaled through town, where charming whitewashed and half-timbered cottages leaned far out of plumb. We continued all the way (about a mile of tough pedaling) to the top of Kinver Edge, where we rested and gazed out over Staffordshire far below.

Under way again, we followed the canal as it continued below a red sandstone cliff that stood nearly 100 feet high. Diminutive, humpbacked Whittington Horse Bridge stood near the ancient, oak-timbered Whittington Inn. Originally a manor house built in 1300, it once belonged to the family of Sir Richard Whittington, three times lord mayor of London and probably the first English millionaire to become the stuff of folk legend. The manor was visited by Queen Anne in 1711, is inhabited by the ghost of Lady Jane Grey, and boasts a 300-yard secret tunnel and hiding holes to shelter priests.

Whittington Lock marks the boundary between Staffordshire and Worcestershire. Its attractive white-brick lock cottage was surrounded with primroses.

The canal wound and ambled like a country lane between fields of green clover and wild carrots and fragrant, deep green woods. Then it grew narrower and narrower until, just after Austcliff Bridge, it was overhung by a massive red rock, its top covered with a thick cluster of oaks, its roots piercing the thin soil. It was strange indeed to be looking *up* at the roots of trees! The canal, meanwhile, tortured itself into a tight horseshoe bend—just the place to meet another boat! (Fortunately, we didn't.) Then the 65-yard Cookley Tunnel pierced the sandstone hill running under Cookley's main street.

Debdale Bridge, a little wooden footbridge on brick pedestals, seemed to lead from one piece of wild country to another. Imagine our surprise, then, at seeing an impeccably dressed Englishman—complete with bowler and umbrella—walk purposefully from one side to the other, going from noplace to nowhere.

Pretty, whitewashed Wolverly Forge Bridge led to an open-roofed, iron-gated sandstone cavern that used to be a pound for stray animals. Nearby, down a one-way road past a red-brick eighteenth-century church, was Wolverly, an enchanting "forgotten" village nestling beside a little stream, with ancient stone cottages and a seventeenth-century grammar school.

There are wide, sky-high fields just ahead, but first this narrow boat, chartered by a family on holiday from Norway, must negotiate a slender underpass near Kinver Lock.

Lockside Horse Opera

Wolverly Court Lock was situated in the middle of a pasture full of frisky horses and ponies, who eyed us with more than a little curiosity. As we entered the lock, Jarrett hopped off on the right bank to crank open the paddles, and the horses edged over to inspect the boat from the left bank. They seemed genuinely friendly, sticking their noses out to be petted. Or were they looking for sugar? Sensing that sugar was what they were after, Jarrett ducked below to find some. It was an immediate success; nothing but caution prevented the shaggy beasts from stepping right on board to find the source of the sweets. One pony actually had one hoof in the cockpit, but Stanley was able to discourage him.

All this was very amusing, but we still had to negotiate the lock—and Jarrett was going to have to work both sides of the lock, horses and all.

Pretending a bravado she didn't feel, she prepared to cross the humpbacked footbridge to the horses' side, where they had gathered in a semicircle to greet her. She had stuffed her pockets with sugar as a protective measure—which turned out to have been a tactical error. The little brown pony and the large white stallion were the greatest sweets lovers, and they followed their noses directly to her pockets and began nibbling away.

Jarrett's fearless facade was cracking. Having closed the gates and opened the paddles on the left bank, she made a quick retreat over the footbridge. One more quick sortie to the pasture to close the paddles and open the front gates, the pony nibbling at her backside the entire time, and she was off again. This, however, was less a retreat and more of a rout; the horses were trotting along after her, whinnying and snorting. Jarrett was plainly relieved to shut the gate and leave that left bank.

And we were off—musing the while that you never knew what you might encounter on the English narrow canals.

From this point the scenery grew more industrial as the suburbs of Kidderminster, renowned as a carpet-making town, swelled around the canal. We kept a wary eye on the water level and looked out for underwater obstructions—of which there were plenty. We ran between Stourvale Iron Works and one of the famous Kidderminster carpet factories, then floated directly under the imposing late-medieval, square-towered parish church.

Kidderminster offered little reason to linger, so we continued over the muddy waters of the Stour on a small aqueduct and entered the lock without delay, descending nearly 12 feet beneath a fantastically busy road intersection. The sheer brick walls of factory buildings rose from the water and towered over our heads.

The Severn Connection

The Stour followed the canal's path along the left bank as we worked our way toward Stourport-on-Severn. This city is a rare example of an English town that owes its entire existence to the coming of the canal, having grown up around the port that James Brindley created there between the Severn and the canal.

Before the coming of the canal, Stourport was nothing but the tiny village of Lower Mitton. When Brindley built his canal port—a series of five connected basins equipped with drydocks and locks leading down into the Severn—the town of Stourport came into existence around the bustling freight activity of the narrowboats and the local sailing barges known as Severn Trows. Today four of the five original basins are still operational, interconnected with locks and short canals and busy with pleasure boats.

York Street Lock led into the town; its gemlike whitewashed Victorian Gothic lock cottage was a former toll office dating from 1854. Here we leaped out to buy some traditional handpainted canal tinware—of the highest quality and craftsmanship we saw in England.

The York Street Lock took us into the first of the basins, surrounded by handsome Georgian warehouses, workshops, and hotel and cottage groups. The Tontine Hotel, a vast red-brick Georgian inn that opened in 1788, was named after the Neapolitan Lorenzo Tonti, who invented an insurance scheme whereby a number of persons invested in a fund that went to the sole survivor among them.

After several twists and turns in the maze of basins and canals, we approached the pair of staircase locks that would lead us down nearly 30 feet to the River Severn, Britain's longest river and one of the oldest navigations in Europe. With its tributary, the Avon, it cuts deep into the heart of England, linking the iron and coal fields of the Midlands with the Bristol Channel and the British coastal trade.

Compared with the Thames, the Severn is a wild and undeveloped river, wide and deep, passing through pleasant pastureland, its high banks lined at times with willow and elder trees and colorful wildflowers. The stretch from Stourport to Worcester—precisely our route—is reputed to be the prettiest on the river.

Our route would take us through a well-defined, verdant valley and three wide, automated locks before turning into the Worcester & Birmingham Canal at Worcester. Our first lock was just a mile downstream, prettily situated under steep hills. Locking through was easy; the big modern chamber was provided with vertical chains, eliminating the need for mooring. The lockkeeper seemed remote in his tower, where he pushed buttons that opened and closed doors and paddles with a soft, efficient hum and a buzz.

Just downstream was the riverside Hempstall Cider House, a thirst-quenching stop for bargemen and the gangs of bow-haulers, men who, until well into the nineteenth century, were employed in place of horses in what Thomas Telford, the famous canal engineer, called "this barbarous and expensive slave-like office."

Further downstream an old church stood alone, high on the wooded hills of the right bank at Shrawley Wood. The wooded heights continued for several miles, rising sometimes straight up from the riverbank. High, imposing banks with crumbling edges led to Holt Lock, five miles below Stourport. Once we were in the lock, the doors, with their massive timber balance beams left from the days when they were run by manpower, closed silently behind us. A gentle rush of water dropped us five and a half feet, the silent doors opened, and we were out again. The entire procedure had taken just two and a half minutes!

Two sweet, white-haired ladies rocked gently on the porch of their cottage, The Briars, looking silently over the hills beyond the river. Soon we slipped under Holtfleet Bridge, a gracefully arched, delicate nineteenth-century iron span. On a hill over the river was Holt Castle, a fourteenth-century tower ruin surrounded by a sixteenth-century mansion trying hard to look like a castle. Nearby Holt Church, a fine late Norman building, sent its discreet little tower shyly skyward.

Just beyond the junglelike junction with the disused Droitwich Barge Canal, we entered Bevere Lock, famous for its colorful, prize-winning gardens. The gates were closed, the tower appeared to be empty, and the traffic light was red, so we tooted our horn gently. The red-shirted keeper sauntered out of his house and over to the tower.

Below Bevere the Severn began to broaden on its way to Worcester, and in the last three miles we moved through meadows and pleasantly wooded country, the banks lined with willows and alders. The only trace of civilization was a glimpse of an occasional farm or an attractive, secluded riverside pub.

Worcester: Cathedral City

As we approached the outskirts of Worcester, large Victorian houses looked out over their gardens to the river. For 900 years Worcester has been known as the Faithful City because of its loyalty and devotion to the Crown. It is a handsome town in one of the richest parts of the undulating Severn Valley. The county town of Worcestershire and the see of a bishop, it is also an industrial center famous for gloves and porcelain. And of course the famous Worcestershire sauce is one of its prime exports!

We soon caught sight of the nearly 200-foot tower of Worcester's magnificent eleventh-century cathedral, which dominates the riverfront from behind terraced gardens. This was one of the most beautiful and impressive approaches to any town we saw in England, its magic enhanced at this sunset hour with the sun's glinting golden over every detail of the town.

The locks leading to the Worcester & Birmingham Canal were closed until the next morning, so we would have to moor here on the Severn—a not altogether disagreeable prospect. Most of the moorings lay between the town's two bridges, bounded by terraces and gardens and the beautiful grounds of the lovely Diglis Hotel. Here we moored in peace as the sun set to the melodies of the cathedral bells.

We took time that evening to explore the irregular Georgian buildings of Fore-gate Street and the fifteenth- and sixteenth-century timber-framed houses and the cathedral of Friar Street. Then we visited the splendidly elaborate Queen Anne Guildhall and, finally, the Grey Friary, once part of a Franciscan Priory and carrying a date of 1480—one of the finest half-timbered houses in England.

Tuesday morning, our fourth day, we made an expensive visit to the "seconds shop" of the Royal Worcester Porcelain Works, famous since 1768 for its elegant wares, and a less expensive tour of the Dyson Perrins Museum, which exhibits the most complete collection of Worcester porcelain in the world. Then, returned to our boat, we cast off, turning into the locks that would take us through Diglis Basin.

During the heyday of the canals, Diglis Basin had warehouses bursting with salt, coal, and chocolate for export and grain and wine for import. Now its only trade comes from pleasure boats.

Ambitious Cut to Birmingham

A simple left jog from the basin, and we were into the Worcester & Birmingham Canal and beginning the third leg of our four-part circular tour of the Midlands. The Worcester & Birmingham is a "second generation" canal; one of the more interesting, arduous, and costly canals, it was built during the period when engineering works were becoming more elaborate as canals entered more difficult terrain. Authorized in 1791, the canal took twenty-four years to complete. It shares with the Trent & Mersey Canal the distinction of possessing the greatest number of tunnels on a single canal in Britain, and it is the most heavily locked cut in the country: in the 30-mile climb from the Severn at Worcester through the beautiful Lickey Hills to the Midlands Plateau at Birmingham, there are fifty-eight locks. Thirty of them are concentrated in a stretch of just two miles—the Tardebigge Flight, the longest flight of locks in Britain.

Gone are the mules that used to pull the narrowboats laden with salt, coal, and chocolate; all commercial carrying ended here about 1964. Today this cut is part of the popular Midlands cruising circuit, winding through mostly rural countryside, a favorite among anglers and naturalists.

Tightly hemmed in by the town of Worcester, the canal ran past the walls of the Commandery, a timbered fifteenth-century building that served as Charles II's headquarters before the Battle of Worcester in 1651. But the town seemed not to have taken advantage of the potential beauty of its little canal, whose banks contrasted sharply and vividly with the water showplace of the Severn below. We were traveling through the dirty, drab, industrial back door of the town, with little of interest to see, and we were very happy to escape it.

At the twin Gregorys Mill Locks and the following duo of Bilford Locks we were lifted a total of 28 feet, up and out of the urban squalor and into somewhat nicer countryside. Blackpole Lock then raised us to pure pastoral bliss, surroundings much more in line with what we had expected from the famed Worcester & Birmingham Canal.

Near Tolladine Lock some of the Gunpowder Plot conspirators—including the infamous Guy Fawkes—lay hidden at Hindlip Hall for a week after their plot to blow up the Houses of Parliament in 1605 was exposed by an anonymous letter. We could still see the spires of Worcester Cathedral some four miles behind us as we began the 56-foot climb to the village of Tibberton. The six Offerton Locks, which completed this climb, took us past reed-lined banks and fields full of newmown hay that lay on the earth like a green and gold quilt.

A short cutting curved past the charmingly named God Speed the Plough pub and into the canalside village of Tibberton. We swept around toward a ridge of hills in the east, but the main Bristol-Birmingham railway line interceded to prevent us from reaching the side of the valley. This railway line would continue to parallel the canal, sending its speeding Birmingham-bound trains shooting past us, all destined to arrive within an hour. We hoped to arrive the following night! We could better understand now, at close range, how the taunting prospect of high speeds must have romanced investors and industrialists away from the peaceful and efficient but slow-poke canals.

We reached Dunhampstead about two o'clock—a mere hamlet of no more than five buildings yet boasting a lively waterfront with a crowded wharf, a popular pub, a shop selling canal wares, and a party and trip boat, *The Cedar.* A pretty wooded cutting led to the 230-yard Dunhampstead Tunnel, the first of five tunnels from here to Birmingham. A handrail ran along both walls—an interesting relic from pre-engine days when work-toughened, rough-speaking boatmen used to hand-pull their boats through the tunnel.

The hills receded behind us, and we ran through flatter countryside to Shernal Green, a pretty residential settlement offering glimpses through the trees of its late-eighteenth-century Hadzor House. This was one of the few straight stretches on the canal, leading through peaceful countryside.

Near Hanbury Wharf stood the town of Droitwich, known as Salinae in Roman times, one of the oldest settlements in England. The Romans appreciated both the curative powers of the salt springs and the salt itself, which was vitally important for preserving meat.

North of Hanbury Wharf the canal wound through pleasant, unspoiled country beneath Piper's Hill Common, a surviving piece of the ancient Forest of Feckenham. This is one of the most charming pieces of woodland in England, full of wood warblers and blackcaps, with dragonflies and damselflies hovering over lonely pools.

It was nearly four o'clock when we entered the first chamber of the six-lock Astwood Flight and climbed 42 feet through pleasant open pastureland. Because of the acute water shortage of 1976, the canal could be used only from 10 A.M. until 4 P.M., so this would be our last lock of the day.

To the north of the Astwood settlement stood the original reason for the town's existence—a huge industrial chemical works. The canal traveled through the heart of the works, which today lie derelict and forgotten, half tumbling into the canal.

Next we arrived at Stoke—first the works, then the town, and finally the wharf. Stoke Works was built in 1828 to pump brine from underground for industrial use, and it once brought considerable trade to the canal. Today the blackened, deserted works do little to enhance the rural landscape, but—happily—it is the only outpost of industry between Worcester and King's Norton, near Birmingham.

Stoke Prior was built as a model village for the salt workers; today the pretty little town lines the left bank of the canal with its back yards, gardens, and greenhouses. Stoke Wharf, just beyond, is a classic canal settlement in the finest tradition: a lock, a wharf and warehouse, a pleasant line of creeper-clad houses facing the canal, and a fleet of narrowboats closely moored at the docks of Tolladine Boat Services. We were forced to stop just 50 yards below the wharf, at the bottom doors of the padlocked Stoke Flight. We had worked twenty-two locks that day—a healthy number for two people—and we were relieved that the water shortage had provided an excuse to call it a day.

Steep, vine-covered cliffs of friable red sandstone line the banks of Cookley Tunnel where it passes under the little village of Cookley. Beyond the tunnel at the next lock near Debdale Bridge, a cave cut into the cliff was an overnight stable for the towing horses that walked the towpath to the right.

Climbing the Lickey Hills

On the fifth day of our journey we woke to the sound of rain on the roof. A steady drizzle fell from dead gray skies, and we just rolled over and went back to sleep. There was no rush to get up; the locks wouldn't open until 10 A.M.

Precisely at the stroke of ten the man from the British Waterways Board arrived and unlocked the gates. We worked the six Stoke Locks in the rain and emerged an hour later in the short pound leading to the thirty locks of the Tardebigge Flight. Tardebigge is truly one of the wonders of the entire waterways system. The flight would take us into pastoral England at its finest, winding through the rolling Lockey Hills while it lifted us 217 feet within a distance of two and a half miles. But we would be several hours in negotiating these miles.

By 1:30 P.M. we had reached Halfway Lock Cottage, a lovely, gabled, white-brick cottage with neat green trim. The drizzle had stopped, leaving us with gray skies and wet decks, but it was the first sunless day of our week-long trip, so we really couldn't complain.

At lock 50 we took a brief excursion over an embankment to view the Tardebigge Feeder Reservoir, a favorite with anglers and naturalists. We would be following the contours of this large reservoir as we worked through the next four locks. The scenery there must be truly magnificent on a clear day, with views spreading far over the surrounding countryside; on our visit the hills were spread with mist, lending beauty of another kind to the scene, while the birds living in the reeds around the reservoir serenaded us sweetly.

After a long pound between the last two locks on the canal, we reached Tardebigge Top Lock, the deepest narrow lock in Britain, with a rise of 14 feet. And, finally, Tardebigge Wharf, overlooked by the elegant spire of the eighteenth-century pale sandstone church that shared the nearby hillside with the small farming village of Tardebigge. Here at the wharf pleasure boats clustered about the wharf buildings, with dozens of old working barges moored on either side of the canal.

This 14-mile summit pound was to be a most delightful stretch of canal, winding tranquilly through the hilly Worcestershire countryside. The flat Severn Valley seemed distant as the canal prepared to plunge first into the Tardebigge and then the Shortwood tunnels. The 580-yard Tardebigge Tunnel was hewn largely from raw stone, its moist, jagged roof glistening in many colors. The scenery here was extraordinary. We seemed to be following the bottom of a deep ravine, the sides heavily wooded, steam rising from the water while raindrops from the trees danced on the surface. Masses of bluebells lined the banks. Far down at the end of the ravine was a tiny speck of light in a hill that blocked our path; the light marked the entrance to Shortwood Tunnel.

Shortwood was slightly longer than Tardebigge—608 yards—and extremely wet. Luckily, we were wearing our foul-weather gear, for the roof of the tunnel drips continually and sometimes streams water down on passing boats.

Beyond the tunnel the canal continued through a countryside of rolling hills and woodland. All along the banks were black and white cottages and charming villages; below was the modest valley of the River Arrow.

In the distance we could see a ridge of hills pierced by King's Norton Tunnel. The ridge serves as an important geographical boundary: to the south is the rolling and open countryside of rural Worcestershire; to the north is Warwickshire and the southernmost indications of the Black Country industrial region.

Plunging into Darkness

As we curved through a wooded cutting we caught sight of the entrance to King's Norton Tunnel, one of the longest in England, more than a mile and a half long. No matter that we had been through five or six tunnels before this; this was a tunnel of a different sort. The small black hole in the hillside looked as though it might be the entrance to almost anything—Hades not excluded—and almost certainly something unpleasant. Once inside, we knew we were committed—there could be no turning back. We were condemned to a mile and a half of inky, echoing blackness.

The light behind us grew pale and gray as the tunnel entrance receded. As our eyes adjusted to the gloom, we began to discern the meager gleam from our head-light, illuminating a small area of tunnel wall and roof in front of the boat but leaving the water itself in blackness. Cascades of chilly water, falling from the ventilator shafts in the roof, doused us. Then, most frightening of all, the pinpoint of light behind us disappeared. Now we belonged to the underworld, "buried" under thousands of tons of rock and earth. We were utterly alone.

An eternity later, another pinpoint of light and hope appeared before us to indicate the possibility of escape. That glimmer gradually became a tiny, bright circle formed by the arch of the tunnel and its reflection in the water. As this slowly grew larger, details of the scene outside formed a complete miniature picture within a circular black frame. It was surprisingly beautiful—especially after the emotional impact of that horrible claustrophobia that had gripped us in the jet-blackness of the bowels of the tunnel. We were both startled to discover that the entire passage had taken only forty minutes.

When we emerged from the tunnel, we were within the Birmingham city limits, though the town around us was known as King's Norton. This former village has been swallowed into the suburbs of Birmingham, but its small village green, grammar school buildings, and the soaring spire of its magnificent medieval church of St. Nicholas ensure that it will survive as a recognizable entity within the city.

Birmingham proper was very near now, and we were about to enter its grimy industrial area, where chimneys belch smoke and hidden machinery roars and steams. The railway joined our waterway, and together we drove through the middle of Cadbury's Bournville Works, otherwise known as the Garden Factory.

On a rainy morning father and daughter tend the gates while mother pilots their narrow boat out of a lock in Wolverhampton on the Birmingham Canal. The crew are at the bottom of a flight of 21 locks. Ahead, beyond the trees, is Aldersley Junction and the Staffordshire & Worcestershire Canal.

This was the creation of the Cadbury family, who in 1879 moved their cocoa and chocolate manufacturing business south from the center of Birmingham to what was then a rural site by the canal. The old canal wharves still remain at the Cadbury works, but it has been a long time since Cadbury ingredients traveled by canal. More recently they have traveled by road and rail, and the shunting engines, painted in the familiar Cadbury's livery, are marked CADBURY'S CHOCOLATE: FOR INTERNAL USE ONLY.

Three miles from the center of Birmingham, the canal and railway together shrugged off both industry and the town and headed off around an embankment to splendid isolation in purely residential countryside. Below, on either side, were the spacious greens, early-nineteenth-century houses, and century-old botanical gardens and woods of the suburb of Edgbaston. The University of Birmingham sent its lofty central tower, a memorial to its first chancellor, Joseph Chamberlain, rising above the many other buildings to a height of 325 feet.

Together the canal and railway squeezed into a steep, foliage-lined cutting, passing under high, charming old bridges.

Through the Looking Glass

The fog, mist, and occasional rain provided a fitting mood for our approach to England's second largest city, an industrial giant and the hub of the Black Country canal network. The railway was our almost constant companion, dipping away here and there only to reappear a short distance further along. Side by side, we ducked into the 105-yard Edgbaston Tunnel, northernmost of the five tunnels of this canal.

Emerging from the tunnel, we arrived in the center of Birmingham, known fondly as Brummagen, or simply Brum. The railway disappeared into another tunnel leading to New Street Station; we made a sudden ninety-degree turn to the left to enter Gas Street Basin, an unassailably authentic piece of canalia and a remarkable relic to find surviving in the center of such a contemporary city.

Here was an old, comfortable, secluded haven surrounded by nineteenth-century canal warehouses and totally unsuspected by the unseen traffic thundering across Broad Street only a few yards away. Delightful old-world narrowboats waited patiently for work orders that might never come, while their crews busied themselves maintaining their spit-and-polish appearance. In this peaceful atmosphere it was difficult to realize that we were just a short walk from the heart of the city, a stone's throw from the Bull Ring and New Street Station. The reason for this sense of total isolation was access—or lack of it. The only way to enter Gas Street Basin was through a small doorway in a high brick wall that, when opened, yielded the astonishing sight of a busy modern city bustling along as though the basin weren't there at all!

Birmingham as the world knows it is one of the great industrial cities, the foremost metalworking center in Britain and the center of an industrial region with a population of more than two million people. A rich and energetic city, Brum has replaced much of its older housing with apartment towers and is in the process of rebuilding its entire central area. In recent years the city center has undergone so many structural alterations that—as the official guidebook of the city says—"there is more of the future to be seen coming into being than there is of the past left to contemplate."

Birmingham's history begins with William de Bermingham, lord of the manor, who could show in 1309 that his ancestors were active in commerce here before the Norman Conquest. The city began its phenomenal growth in the late eighteenth century, when abundant supplies of coal, iron, and wood were exploited, thereby attracting a multiplicity of trades. In the first fifty years of the nineteenth century its population tripled; in 1835 Tocqueville described the city as "an immense workshop, a huge forge, a vast shop. One only sees busy people and faces brown with smoke. One hears nothing but the sound of hammers and the whistle of steam escaping from boilers."

Around this boom town grew an astonishingly extensive network of canals, serving the Black Country and all England. In fact, if you include all the now-abandoned waterways, the city has more miles of canal than Venice.

We took a walk through that obscure little door in the wall, to discover the famous Repertory Theatre, established in 1913, and, nearby, an enticing restaurant, neither cheap nor informal, that—although we were still in boating clothes—we felt was our richly deserved reward for a thirty-six-lock, nine-hour work day on the Worcester & Birmingham Canal.

After a leisurely, sumptuous meal we somehow stumbled back through the unmarked, inconspicuous-looking door that led to the other side of the looking glass —back into Gas Street Basin. Despite our having missed entirely the Corporation Art Gallery and Museum, second in England only to the galleries of London; the Museum of Science and Industry, which is probably second to none in England; and the cathedral with its famous stained-glass windows, we probably saw Birmingham in a way few visitors have ever seen it. And what we saw was perfectly in keeping with our nineteenth-century manner of snail-paced travel.

The Melancholy BCN

Thursday morning it continued to rain steadily. We left Gas Street Basin to dive under a bridge, beneath Broad Street and the Church of the Messiah, squeezing between the cavernous brick walls, twin grassy towpaths, and blue-brick embankments of the Birmingham Canal Navigations—the BCN.

The Navigations are composed of several routes which, in their heyday, comprised more than 160 miles of working waterway, including 212 narrow locks, more than 550 private side basins serving factories, three exceptionally long tunnels, numerous bridges, aqueducts, pumping stations, railway interchange basins, maintenance yards, toll-collection booths, cottages, and other structures. The web of lines forming the BCN became the veins of the Black Country, carrying the lifeblood of its commerce and wealth.

What survives today—just over 100 miles of navigable waterway—constitutes the most concentrated and vivid reminder of urban canal navigations in Britain. Although the surviving canals here are not all ideal for leisure cruising, they represent a living monument to the Industrial Revolution.

Architecturally, the BCN spans nearly the entire history of British waterways. Originally designed and engineered by James Brindley, the BCN had all the twists and turns of that first phase of English canal building. Later, with increasing competition from the railways and the need for greater speed and economy, canal engineers reached the peak of their achievement in what is generally regarded as the third phase of English canals. The name of Thomas Telford, later a giant in the canal field, first surfaced with his work on the BCN in 1825. Telford surveyed and revised the outdated and overloaded BCN Main Line, which had remained virtually unimproved since its construction. The result was a straightened, faster canal, with fewer locks and larger cuttings.

By the end of the nineteenth century, trade on the BCN was topping 8.5 million tons annually. Railroad domination, rather than sounding the death knell of this canal (as it did for others), resulted in expanded use of the BCN system: a large number of interchange basins were built to promote outside trade by means of rail connections. As late as 1950, despite the general worldwide decline of canal transport, there was still a million tons of trade here, and the entire system continued to operate until the end of the coal trade.

As might be expected, there is little natural beauty on the BCN. Without its teeming traffic of colorful barges it seems neglected and forlorn. Daisies and willow-herb grow along the horseless towpaths; obstructions block the less frequented bridge holes, scum and timber float on the water, and abandoned workboats rot silently and somberly by the banksides. At night there are lonely bonfires of oil-soaked timber and tires that blaze unattended on the cobbles of the lockside; by day shafts of bleak light strike the pea-soup water deep between the blackness of the derelict warehouses. A wealth of ironwork, ribbed courses of brick where the towpaths rise at each lock, signposts, bollards, and lamp brackets recall a vanished period of bustling, round-the-clock activity and prosperity.

Yet all these very properties give the BCN its special, near-gothic melancholy —and convince us that there is no more poignant way to discover the Black Country of England or to experience the heart and soul of England's canals than by cruising the BCN.

We followed Thomas Telford's New Main Line, straight as a Roman road, while little loops—remnants of Brindley's Old Main Line—shot off in various directions, indicating just how meandering the old contour canal course had been.

At Smethwick we entered Telford's great, 70-foot deep, steep-sided cutting that parted the hillside and eliminated the need for several of Brindley's locks. The sides of the cutting were richly clothed in wildflowers and blackberry bushes; the entire secluded area has become an unofficial nature reserve. The densely urbanized area above our heads seemed far away as we traveled through this peaceful haven.

Telford's celebrated cast-iron Galton Bridge, once the largest canal bridge in the world, soared across the cutting in one magnificent, 150-foot lacy span.

Near Dudley the pleasant, semirural isolation of the cutting ended with a complex meeting of rail, canal, and motorway. The Steward Aqueduct carried Brindley's Old Main Line over our heads toward the south; the M5 motorway swung in from the east, carried high over our heads on slender concrete pillars; and the railway joined our march toward Wolverhampton. The New Main Line continued unperturbed as four different waterways shot in from every direction to connect with it.

Just before noon we stopped for lunch in Dudley Port, little more than a single street with a post office and a general assortment of shops. Here we sniffed out an authentically raunchy fish and chips shop where, for the equivalent of sixty cents

At Farmers Bridge Junction in the center of Birmingham handsomely restored canals lead to Coventry, Worcester and Wolverhampton. The Gas Street Basin is usually filled with colorfully restored craft and at Cambrian Wharf an attractive modern development has preserved the old brickwork locks, bridges and towpaths.

apiece, we received large portions of codfish and chips. We took our greasy paper bag lunch through the ceaseless rain back to our muddy narrowboat, where we added liberal American quantities of ketchup and tartar sauce.

After lunch we negotiated the three Factory Locks leading to Factory Junction, where the Old Line returned to us again from the south. North of Deepfields Junction we passed through the middle of Bilston Steel Works. Furnaces and cranes filled the sky; railroad cars laden with iron ore lined the banks. Towers belched smoke, fumes, and steam into the rarefied air above our heads, while little white wildflowers struggled for survival among the heaps of scrap metal on the left bank.

Capital of the Black Country

In mid-afternoon we reached the industrial heart of Wolverhampton. Factories surrounded the cut and shut us off from the rest of the town, though we could see the impressive square tower of the Church of St. Peter rising over the industrial mélange. The skies were very gray, but—mercifully—the rain had stopped.

Wolverhampton, capital of the Black Country, was first recorded in a royal charter in 985 A.D. Its name comes from Wulfruna, a sister of King Edgar II, who later endowed a collegiate church in the town. Today, with a population of nearly 300,000, Wolverhampton is a modern industrial city noted for its ironworks and its fine hardware—famous since Elizabethan times.

Beyond Horseley Fields Junction we reached the center of the city and, at the same moment, the top of the twenty-one-lock staircase leading from Wolverhampton down to Aldersley Junction on the Staffs & Worcs Canal. Once again, having arrived at just four o'clock, we found the gates padlocked and no further progress possible. Thus we moored in the center of the city and settled down for the night.

The sun returned to us early on Friday, the last day of our cruise, and at exactly 10:01 A.M. we entered the first of twenty-one locks that carry the canal from industrial Wolverhampton down to the peaceful, quiet, open countryside of the Staffs & Worcs. The lockkeeper, a slightly pudgy, good-natured canal character in his mid-forties, said he had a job to do at the bottom lock and would "lockwheel" us down. What he meant became clear as he ran ahead to fill the lock for us, then opened the upper gates; while we worked the lock, he ran ahead to prepare the next. It was incredible just how fast we progressed with that kind of energetic assistance: we finished the twenty-one-lock flight in just under two hours—considerably faster time than we had made on the Tardebigge Flight.

Rejoining the Staffs & Worcs Canal, we turned north in pleasant surroundings for the final, eight-mile run to Gailey. It had been an unexpectedly different trip, one that had given us a personal glimpse of England's vital industrial past. The small size and human scale of the Midlands waterways flavored them with an intimacy and homeyness that was very much with us as we neared the final stretch of our unforgettable, week-long English canal cruise.

Some Practical Information

The canal system of England, comprising some 1,500 miles (2,400 km) of commercial "highways" and flowing through both the rural heart of England and the birthplace of the Industrial Revolution, is perhaps the most unique of waterways. The narrow canals, whose locks measure a startling seven feet (2 m) in width, limit navigation to the narrowboats with their 6'10" beam and maximum length of 70 feet (21 m). Viewed from above, these amazing vessels resemble a long pencil, pointed at one end, with a tiller and a diesel engine at the other.

Nearly all the canal locks are unmanned and must therefore be operated by the crews themselves, just as the commercial boat people have been doing for decades. This gives all hands an opportunity to enjoy the fresh air and scenery while getting good physical exercise.

The narrow canals offer an interesting contrast: one floats past quiet, pastoral countryside at one hour, and a bit later one finds oneself engulfed in a region of warehouses and factories, littered canals and grimy air, and total industrialization as far as the eye can see. This is the real heart of England, and canal cruising offers the best means of experiencing it firsthand.

The canal enthusiast has the choice of some attractive options:

SELF-DRIVE BOATS, 6'10" wide and from 28 feet to 70 feet long, accommodate from two to ten persons and are available from hundreds of charter bases throughout the canal system. The boats are generally diesel powered and are steered by a tiller. Although modest in their accommodations (due to the narrow beam), they do allow comfortable and happy cruising.

Typical weekly charter costs are:

		June-August	Other
42-footer (13 m)	4 berths	$250–325	$150–250
52-footer (16 m)	6 berths	$300–400	$225–300
58-footer (17.5 m)	8 berths	$375–475	$300–375

Rather than try to list some of the hundreds of hire firms, we would suggest that interested travelers write to any one of the major booking firms, representing the individual hire fleets, for advice and literature:

Floating Through Europe, Inc.
501 Madison Avenue
New York, N.Y. 10022

Bargain Boating
Morgantown Travel Service
127 High Street
Morgantown, W.V. 26505

Skipper Travel
210 California Avenue
Palo Alto, Calif. 94306

Hoseasons Holidays Ltd.
Sunway House
Lowestoft, Suffolk NR32 3LT

Blake's International Holidays Afloat
Wroxam, Norwich NR12 8DH

Boat Enquiries Ltd.
7 Walton Well Road
Oxford OX2 6ED

HOTEL BOATS operate on many of the interesting canals. Limited to a 6′10″ beam and usually 70 feet long, the hotel narrowboats frequently operate in pairs, the first boat (the "motor") containing the crew quarters, the galley, and the salon; the second boat (the "butty"), towed behind the "motor," containing the passengers' sleeping cabins. The very narrow beam limits the comforts and amenities considerably, and there is a certain amount of climbing necessary—as when the two boats are moored alongside and passengers must climb from one boat to the other. (Elderly travelers should consider this before booking such a trip.)

Information and booking can be obtained from:

Floating Through Europe, Inc.
501 Madison Avenue
New York, N.Y. 10022

Boat Enquiries Ltd.
7 Walton Well Road
Oxford OX2 6ED

In addition, the Inland Waterways Association, 114 Regents Park Road, London NW1 8UQ, operates hotel narrowboats on the canals.

PURCHASE OF AN "INVESTMENT BOAT" and registering for charter with a broker or hire firm is a growing form of boat ownership in England. Under such an arrangement, the owner has the use of his boat for a specified period (as per agreement with the charter agent), and he receives an income during those weeks when the boat is chartered to others. For additional information, write to:

The Association of Pleasure Craft Operators
26 Chaseview Road
Alrewas, Burton-on-Trent, Staffs

The Inland Waterways Association
114 Regents Park Road
London NW1 8UQ

Books, maps, and guides to the canal system are available from Floating Through Europe, Inc., 501 Madison Avenue, New York, N.Y. 10022, which maintains an extensive inventory of these materials.

Part II

Planning Your Cruise

10

Booking Aboard a Crewed or Passenger Boat

The traveler who desires to tour aboard a crewed or passenger vessel will find a wide range of boats available, from the private yacht skippered by its owner for a small party or a family to an 18-passenger, 100-foot (30 m) hotel barge with a crew of five, to a sleek, modern 320-foot (98 m) Rhine steamer carrying some 200 passengers. Trips range in length from a day excursion to an eight-day cruise across eight countries and through five capital cities.

1. *Taking a crewed cruise.* Imagine yourself floating down a peaceful, historic river or canal, seated in a lounge chair on the outdoor deck, with camera or sketch pad in hand. At another moment you may be disembarking at a quiet rural lock and walking or bicycling the towpath while the boat chugs softly alongside, ready to pick you up again at the wave of your arm. Each year more and more discerning travelers are discovering the joys and the convenience of this kind of cruising. Since bookings for these cruises can be made weeks or even months in advance, such a cruise can easily be scheduled as part of a longer European holiday. There exists generally a fine spirit of camaraderie on many cruises; one can enjoy the companionship of travelers from many parts of the world and at the same time have the opportunity to meet local people in attractive and informal settings.

Hotel barges, ranging in size from 60 feet (18 m) to 126 feet (38 m) and carrying from 6 to 28 passengers, are becoming the most popular form of crewed waterway travel. They offer a variety of accommodations: single, twin, and double staterooms and an occasional large suite. While individual cabins can be booked, families and groups can charter an entire hotel barge at a proportionately reduced rate. The better hotel barges offer spacious and comfortable accommodations with private showers and toilets, a high standard of continental cuisine, three-speed geared passenger bicycles, and chauffeured minicoaches for passenger touring and shopping excursions.

2. *Chartering a private captained yacht.* For those seeking a personal type of waterway cruise without the responsibility of a bareboat (sail-it-yourself) charter, chartering a private captained yacht for a week or two presents an intriguing possibility. It offers many of the advantages of both the large excursion boat and the sail-it-yourself boat. The private chartered yacht will generally carry four to six persons, depending on its size and accommodations, and it will be skippered by the owner or his crew, who will invariably be native to and familiar with the region in which you are traveling. Many people consider this the ideal way to cruise the waterways, for

the skipper can show you his country in a personal and characteristic way that would not be available on an excursion boat or a bareboat charter. Our Dutch odyssey was such a trip; George Van Dam Merrett, owner of the motor yacht *Sirene,* brought to us a lifetime of local knowledge and boating experience and personally introduced us to Holland's waterways and its people. We spent some memorable evenings along the way, occasionally dining and socializing with George's friends in their homes, getting to know them as friends. He was also able to show us the back yards and playgrounds of Holland that only the Dutch generally see.

This type of cruise can be relatively expensive, since you will be paying for the services of the skipper as well as for the boat. The additional expense quickly averages out, however, when the cost is shared between two couples. If you do decide to cruise with another couple, be sure that you're all thoroughly compatible; a week or more in the tight quarters of a small craft can strain untested relationships.

One of the memorable aspects of our various captained cruises has been the provisioning during the trip. One's first provisioning excursion can be a marvelous experience—or a disaster (especially when you don't speak the language). By all means, ask your skipper to accompany you (he will usually be glad to do so) and solicit his suggestions concerning the trip menu and purchasing. He may not know a ripe melon from a green one, but he'll be familiar with the foods and the eating habits of the region, and he can show you how to enjoy the local specialties and where to find the best prices.

While we've found some foods to be much cheaper in Europe than they are in the United States, on balance our provisioning costs have approximated prices in the United States. But that's only if you eat local products and plan meals as local families do—otherwise food costs can skyrocket. On one of our first waterway trips, where we had been eating and enjoying local fish meals purchased quite moderately from quayside fishermen, we passed a small poultry market and spontaneously decided to buy a fresh duck. We should have first asked the price, but being unfamiliar with the language and inexperienced at foreign marketing, we simply ordered one duck. After it had been cleaned, prepared, and wrapped, we got the startling news: our not-very-large duck cost the equivalent of $17. It sure was good, but we could have had three excellent fish dinners for the price of that one duck.

3. *Availability of boats.* The matter of boat selection resolves itself quite logically, for the size and scope of the waterway largely determines the type of craft available. Understandably, the larger excursion steamers operate on the major continental rivers, such as the Rhine, the Rhône, and the Danube, where distances are great, commercial traffic is heavy, and currents are swift in places, rendering navigation tricky. At the same time, there are many smaller waterways, such as the Canal du Midi in southern France, the rivers and canals of Burgundy and the Loire Valley, the charming and picturesque waterways of Holland, and the narrow canals of England, where one finds a large assortment of smaller crewed boats ranging from

luxury hotel barges carrying 6 to 24 passengers to skippered 30-foot (9 m) craft for just 4 persons.

The sections of practical information that follow each of the cruise chapters provide details concerning available boats and where and how to book them.

4. *Costs of cruising.* Costs of booking passage vary widely, according to the duration of the trip, the country or region, the size of the boat, and the accommodations selected.

DAY EXCURSIONS. Certainly the least expensive crewed cruise will be the day or half-day excursion on a lake or river, where the price of your ticket covers a seat or standing room at the railing. Most day boats offer a snack bar or a restaurant onboard, but many passengers prefer to carry picnic lunches and purchase beverages en route. The cost of an excursion aboard one of the day boats that ply the waters of nearly every large European lake or river ranges from $3 to $8, the full-day trip at the upper limit. Our habit, whenever we travel to a town with a lake or a riverfront, is either to inquire at the local tourist information office about boat trips or to drive to the waterfront to see for ourselves. An afternoon's minicruise on a lovely European lake or river makes a welcome, often unforgettable change from the standard auto trip or bus tour.

LARGE PASSENGER BOATS. The next most economical passage on a crewed cruise may be tourist accommodations on a large passenger ship, where the modest cost will certainly be matched by the modest cabin facilities. A double cabin, for example, will include two narrow berths, some shelf space for clothing, and a washbasin—that's all. There are no dining distinctions, however; all passengers take meals together in the ship's dining room.

As the cabin accommodations increase in quality, so does the cost. You could find yourself in a deluxe stateroom paying deluxe prices—well over $100 per person per day. If you book a tourist-class cabin in a steamer and then, once aboard, decide you want to switch to a better cabin, you can upgrade if space is available. Traveling once on the overnight steamer from Gothenburg to Kiel, we found our cabin was tiny and without windows; we were able to change to a better cabin by paying the prevailing supplement.

CAPTAINED YACHTS. The cost of chartering a private captained yacht for one or more weeks varies widely, according to the size and quality of the yacht and its accommodations. Generally, the charter fee covers the yacht, the services of the skipper, and the direct expenses of boat operation such as fuel, maintenance, and repairs. The fee does not include docking costs and bridge or lock tolls, all of which are very modest. It also does not include food and provisioning costs, for which you are responsible, including the feeding of the captain. And if you invite the captain to join you at a restaurant, he will go as your guest.

We've seen captained yachts ranging from 30 feet (9 m), accommodating 3 to

4 persons, to 60 feet (18 m), accommodating 5 to 6 persons. Typical weekly charter costs run about $600 for a 30-footer, to $1,200 to $1,500 for a 55- to 60-footer.

The following are examples of the per-day costs (during high-season in midsummer) for three different categories of cruises—a private skippered yacht (the 56-foot *Sirene,* in Holland), a luxury hotel barge (the *Beverly K.,* in Shakespeare country in England), and an excursion steamer (on the Rhine):

	Modest Cabin	Best Cabin
Yacht *Sirene* (no meals)	$46	$46
Hotel barge *Beverly K.* (with meals)	$68	$83
Rhine steamer (with meals)	$90	$110

5. *Shoreside activities.* We've generally enjoyed the excursions organized by steamer lines and hotel barges, and we would encourage you to take advantage of them. The tour schedules are generally announced well in advance, so you will have sufficient time to consider each excursion versus the possible alternatives. If you are not interested in a particular tour, you should certainly tour independently during that time, on foot, by bicycle, or by hired taxi (which can be arranged by the skipper or ship's purser.) You may plan to rendezvous with the ship further along the waterway; if so, be sure you know exactly where and when to meet.

6. *Ship's personnel.* Make an effort to get to know the ship's officers. We've always found them to be hospitable, friendly, accommodating, and invariably multilingual. One of the highlights of our Göta Canal trip was getting to know the captain, an amiably delightful professional mariner in his early thirties. On our final day of the cruise we were thoroughly delighted when he invited us to dine with him and his family at their home. Captain Sven Karnehed and his wife Eva treated us to one of our finest experiences in Sweden, and we have developed a lasting friendship over the years.

7. *Meals aboard and ashore.* Meals will be taken in the ship's dining room; upon embarking you'll be asked to meet the head waiter in the dining room to learn your table assignment. Sometimes meals are served in two sittings, so you may have an opportunity to specify first or second sitting. If you've booked aboard one of the larger excursion steamers, your menus will be predetermined for you. You can expect to be served wholesome and well-prepared foods, and very likely you will be introduced to new and interesting variations by the chef. If someone in the family won't eat a particular meal, you can probably obtain a substitute dinner. You will also find occasions to have a meal or a snack ashore, and here you can indulge yourself as adventurously as you like. The free literature furnished by the national or local tourist offices will tell about regional food specialties; the ship's officers are also a good source of information. Even when you don't speak the language, you can usually find someone in the restaurant—the waiter, the proprietor, or perhaps another diner—who can assist in menu selection.

8. *What to take along.* Decisions concerning what to take with you on your cruise will depend very much on the ages and interests of your family members. There may also be baggage restrictions imposed by your means of transportation; when flying transatlantic, for example, you are limited to 44 pounds (20 kilograms) per person, which includes the weight of your luggage.

We have found that large, well-made zippered duffel bags—one or two to a person, with the owner's initials marked boldly—make ideal luggage for boat-involved travel. They are lightweight, nonbreakable, simple to carry, store flat when empty, and have no hard or fixed corners. You'll find, too, that you can live out of a zippered duffel when space is really tight, as on a small boat. Many sailmakers carry duffels, made in their own canvas shops; these are far stronger and more durable, albeit a little more costly, than those sold in discount and department stores.

Breakables and valuables, such as cameras, binoculars, radios, and tape recorders, can be carried as cabin baggage in either zippered airline shoulder bags or in canvas tote bags. The best advice we can give is to travel as light as possible; it's been our observation that most people pack to an excess—much to their subsequent regret.

Comfort and informality should generally dictate your choices of clothing. Clothing for children is discussed in Chapter 14. Men should include a sports jacket and coordinating trousers (two sets if traveling on one of the larger cruise ships, for jackets will be worn to all dinners). Women's clothing should include more dress-ups on the larger steamers than on a small captained yacht. When you cruise, particularly on the smaller boats, leave the high, leather-soled shoes at home. Rubber soles and boating shoes, plus comfortable walking footwear, will be appropriate. Finally, you will probably be thankful if you have the foresight to pack lightweight foul-weather gear or raincoats.

11

Chartering a Self-Drive Boat

There is one danger inherent in chartering a self-drive boat on any of the European rivers, canals, or lakes: it's a trap! We know; we succumbed to it. Our very first waterway trip was aboard a self-drive 34-footer on the Canal du Midi in southern France—and we've never recovered from it. Today, thirteen countries and several thousand miles later, having enjoyed all our cruises, we would still opt for a self-drive trip if we had to select a single favorite.

For us there is something marvelous about being able to plan and organize your own independent holiday, to choose the country and the waterway and then to select your own boat from the several thousand available. From the moment you hit the starter button and pull away from the dock, you experience a continuing freedom of decision: to select your own itinerary and to change it at will, to set out at the crack of dawn or laze until mid-morning, to stop along the waterway as you like for lunch, shopping, touring, picture taking—even to take a little "siesta." Ready to tie up for the night? Sure; where would you like to stop? Your charts and touring material (these are abundantly available) will provide all the information you need. Your boat, and the wonderful people and situations along your route, will readily provide all the excitement, color, and culture you could hope for. All you need are family or friends, a modest budget, a keen sense of curiosity and adventure—these are the elements of an unforgettable dream holiday!

1. *Arranging the charter.* Self-drive boats are widely available in Britain, Scotland, Ireland, France, Germany, Holland, and Sweden. The boats range in size from 16 feet (5 m) to 50 feet (15 m)—and up to 70 feet (21 m) on the British narrow canals. They can accommodate from 2 persons to as many as 8 or 10 persons.

Charters can be booked through individual charter agents in Britain or on the Continent or through major booking agents. Their names and addresses will be found in the sections of practical information that follow each of the cruise chapters in this book. These sections also provide details concerning available boats, charter costs, where to write for brochures and additional information, and how to book.

ONE-WAY VERSUS ROUND-TRIP CHARTER. Some travelers prefer to retrace their route on the return trip, for this allows them to study the area in greater depth and to catch what they may have missed on the outgoing leg. Others prefer to retrace no part of their route, to spend their entire holiday covering new territory and experiencing new adventures. We have enjoyed both one-way and round-trip charters, and we find much to recommend for each.

If you have a preference for a particular trip, discuss this with the charter agent before you book. If you don't want to retrace any of your route, you might book with a firm that has more than one base, such as Blue Line Cruisers on the Canal du Midi, or you might book a circular route, as is possible on many of the British narrow canals. The very interesting Stratford Ring in Britain can be done in two leisurely and rewarding weeks; other circular cruises can be done in one week.

THE COSTS OF CHARTERING. The air fare for your passage to the embarkation point will be the major cost of your waterway trip, so you may want to make your cruise part of a longer European vacation. Charter rates vary, depending on the season (June, July, and August are generally considered high-season; April, May, September, and October are off-season). During off-season two to four people can charter a 25-footer, for example, for as little as $125 per week in many areas; a family of six can charter a comfortable 35-footer for less than $300. These costs usually include fuel and cooking gas or alcohol. Extra amenities such as bicycles ($4 each per week) and television sets ($5 per week) are generally available. In any event, it is important to have a clear understanding with the charter broker as to what is included with your boat and what optional extras will cost.

Once you have signed the contract and sent in your deposit, you are obligated for the full balance of the charter fee. If you must cancel, you should notify the charter agent immediately. He will then attempt to recharter for that period. If he is able to recharter, you will forfeit only your deposit; if he is unable to resell the booking, you must pay the full amount. Cancellation insurance may be available; we discuss this later in the chapter.

NO EXPERIENCE REQUIRED. One of the delights of waterway cruising is that little or no experience is required for many trips. Although pilotage on some of the larger rivers, with their swift currents, deeper waters, and heavy commercial traffic, could be tricky for the inexperienced boatperson, cruising on the smaller canals should pose no problem for any adult with the desire to do it. These smaller canals are generally quite narrow—frequently no more than 40 feet (12 m) to 60 feet (18 m) wide—shallow enough to walk across in many places, and your boat speed will not exceed four or five miles per hour. How formidable does that sound? On our Canal du Midi cruise, teenage daughters Laura, Beverly, and Janet did most of the steering; Janet, at ten the youngest, had proudly mastered even steering under bridges by trip's end.

Before you begin your cruise the charter agent will go over the boat with you, provide a thorough orientation, and probably furnish you with a cruising manual that covers operating procedures in detail. Finally, he'll go out with you for a trial run, standing at your side until you are confident that you can properly operate the boat. Then you'll return him to his dock—and you're on your way!

DOCUMENTS AND INSURANCE. The details of chartering are quite simple; no document or paperwork is required other than the Booking Form, which you will complete and mail to the charter agent, along with your check and the signed charter agreement that you will have received from the charter agent. The charter agent will send you his Conditions of Hire, and it is important that you read this carefully. It includes information regarding hire period and terms, deposit, cancellation, restrictions and limitations, and responsibilities of the charterer. The boat will have been registered with the appropriate local authority by the charter agent or the owner, and the registration papers should be kept permanently on board. (This will be explained to you during your orientation.)

Aside from a modest deposit (generally less than $100) that you must leave with the charter agent to cover loss or breakage of equipment, you will have no financial responsibility for the boat.

You may want to have your luggage and personal belongings insured, and these can usually be covered as part of your personal or travel insurance. It might be advisable to consult your regular insurance agent prior to departure.

Cancellation insurance, available through the major booking agents, will cover you for the charter fee in the event you must cancel your charter due to illness, death, or injury of any member of the charter party or a close relative. The cancellation policy is written by a commercial insurance company, and the premium, covering a maximum of $750 per claim, is about $10 for a week's charter.

2. *Setting up and provisioning.*

WHAT YOU WILL FIND ON THE BOAT. In addition to a full tank of fuel (which is generally included in the charter fee and which should last you at least a week), you will receive with your boat a full tank of fresh water and sufficient gas or alcohol for cooking. The fresh water capacity will vary from boat to boat (be sure to use it sparingly), and you can count on having to fill your tank one or more times along the way. Your boat will probably be equipped with a length of hose for refilling the water tank, and the charter agent will explain where and how to fill up.

Your galley should be completely equipped with dishes and flatware, pots and pans, and cooking and serving utensils. Be sure to inventory these items, and check to see that you have can opener, bottle opener, and corkscrew aboard.

Cooking and galley facilities aboard our various self-drive boats have ranged from very adequate—a gas stove and refrigerator, hot and cold pressured water, and lots of storage and counter space on our Canal du Midi cruiser—to very primitive—a two-burner alcohol cooker and a tiny sink with a foot-pump-operated cold water faucet on our Kiel Canal craft. The latter had no refrigerator or ice box; we bought a small ice cooler and then couldn't find any ice. (The "galley" on this boat was located in the canvas-covered cockpit, the cooker and sink *under* the helmsman's seat.) We had a thoroughly marvelous time on the Kiel Canal, notwithstanding the extremely modest facilities, in part because we knew in advance what to expect. If your charter brochure isn't sufficiently specific concerning any of the boat's facilities, you will want to write and ask questions.

You'll need towels and bedding (pillows and blankets), though sleeping bags frequently serve as bedding. These items are not always supplied with your boat (sleeping bags are frequently rented for $2 each per week); discuss this with the charter agent well in advance, and be prepared to pay a modest supplement for them.

Docking lines, mooring stakes, and a hammer (for mooring to the banks), an anchor and line, and lock handles (for opening untended lock gates in certain regions) should be furnished, but it's prudent to inventory them with the charter agent before setting out. Life preservers are sometimes supplied, sometimes available at extra cost; you should at least have life preservers for all children and nonswimming adults. The boat will have a bilge pump, and this, too, should be checked during your orientation.

WHAT TO BRING FROM HOME. Aside from clothing—don't forget the rubber-soled boating shoes and waterproof slickers—and family recreational items, discussed in other chapters, you'll need to bring very little from home. The one essential item is a medical kit, the extensiveness of which will depend on the size and age of your family. Don't count on finding any medical or first-aid supplies on board; you must bring along your own kit, including bandaids and bandages, an antiseptic cream or fluid, aspirins and cold tablets, your regular nose drops or spray and, of course, a reliable fever thermometer.

PROVISIONING THE BOAT. Some charter agents will provision your boat for you if you advise them in advance regarding your needs. While we've always enjoyed our little marketing adventures, it does make a lot of sense to come aboard and find your galley already stocked with items of your choice—particularly if you just arrived from overseas a few hours earlier.

Besides stocking up on food for the trip, you'll need to buy such staples as paper goods, condiments, and basic cleaning, laundry, and toilet products. For a typical one-week cruise, you probably shouldn't shop for more than three dinners at the outset; you'll want to allow for dining at shoreside restaurants (the "cook" is on vacation, too) and marketing along the way. You're not likely to have a freezer (some of the better-equipped boats will have small ice-cube sections in the refrigerator), so forget about frozen foods until you return home.

What will it cost to provision your boat? If you try to eat as you would at home, with prime cuts of beef and packaged foods, look out—you'll have a very expensive cruise. On the other hand, you'll enjoy a much more rewarding holiday—and spend far less—if you shop as the local housewives do, buying the more plentiful cuts of meat, fowl and fish, and the vegetables, fruits, cheeses, and wines of the region. If you can't speak the language, don't worry; ask the charter agent for advice on provisioning. Besides, after just a few minutes inside any European meat or produce market, you'll be sniffing out food bargains like a native.

12

*Cruising
Aboard
Your Own
Boat*

Anyone who has operated a self-drive boat on one of the waterways has probably nurtured a dream—as we have—of returning some day for an extended cruise aboard his or her own boat. Such a dream need not be unattainable, but it takes time (you shouldn't consider having your own boat unless you can spend at least several months cruising) and it takes money—though a family, or two families sharing expenses, can accomplish this dream for less money than you might think.

1. *Suitable craft for the waterways.* Let's begin with the profile of an "ideal" boat for live-aboard waterway cruising. We favor a power boat with a heavily built displacement hull and a large, slow-turning diesel engine. We recommend a single engine because of the greater protection afforded the propeller behind the central skeg of the hull.

MAXIMUM DIMENSIONS. The principal limiting factors are the draft and air height. Although we know of vessels that have successfully cruised through Europe with as much as a six-foot draft, you'll have a greater selection of waterways to choose from, and you'll have a more enjoyable cruise, if you can limit your draft to four and a half feet and your air height to ten feet. Length and beam? For cruising most of the continental waterways, you are generally limited to 126 feet (38 m) by 16 feet (5 m) —not very restrictive dimensions. In England, however, the rules are quite different. Although the larger British rivers can accommodate vessels with a 14-foot (4 m) beam, the wonderful canal network is much narrower, with locks just 7 feet (2 m) wide. This limits English canal cruisers to a maximum beam of 6'10", and a length of 70 feet (20 m). Therefore, whenever the call of the English canals strongly exterts itself, you will have to leave your boat at a convenient Thames boatyard and charter an inexpensive self-drive narrowboat for a cruise.

OPTIMUM DIMENSIONS. One way to determine the size boat that would best accommodate your family or crew is to make your own estimate and then add an additional 10 or 15 percent. There's hardly any disadvantage in cruising a slightly-too-large boat on the waterways; but a boat that's even a few feet too small could detract significantly from any long-anticipated cruise. Although we've seen as many as six persons seemingly cruising happily on a 24-footer, we would recommend, for a power boat, a minimum length of 25 feet for two persons, 30 feet for four, and 36 feet for six. For sailboats, which invariably contain less living space than the same size power boat, add a few feet to the above recommendations. And bear in mind that we're talking about boat sizes for a several months' live-aboard cruise; on shorter holiday trips, you can do very nicely with smaller boats.

PRIVACY. In determining boat size, perhaps the most important condition for a successful full-season waterway cruise is that the boat offer adequate privacy for the entire crew, even when the entire crew is husband and wife. People living on a boat for an extended period need a certain amount of privacy plus the ability to "get away" at times; when that isn't possible, conditions soon become strained. A private cabin for each couple is a necessity on a long cruise. And when two couples are involved, the old adage, "two heads are better than one," applies to toilet facilities.

CHOICE OF POWER. This will probably be the simplest of all your decisions if you plan to buy a motor boat. Use diesel. A diesel engine is considerably safer and more reliable than a gasoline engine, diesel oil is less expensive and far more economical, and it is generally much easier to get a diesel engine serviced or repaired in Europe. Carry as complete a set of spare parts as possible; your local diesel dealer can advise you and secure parts for you.

If your dream boat is a sailboat, you'll have the added inconvenience of having to pull the masts and carry them on deck. And if your mainmast overhangs much, look out—it's a potent weapon in a crowded lock. If you'll be returning to the same port where you had the masts pulled, you can arrange for them to be stored there, but this will limit your itinerary options on the return leg.

HULL CONSTRUCTION. It doesn't matter appreciably what your hull is constructed of, so long as it is solidly built with heavy scantlings. The waterways are no place for a lightly constructed boat. After your first few forays in crowded locks, where you may be pinned between a 150-ton barge and the stone lock wall, you'll fully appreciate strength and weight in your hull.

2. Getting a boat on the waterways. Basically, there are three approaches to establishing your own boat on the waterways: sail or ship your boat to Europe; buy a new or used boat in Europe; have a boat built in Europe.

SAILING OR SHIPPING A BOAT TO EUROPE. If your boat is in the United States and you want to get it to Europe, you can either sail it or ship it over as deck cargo on a steamship. A power boat, unless designed for transoceanic passages (at least 60 feet long, deep draft, and carrying fuel for a minimum 3,500 miles), will have to be shipped over. This is not difficult to arrange; freighters carry deck cargo across oceans daily. However, you should query several shipping lines and compare the rates, for we've heard widely differing quotations for shipping the same boats from New York to Le Havre. (When you do connect with a steamship line, you might very well be able to arrange passage for yourself and your family aboard the same ship.) You may have to provide a wooden shipping cradle for your boat; this should be ascertained well in advance, so that you can obtain one. And, since this project will obviously go beyond your normal marine insurance coverage, be sure to arrange new coverage that includes the transatlantic passage.

The principal European ports of entry are Southampton, Rotterdam, Le Havre, and Marseilles. The choice between the northern and southern starting points for your cruise should be determined by the time of year in which your trip commences. Perhaps the ideal situation would be to have your boat shipped to one of the northern ports—Southampton, Le Havre, or Rotterdam—in the spring; you can then cruise southward through Europe during the summer, arriving in the Mediterranean in autumn. Winter in the Med? Well, how much time did you say you had?

Sailing a boat across the Atlantic is probably every sailor's dream, and you really don't need a huge yacht and a big crew to make that dream a reality. Sure, we've all read about someone's sailing a 13-footer singlehanded across the Atlantic—and then there were the two Britons who actually rowed across. As a practical matter, almost any sturdy, well-designed, well-constructed, and well-rigged sailboat of about 36 feet (11 m) or larger can probably make the passage. Such an undertaking is beyond the scope of the present discussion, but there are a number of excellent books, many of them written by people who have sailed transatlantic in small boats, that go into great detail about long-distance ocean cruising.

BUYING A BOAT IN EUROPE. Yachting is a popular and widespread pastime throughout much of Western Europe, and anywhere people own boats, there will exist an active secondary market. A number of European-made boats, both power and sail, are sold in the United States, and it is a routine matter to order one through a dealer in the United States for pickup in Europe. And you'll save money by buying this way.

Used boats are also offered for sale, both privately and through brokers, in many European yachting centers, notably in England, France, Holland, Germany, and Sweden. British and French yachting magazines that list both privately offered and brokerage boats are available in the United States. Correspondence with the advertising parties could result in some good leads, although of course a personal inspection will be necessary before buying any boat.

Bear in mind that any boat purchased in Europe will be paid for in the local currency. This may be either a benefit or a disadvantage, depending on the then-existing parity between that currency and the dollar. When a currency is depressed relative to the value of the dollar, you can buy more of it with the same amount of dollars—which would be favorable for you in purchasing a European boat. Your banker can give you advice concerning the currency aspect of the transaction.

HAVING A BOAT BUILT IN EUROPE. If you know what you want but can't find it in an existing boat, you might consider having your boat built in Europe. If you do it right, your boat can end up costing no more than a stock boat purchased in the United States—and you can get it just the way you want it.

First you must decide realistically on the kind of boat you will need. Will it be used solely for cruising inland waterways? A flat-bottomed steel barge will do the job. Will you want to cruise it offshore? That will involve a more complicated design and construction project. Will you ultimately want to sail or ship it to the United States? Will it be a sailboat or a powerboat? Do your experimenting and make your mistakes on paper before any construction is undertaken. It's a lot easier—and cheaper—to rectify problems before the keel is laid.

The authors did just this. From the time we made our first waterway trip, we dreamed of designing and building our own inland cruiser—in our case, a barge-type vessel. In 1976 we finally completed our design and, after speaking with several builders, selected an established boatyard in the English Midlands to build our boat. We had the pleasure and excitement of designing our own 72-foot (22 m) waterway barge and watching it being built. Our *Bonjour* was launched on the River Thames in May 1977 and, much to our satisfaction, is still plying that historic river.

3. *Documents and formalities.* If France is where you'll first enter Europe with your boat, you'll find the formalities quite simple. The *Permis de Circulation,* formerly required, has since June 1974 been discontinued. The sole requirement now is that the owner or captain go to the customs office at the port of entry, bearing the ship's papers, a list of all crew members aboard the vessel, and their passports. He will receive a green card *(carte verte)* stamped with his boat's name and date of arrival. He may keep his boat in France for up to six months without being subject to customs duty. He must remove his boat from France before the expiration of the six months —or store the boat in an approved customs port—and surrender the green card. The following year he can return, eligible for another period of six months.

The formalities for taking a yacht into Great Britain are just as simple. Nonresidents can take their yacht into the country for up to twelve months without being subject to tax or duty. Upon entering the first British port, the captain should report to the customs office with the ship's papers, a passenger list, and all passports. He will fill out and have validated an entry form—and that's it.

When taking a boat into Holland, no frontier documents are required so long as the boat will be used for private touristic purposes. Upon entering Holland, the captain will report to the customs office with his ship's papers and crew passports. He must also clear customs upon leaving the country.

4. *Equipping your vessel.* Unlike chartering, where the owner or his agent will ready and equip a boat for you, as an owner you'll have to equip your own boat. For the boat purchased or built in Europe, you can count on finding it already set up with European fittings and much of the gear that you'll need for waterway cruising. And your builder or yacht broker will be able to advise you and then order any equipment that you may need.

When you take to Europe your own boat from the United States, however, you'll have to convert and equip it for waterway cruising. Your American boat is probably wired for 110-volt shore power, but European voltage is 220. Before shipping your boat, consult your electronics man about the feasibility of your being able to use 220-volt shore power; if you can work that out, you'll need an adapter to plug into the European box. If an adapter is not available at home, you can probably get a boatyard at your port of entry to make the conversion. Another important consideration is your gas bottle (if you cook with gas); both the shape of the bottle and the threads on the connection will be different on continental bottles. You'll have to get a European yard or gas distributor to change the fitting on your bottles, or you'll have to switch to a European bottle and adapt it to your boat's fitting.

Most European waterways have strict prohibitions against the overboard flushing of toilet wastes. If you don't already have a holding tank system, you should have one installed before shipping your boat. Pump-out stations are located on the waterways.

One aspect of waterway cruising in Europe that differs from cruising at home is that you'll need fenders virtually all around your boat to protect it from the ravages of heavy contact in locks and crowded harbors. (Since many of the popular harbors are very crowded at times, it is common for boats to raft together, sometimes as many as three and four deep.) Unfortunately, the white cylindrical fenders commonly found on most yachts are not adequate for heavy-duty use around locks; they quickly become black and greasy, and this gook will spread onto your topsides. A better solution is to carry several old automobile tires covered with heavy canvas covers (from your sailmaker) tied to your lifelines or stanchions with dacron lines. For added protection, hang some heavy fenderboards outside of the tires.

Other equipment that you'll need are: a long boathook; a long, stout pole (the longer the better—and no sharp ends) for poling yourself off mudbanks and lock walls; mooring stakes and a heavy hammer (for mooring up to river and canal banks); a long water hose for filling your tanks (buy it in Europe; their hose fittings are different from your own); and a long, stout plank for use as a gangplank when you can't moor up close enough to shore.

5. *Can you really do it?* Although cruising the waterways in your own boat involves some complicated logistics, such an undertaking is becoming increasingly feasible for more and more Americans—particularly those who establish a joint ownership of two or more partners. This arrangement offers the dual advantage of sharing both the expense and the cruising season, which lasts at least five months per year (May through September, with some extra weeks at both ends of the range). It is a particularly intriguing project; the authors have certainly enjoyed designing and having built their own waterway barge, and we would welcome hearing from any of our readers who would like our comments or suggestions regarding their own cruising projects.

13

Skippering Your Own Cruise

Who skippers boats on the waterways? In our four years of cruising, we have seen boatmen as young as ten years (mostly skippering little daysailers), octogenarians at the helm of a variety of cruising and fishing craft, and every age in between. Skippers come from a wide range of occupations, for in many regions the waterways offer the best available means of transportation. The people of the waterways use their boats to deliver mail and morning milk, to transport cows to pasture and people to their daily marketing, and to take a crowd of teenagers on a hayride.

1. *Planning the trip.* On a self-drive cruise your selection of a charter agent should be based on the waterway you want to cruise and the fleet with the most suitable boats in that region. Although advance planning will help to ensure a successful trip, you should try to avoid overplanning; much of the joy of your cruise will come from the spontaneity of events, the little occurrences and circumstances that cannot be predicted and that you will never forget. One of our favorite self-drive cruises was our Schleswig-Holstein trip; we had chartered a 25-foot cruiser at Kiel and planned to visit the Danish islands in the Baltic before transiting the Kiel Canal, but on departing Kiel we encountered extremely heavy headwinds and high seas on the 35-mile offshore passage. So we decided to turn northwest, hugging the German coastline, and to visit instead the lovely Schlei River and the province of Schleswig. We also enjoyed a short hop up the Baltic coast under comfortable and pleasant conditions in the lee of the mainland. Although we hadn't actually prepared for *this* trip, we had packed our touring guides and spent some hours boning up during our passage to the mouth of the Schlei. The result? We had a wonderful and unexpected four-day visit to an area that we had only read about, but which afforded us far more pleasure in actually visiting.

2. *How much distance should you cover?* We have seen waterway cruisers who travel just three or four hours daily, covering no more than ten or a dozen miles. We have also seen the waterway equivalent of jet travel, with crews pushing along twelve and fourteen hours daily, squeezing in at crowded locks and, on waterways with untended locks, as on the English narrow canals, sending crew members on foot one and even two locks ahead to open the lock gates for their "speedboat."

We have learned to enjoy a leisurely cruising pace in which, on an average day, we may travel six or seven hours, perhaps running from 9 A.M. to noon, stopping a few hours for lunch and a little excursion, then resuming our cruise from 2 P.M. until 5 P.M. or 6 P.M.

It's a simple matter, using the concept of the lock-mile, to calculate the approximate distance you can cover on any particular waterway. If you consider going through a lock as the equivalent of traveling half a mile, you need only add miles and locks (divided by two) for any cruising route to determine the total number of lock-miles. For example, 30 miles of waterway plus 20 locks would equal 40 lock-miles. You may be able to average four miles per hour under ideal conditions on canals (you can probably average six miles per hour on rivers). We have found that we can cover between 20 and 30 lock-miles per day. (The actual distance in miles will always depend on the number of locks and the extent of delay at each lock). On the English narrow canals, with their slower boats and smaller waterways, you probably won't average better than 20 lock-miles per day.

How much distance can you cover in a week's cruise? If you can average 6 hours of cruising daily, for six days, you'll have run 36 hours, equal to between 130 and 150 lock-miles. For the neophyte, 36 hours of cruising will equal perhaps 80 to 100 miles of actual distance. Our record distance was some 150 miles in a seven-day week, but that was on the Thames, where the few locks were all automated. We had to push a bit to make the round trip between Staines and Oxford within a week.

3. *Navigating the locks.* The invention of the pound lock, which lifts or lowers boats from one level of canal to another, finally made possible the navigation of waterways that climbed into the mountains. Locks can also be used to control tidal flows; in England, for example, the big lock at Teddington separates the tidal and nontidal sections of the Thames River. The basic concept of the pound lock was known in Europe as early as the fourteenth century, and our twentieth-century pound lock does not differ markedly from those designed in the fifteenth century by the duke of Milan's engineer, the versatile Leonardo da Vinci.

The navigation of the lock is straightforward and soon mastered. The following sections, which we offer as a concise manual of lock navigation and operation, describe the procedures involved.

APPROACHING THE LOCK. Approach the lock at low speed, but with sufficient forward motion to maintain effective steerage control, and try to assess the situation at the lock as early as possible. Ideally, the gates will be open and you will slowly motor into the lock, advancing as far as is practicable. On the approach there is frequently a strong eddy or sidewise current coming from the weir stream (the embankment or diversion from the main stream, designed to prevent flooding of the river); the helmsman must be alert to react quickly with helm and throttle to correct the course.

When the lock gates are closed and it appears you may have a long wait, or if there are boats ahead waiting to lock through, you should moor up and wait your turn. You will find moorings at both ends of the lock, either alongside the quay or against heavy wooden pilings sunk into the river or canal bed. You'll be more secure tied up than you will be floating around in front of the closed gates, trying to stay clear of other boats and the banks. If there are already several boats at the moorings and you can't find a spot, ask another boatowner if you may raft up to him, putting out plenty of fenders in advance. We've done this countless times, and we have always been invited to raft up.

UNTENDED LOCKS. Entering an untended lock when descending is easy; your boat will enter at the level of the embankment, and your crew can jump ashore to tend lines. When ascending, however, your boat will be coming into the lock five, ten, or even fifteen feet below the embankment level, and you'll need a crew member up on the lockside to receive lines. You can do this in either of two ways: fifty yards or so before the lock, nose over to the towpath so that a crew member can jump ashore and run up to the lock to catch lines thrown by another crew member; or enter the lock very slowly, having one of your more agile hands scamper up the ladder or stone steps built into the lock wall. Both procedures are simple; you'll get the hang of them after just a few times.

Operating an untended lock is an easy and an interesting procedure in which the entire family can participate. You'll have your own lock key (obtained from the charter agent) to operate the windlasses. And, when possible, you'll always share a lock with other boats; this helps conserve water and speeds up the locking operation. The detailed locking procedures and diagrams that follow are provided courtesy of the British Waterways Board.

When ascending:

1. Make sure that the top gates and paddles are closed.
2. If the lock is full of water, empty it by raising the bottom paddles.
3. Open the bottom gates and slowly enter the lock.
4. Close the bottom gates behind you and lower the paddles.
5. Open the top paddles to fill the lock.
6. Open the top gates and slowly maneuver your boat out of the lock.
7. Close the gates behind you and lower the paddles. Don't forget to retrieve any crew member still ashore.

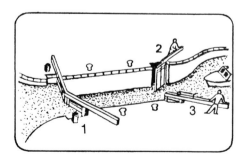 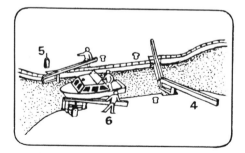

When descending:

1. Make sure that the bottom gates and paddles are closed.
2. If the lock is empty, fill it by opening the top paddles.

3. Open the top gates and slowly enter the lock.
4. Close the top gates behind you and lower the paddles.
5. Open the bottom paddles to empty the lock.
6. Open the bottom gates and slowly maneuver your boat out of the lock.
7. Close the gates behind you and lower the paddles. Again, don't forget any crew members ashore.

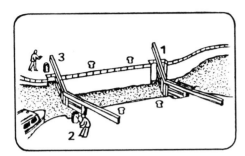 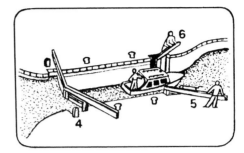

ATTENDED LOCKS. When you enter an attended lock, the lockkeeper will probably receive one of your lines, so you'll be tying up on the side where he is standing. If the lockkeeper isn't present, tie up on whichever side is more convenient for your crew member to get ashore to receive lines. In tying up in the lock you'll need two lines, one from the bow and one from the stern. When you are ascending, the water will be flooding the lock, raising your boat several feet in just a minute or two. Station a crew member at each line to take in slack as the boat rises in order to maintain the boat's position in the lock. When you are descending, your boat will be dropping rapidly, and you must be sure that neither line is tied or fixed. If the line jams on your cleat as the water level drops, your boat will be left hanging by just the two lines—until both cleats break off. (That could ruin your entire day!) How should you handle this problem? Just take some turns around your cleats, playing out the lines slowly as the boat descends.

When you're in a crowded lock, station a crew member on deck with extra bumpers to fend off other boats as required. Never use your boathook or long pole to push off another boat—it's a sure way to lose friends.

ASSISTING THE LOCKKEEPER. The procedure here is similar to that at an untended lock—except that you only have to do half the work. Where a lockkeeper is on duty, as on most French locks, a crew member is expected to assist him, and it's simply a case of "monkey see, monkey do." The lockkeeper will operate a set of gates and paddles on one side of the lock, and your crew member will do the same thing on the other side. As your boat is leaving the lock, the keeper will sometimes wave your crew back aboard, indicating that he will close both gates himself. In that case, thank him and be on your way. Otherwise, as he closes one side behind the boat, your crew will be closing the other. When you have maneuvered out slowly, wait to pick up your crew from the towpath just past the lock.

LOCKING THROUGH AN AUTOMATED LOCK. The first time through a completely automated lock must surely be one of the weirdest experiences of waterway cruising. You may not even see the lockkeeper in his glass-walled control station high overhead. On some of the really big automated locks he may not even see you—but you can be sure he's up there, watching you enter and tie up on his closed-circuit television screen (a development that da Vinci and Riquet never contemplated).

HOURS OF LOCK OPERATION. The hours during which the locks may be used will vary from country to country and with the time of the year. Hours are posted at each lock; generally you can lock through from sunrise to sunset. Bear in mind that, on attended locks, the keeper may close down for breakfast around 9 A.M. and will certainly close for a one-hour lunch, between noon and 1 P.M. You should plan your own meals around these times.

LOCK STOPPAGES. Perhaps we have been lucky, but in four years of cruising we've never been held up for more than one day by a lock stoppage. The fact is that many locks are antiques; the gates, sluices, and paddles are sometimes fifty or even one hundred years old, and they do break down. If you are held up by some such problem, ask the keeper when he expects to begin operating again—and, if necessary, consult your waterway map for an alternate route. Besides closing for breakdowns, locks close for annual cleaning or maintenance, but announcement of these stoppages is usually made weeks or months in advance. When taking a self-drive boat, always show the charter agent your intended route and ask if there are any stoppages scheduled along the way. It's easier to alter your itinerary at the start than it is to make changes once you're halfway along on your trip.

There is one other potential problem that may cause lock closures. In the event of a severe drought, such as the one experienced in Western Europe during the summer of 1976, certain portions of canals or rivers may drastically restrict the hours of lock operation. On the Worcester & Birmingham Canal in June 1976, we found the locks open only between 9 A.M. and 4:30 P.M., which forced on us a severe push to return to our hire base by the appointed day.

LOCK FEES. During our first waterway holiday, on the Canal du Midi, we were surprised to learn that private pleasure boats, including chartered self-drive boats, travel the waterways free while commercial barges generally pay locking fees. In our four years of cruising, the only places we were asked for payment were some of the smaller Dutch swingbridges—and the fee was just a small coin. About the only cost of cruising, other than food and personal expenses, is an overnight docking fee, generally fifty cents, that is sometimes charged at private or municipal moorings.

What about gratuities to a lockkeeper who performs some special service, such as helping you tie up or giving you directions or touring information? Lockkeeping in Europe is an old and honored tradition; lockkeepers are frequently members of families that have held the same job for several generations. These men and women take great pride in their work and are invariably efficient and helpful. Although there is no set rule regarding tipping, we prefer to offer a small token, such as an invitation to come aboard for a cold beer or a glass of wine. Even if you don't speak the language, do it anyway; hospitality and good fellowship are universal languages in themselves, and a warm smile and friendly gesture will make friends anywhere. And if you carry a supply of candy for the lockkeeper's children, you'll be very popular. One other little gift is a surefire winner every time: with a Polaroid-type camera, you can take a photograph of the lockkeeper or his family and present them with it.

4. *Rules of the road and boat handling.* The basic rule of the road is that boats travel on the right-hand side of the waterway. When overtaking, you pass on the left, at a speed slow enough that your wake doesn't upset the overtaken vessel. The exception to this rule occurs when you are passing or being passed by a large, deep-draft vessel, such as a barge. Here priority belongs to the deeper and larger boat; it will indicate, usually by putting out a blue or green flag, where it wants you to pass. You, being small, shallower, and more maneuverable, will yield right of way. On bends or curves the deeper water is usually found on the outside of the curve; if you encounter a laden vessel there, it will probably signal that it wants the outside of the curve. When being overtaken by another vessel, you should move to the right and slow somewhat, to allow the overtaking vessel to pass unhindered.

SPEED LIMITS. Speed limits, posted at locks, should be strictly followed. You must also be sure not to churn out a strong wake; it will not only bounce moored craft and perhaps swamp small boats, it will disturb wildlife and erode the banks, thereby destroying some of the beauty you are privileged to enjoy. The limit is generally four miles per hour on the smaller canals and rivers. On very shallow canals even this speed will be excessive. On the larger rivers, where there is deeper water, you can do six or even eight miles per hour safely—but again, watch your wake.

NAVIGATIONAL SIGNALS. Because waterway cruising is a very informal kind of boating, you will not normally be involved with navigational signals. However, you will want to be familiar with the four horn signals because in certain maneuvering or dangerous situations they will be used. The signals are:

1 short blast:	I am turning to starboard (right)
2 short blasts:	I am turning to port (left)
3 short blasts:	My engine is going astern (reverse)
4 short blasts:	Danger; or, I am unable to maneuver

The visual signals are simple and are largely a matter of common sense. You probably won't be using any visual signals yourself, but when you approach a laden barge, it may extend a blue or green flag from either side, indicating that you are to pass on that side. The visual signals that you will encounter at the larger locks are just like traffic lights: green means enter the lock and red means stay out.

MOORING YOUR BOAT. Being able to moor your boat at interesting or attractive places is one of the pleasantest aspects of waterway cruising; only a little practice will be needed to make you quite proficient. The most important thing to remember is that, whenever possible, you should approach the mooring by heading into the wind or current, whichever is dominant, as this will help slow your boat. If you must approach with the wind or current from behind, you should come in very slowly, using short bursts of reverse to cut your forward motion.

When you're uncertain about the depth of the water near the bank, station someone on the bow with a pole or a boathook to sound the depth. Make your approach bow first, at an angle to the shoreline, so that if you do hit a shallow spot, your propeller will still be in deeper water—and a strong burst of reverse should free you. Normally, when you approach a mooring, there won't be anyone ashore to receive your lines, so you should nose in gently and have a crew member jump from the bow to receive bow and stern lines. (The person who jumps ashore should avoid any thick, grassy patch; there may be an unseen hole underneath.) Be sure not to stretch your lines across the towpath—cyclists and occasionally motorists travel the towpaths, and your lines could endanger them. If there isn't a handy tree for tying lines, hammer in the two steel mooring stakes (normally supplied with the boat) with the heavy hammer (also supplied) and tie onto them. Be sure to test your stakes for holding power before leaving the boat unattended.

5. *A typical day on the waterways.* From the moment you untie your lines and pull away from the dock, waving farewell to the charter agent, your days and nights will be entirely immersed in a new adventure. Your first afternoon afloat will be filled with revelations, and in the evening everyone will be anticipating the excitement of a first night on the water.

SHORESIDE EXCURSIONS. One of the regular highlights of our cruising was the daily shoreside excursion in search of adventure. Each morning, before getting under way, we would consult our waterway chart and note the towns and villages on the day's route, blocking out stops and excursions at particularly interesting places. Yet some of our most memorable excursions were totally unplanned. We would be rounding a lovely bend of the canal or approaching a particularly scenic village, and, quite spontaneously, we would decide to moor up and explore. Our lines were no sooner secured than we'd find Laurie, Bev, and Janet waiting impatiently on the bank or quayside, canvas tote bags in hand. Some time later we'd return to our boat, our gait noticeably slower, our canvas bags bulging with fresh, crusty bread or croissants, milk, some of the local cheese, crisp salad vegetables, meat or fish for dinner, and—most coveted prize of all, which the youngest usually got to carry—the just-baked pastry, chosen by majority vote.

LAUNDRY, MAIL, AND CURRENCY. Getting laundry done in Europe, especially in the smaller towns and villages along the waterways, is very different from doing it at home. You should pack a minimum of items that require dry cleaning, because when you're lucky enough to find a dry cleaning service, it can take as long as four days. For those indispensables that must be cleaned, bring along a do-it-yourself kit, with a good cleaning fluid and a small stiff brush. Washing is another matter. Machine laundromats are generally available in the larger towns, and where you can't find a laundromat, you'll probably find someone who will do handwash.

Sending mail off is a simple matter; we've hardly spent a day on a waterway, outside of weekends and holidays, when we couldn't post a letter. However, it is sometimes difficult to buy stamps, and for that reason you should carry with you a supply of postage stamps sufficient to airmail your post cards and letters back home. Receiving mail may seem complicated, but it isn't—so long as you can give your correspondents your approximate itinerary. Letters addressed to you, c/o Poste Restante, at a given town, will be held. Alternatively, you can have your mail forwarded, with the name of your vessel, care of any lockkeeper along your route.

In the larger cities, both travelers checks and foreign currency are easily converted into the local currency. In the outlying regions you must be prepared to deal in the local currency. Thus you will be better off purchasing extra currency at the outset.

6. *Expecting the unexpected.* There are a number of unexpected things that sometimes occur during a cruise. Consider, for example, the perennial controversy between the boatman and the fisherman over who has priority. You'll be cruising down a canal, and ahead of you there will sit a relaxed fisherman, his long poles and lines extending clear across the canal. It seems as though he wants you to stop and detour around him! You don't want to pass over and cut his lines, yet you must pass. We have faced this situation many times; we have found that if we slow down and call politely for the fisherman to withdraw his lines, we will get a clear channel.

The waterways are filled with all kinds of craft, including small sailboats, tacking back and forth like bees before a hive. This may exasperate you, but sailboats have right of way, and you must maneuver clear of them. In addition, you'll frequently encounter dredges and ferries, both of which have right of way before you.

What about running aground? Remain calm and try to maneuver off with your engine, being careful not to damage the propeller on tree stumps or other underwater obstructions. Most self-drive boats carry a very shallow draft—three to four feet at most—so if you do get stuck, it means you're in really shallow water. If you can't easily get off with your engine, you must try to pole off, with the long wooden pole that will be aboard your boat. Failing that, you can probably get a tow.

Mechanical problems with the boat? Remember the old saying, "When all else fails, read the instructions." Self-drive boats carry a manual that includes a good set of troubleshooting suggestions. However, if you can't cope with some malfunction or breakdown, phone your charter agent or his boatyard, and they will either explain how to solve your problem or dispatch someone to fix it for you, at no cost to yourself.

14

Cruising with Children

Perhaps the richest of family experiences is the sharing with your children the joys and adventures that not only last a lifetime but improve and broaden with the passage of time. A well conceived and executed holiday trip through Europe's inland waterways offers just that opportunity. For the child such an experience can open new paths, outlooks, and expectations. If you resolve to remain "tuned in" to your child's feelings and attitudes and to maintain an approach tailored to his or her specific needs, personality, and interests, you're sure to keep your child inspired.

1. *Planning the trip.* It is important to include the entire family in the discussion and planning at the outset. That is the ideal time to spread a large, detailed map of Europe on the dining room table and to trace the paths of major rivers and canals. Even before discussing specific waterways, you might present the overall concept of Europe as a single landmass absolutely criss-crossed with navigable waterways.

In addition to planning the area you'll want to visit, you should consider together the various forms of travel. You'll probably find that the younger your children are, the more appropriate a bareboat charter will be. With younger children (pre-teens and under), the privacy and flexibility afforded by a sail-it-yourself cruise will be appreciated by all hands. The children will find much more to do on a family-operated boat, and—perhaps most important—you'll have ultimate control and flexibility concerning schedules, stops, and all activities.

It is after the decisions have been made regarding how and where to travel that children will really become involved. You'll want to furnish your youngsters with books, articles, maps, and other references—better yet, if they're old enough, show them where and how to obtain these items, and let them collect the materials themselves. You may be amazed at how quickly and creatively your children establish their own ideas, outlooks, and expectations. Your role is to encourage, to lead, and to inspire. Just be sure to allow the child full rein and responsibility.

Plan to sustain the children's interest and to increase it gradually as the trip nears. From time to time you might suggest such projects as referencing a particular aspect of the trip, finding a map or chart for presentation to the family, and, by all means, writing to the various government and tourist agencies of the area you'll be visiting, for additional information. The wealth of free information available is considerable —but remember to begin writing well ahead of time to allow for delays in mail and shipping.

Once the trip has been determined, you might talk with each child's teacher and solicit suggestions on tying in the trip with other academic activities or with ongoing hobbies. It's one thing to announce to a child, "We're going to France this summer"; it's quite another thing—and one considerably more effective and provocative—to say, "Let's follow in the path of the Roman legions across Europe by cruising down the Rhine."

Keep in mind that most kids function best when they understand in advance what's in store for them. Surprises may be fun, exciting, even desirable in many instances; but in terms of pre-trip planning, the more involved the children are, the more they'll know what to expect, and the more they'll be able to appreciate the experience.

2. *What to take along.* Packing for the children for a cruise will be a lot like packing for any other vacation. Boat shoes or sneakers, sweaters, a windbreaker, a good poncho for inclement weather, shorts, polo-type shirts, and some pairs of jeans or denim trousers should fill the duffel bag. Wash-and-wear items will be the order of the day, as quick-service laundry facilities will not generally be available.

Infants and very small children will of course require their usual paraphernalia: baby foods, disposable diapers or diaper liners, and baby formulas. These will be available in the major cities, but you cannot expect to find them in the smaller towns along the waterways. Unless you're certain to have sufficient time to shop for them in a large city—and a delayed flight could easily disrupt your schedule—you will be better off packing them from home.

As for toys, games, and other diversions, you should bring the very minimum. But don't overlook the necessities: a favorite doll, a much-hugged blanket, a few decks of cards, and notebooks, sketch pads, and coloring materials for each child. On our waterway trips we have always been able to find a toy or stationery store in even the smaller towns. And what child wouldn't be absolutely thrilled to wander through a small French or Dutch toy store, ready with a, "Mom, may I have this?"

3. *Children as active crew participants.* Children of all ages can participate in waterway cruising, though the extent of participation will depend on the imagination (and perhaps the patience) of the parents, as well as on the type of boat involved. Stan's three daughters did much of the steering of our chartered 34-footer on the Canal du Midi, with Janet, at ten the youngest, doing her share. Although it wasn't until the last few days of the trip that Janet was willing to steer through narrow bridge openings, she did qualify finally as a "certified under-bridge steerer" by trip's end.

Besides the steering, which does require close supervision, kids can be assigned such crew jobs as navigator, shopper, trip photographer, and even ship's purser (in charge of expenditures en route). Children should share the responsibility for routine boat and engine maintenance, including inspecting the engine oil and water level (just like on a car) each morning. They should also assist with line handling when tying up or getting under way. Even very young children can perform many of these jobs;

in addition, they can serve as ship's lookout, "alerting" the helmsman to approaching boats, nearby bridges, and even cows and horses in the fields. Windmill counting in Holland can sustain a younger child for long stretches. Children should also assist with meal preparation and clean-up and in keeping the cabins neat and orderly.

4. *Keeping children interested.* Perhaps your best investment of the entire trip, after the cost of charter or passenger fees, will be the modest cost of lined-paper notebooks and pencils. Label the notebook covers "Diary," present one to each child (with his or her name on the cover), and your children will take to it like a slice of chocolate layer cake or a three-day weekend. And don't be surprised if you find a thirty or forty page "document" after just a single week of cruising—complete with sketches in color, no less. You may be amazed at what your children consider significant; if they permit you to read each day's entries, it might just open your eyes to things that you had been missing. If the child can't write yet, he or she can draw, sketch, or doodle.

Another really super ongoing project is collecting for a scrapbook (some kids will want to incorporate this in their diary). Most likely the scrapbook will be put together at home after the trip, but children who are enthusiastic about the project will collect all sorts of things for it: picture post cards, tourist pamphlets, maps, ticket stubs from shoreside activities, menus, restaurant checks, and photographs.

Are your children science-oriented? They might love to build a model of a canal lock, the degree of sophistication depending on age, talent, and perhaps adult help. A talk with a school science teacher well before the trip may enlist both technical assistance and encouragement. The actual construction will be done at home or in school following the trip, but the child will have to sketch, photograph, and measure (by pacing) the lock dimensions. Anyone in the family who speaks the lockkeeper's language will be a valuable source of information concerning the lock and its operation. Whether the finished product is a rough replica crafted in modeling clay or an accurate scale model complete with movable lock gates and changing water levels, you'll feel a glow of satisfaction as you inspect and admire the proud offering.

Children who are (or will be) studying a foreign language will benefit tremendously from traveling within the respective country. Unless children are quite experienced with a language, they will be shy and quite reluctant initially to converse. On our first French canal trip, Laurie, even with two years of French, had a difficult time as ship's translator; on her next visit to France she was very relaxed with the language, quite fluent, and quick to improve. Beverly, studying Spanish in junior high, wanted us to find waterways in Spain, yet she did manage to gain pretty good comprehension in French. Janet, about to begin her first year of French, improved more than any of us. It would be helpful to take along some language materials to augment the children's conversational experiences; books and language cassettes, available at many libraries, are recommended.

Will a birthday or a special holiday occur during the trip? A little advance planning may be required here—perhaps a box of birthday candles and some party decorations stashed at the bottom of your duffel. You should be able to order or buy a birthday cake along the way, but if that seems unlikely, you could include a simple boxed cake mix in your stash, for a real "homemade" birthday cake.

In addition to the projects discussed above, you can depend on the familiar vacation standbys that always work for your children: family singalongs, reading, story-telling for younger children, and alphabet and other guessing games that readily absorb a child's attention. Most exciting will be meeting people along the way, perhaps offering a dinner invitation or, if time permits, a few hours' cruise some sunny afternoon. Don't overlook the possibility of your child's establishing "pen pal" relationships with other children; it's amazing how language barriers recede when children get together.

5. *Waterway safety.* Safety on a waterway holiday is very much a matter of common sense; above all, it involves explaining to children, at the outset of the trip, what the safety rules will be and why they are important.

Nonswimmers and younger children should wear properly fitted life preservers when out on deck, particularly when they are not under direct supervision. When tying up or leaving a dock or pier, instruct all hands against carelessly allowing arms or legs to get caught between the boat and the dock; there are far too many instances of easily avoidable bruises and sprains resulting from such inattention.

We've suffered our share of "lost" children ashore, and we have necessarily developed some rules to prevent such uncomfortable situations. When children are permitted to wander away from the family—that's certainly a normal situation—you should have them team up (a "buddy" system) and insist that each pair stay together. If one of the children has a watch, you might ask that they return by a certain hour. In the event the children are exploring wooded or undeveloped areas, provide each of them with a whistle on a string lanyard, so they can signal you should they be in distress. And equip yourself similarly; when you want them to return to "base," you can signal them with two or three pre-arranged blasts.

Children should be taught that if they do become separated from the family, they shouldn't panic or act rashly. Assure them that they will soon be reunited and that they should ask other adults, or even children, for assistance. Everyone responds to a lost child.

6. *Sniffles and sneezes.* On our very first waterway trip, Beverly, then eleven years old, came down with a fever and had to be confined to bed for three days. Had we been traveling by any other means, our holiday would have been disrupted, with both the child and a parent confined to a hotel room for several days. In our case, though, after determining the malady and administering medicines from our first aid kit, we set her up in the bed with the largest outside window. Continuing the journey, we brought mile after mile of French countryside past her appreciative eyes.

Bibliography

Benest, E. E. *Inland Waterways of France.* Saint Ives, Huntingdon, England: Imray Laurie Norie and Wilson, 1978.

Bolland, R. R. *Victorians on the Thames.* Tunbridge Wells, Kent, England: Midas Books, 1974.

Bristow, P. *Through the Dutch Canals.* Lymington, Hampshire, England: Nautical Publishing Company, 1974.

Bristow, P. *Through the French Canals.* Lymington, Hampshire, England: Nautical Publishing Company, 1972.

Bristow, P. *Through the German Canals.* Lymington, Hampshire, England: Nautical Publishing Company, 1975.

British Waterways Board. *Nicholson's Guides to the Waterways.* Volumes 1 through 5. London: Robert Nicholson Publications, 1978.

Gabrielson, J. *Göta Canal.* Stockholm: Generalstabens Litografiska Anstalts Förlag, 1973.

Gladwin, D. D. *The Canals of Britain.* London: B. T. Batsford, 1973.

Hadfield, C. *Introducing Inland Waterways.* Newton Abbot, England: David & Charles, 1973.

Hankinson, J. *Canal Cruising.* London: Ward Lock, 1974.

Hogg, G. *The Shell Book of Exploring Britain.* London: John Baker, 1971.

Inland Waterways Association. *Inland Waterways Holidays.* Epsom, Surrey, England: Boat World Publications, 1977.

Johnson, I. and E. *Yankee Sails Across Europe.* New York: Norton, 1962.

Kimbrough, E. *And a Right Good Crew.* New York: Harper & Row, 1958.

Kimbrough, E. *Better Than Oceans.* New York: Harper & Row, 1976.

Kimbrough, E. *Floating Island.* New York: Harper & Row, 1968.

Kimbrough, E. *Water, Water, Everywhere.* New York: Harper & Row, 1956.

Lewery, A. J. *Narrow Boat Painting.* Newton Abbot, England: David & Charles, 1974.

Liley, J. *France—The Quiet Way.* London: Stanford Marine, 1975.

Malster, R. *Wherries and Waterways.* Lavenham, Suffolk, England: Terence Dalton, 1971.

Marsden, W. *The Rhineland.* New York: Hastings House, 1973.

McKenney, R. and Bransten, R. *Here's England.* New York: Harper & Row, 1971.

McKnight, H. *The Shell Book of Inland Waterways.* Newton Abbot, England: David & Charles, 1975.

McKnight, H. *A Source Book of Canals, Locks and Canal Boats.* London: Ward Lock, 1974.

Morgan-Grenville, G. *Barging into France.* New York: Van Nostrand Reinhold, 1973.

Morgan-Grenville, G. *Holiday Cruising in France.* Newton Abbot, England: David & Charles, 1972.

Nelson, N. *Holland.* New York: Hastings House, 1970.

Pilkington, R. *Small Boat on the Thames.* London: Macmillan, 1966.

Pilkington, R. *Small Boat Through France.* London: Macmillan, 1964.

Pilkington, R. *Small Boat Through Holland.* London: Macmillan, 1959.

Pilkington, R. *Waterways in Europe.* London: John Murray, 1972.

Price, P. V. *Eating and Drinking in France Today.* New York: Scribner, 1974.
Ransom, P. J. G. *Waterways Restored.* London: Faber, 1974.
Rolt, L. T. C. *From Sea to Sea.* London: Allen Lane, 1973.
Rossiter, S. *England. The Blue Guide.* London: Ernest Benn, 1976.
Row, V. *The Loire.* London: Eyre Methuen, 1974.
St. George, G. *Russia.* New York: Hastings House, 1973.
Savage, G. *The Languedoc.* London: Barrie & Jenkins, 1975.
Sitwell, S. *The Netherlands.* New York: Hastings House, 1974.
Van Doren Stern, L. and P. *Beyond Paris.* New York: Norton, 1967.
Van Wel, F. *Holland.* Munich: Knorr & Hirth Verlag GMBH, 1970.
White, F. *West of the Rhone.* London: Faber, 1964.

Illustrations on Title Pages

Page iii Pastoral on the Thames at Wargrave: cattle grazing in the fields; old homes under tall trees; rowing, sailing and powerboating on the river; boatyards on the riverbank; and the George and Dragon hostelry for the sailors' rest.

1 The busy lock at Kampen in the Netherlands opens to connect the great Ijsselmeer with the River Ijssel, which meets the Rhine past Arnhem. A fleet of yachts can be packed in with a big commercial barge, gunwhale to gunwhale. There is much good natured fending off, heightened by concern for hulls and rails when the craft are squeezed together.

3 The nearest of the four bridges is the Pont Canal carrying the Canal du Midi over the River Orb at the 2000-year-old city of Béziers. Red-tile roofs contrast with the surrounding green vineyards. Béziers lies in the plain between the Mediterranean and the Monts de l'Espinouse, blue hills in the distance over the Cathedral of St. Nazaire.

33 The jolly *Palinurus* on the tree-lined River Yonne shows the characteristics of a hotel boat: on the stern, bicycles for the guests, at the helm an attentive crew, amidships a large salon for gourmet dining, a sun deck forward for comfortable viewing, sleeping cabins below and a boom ready to swing the gangplank when the barge moors along the bank for excursions ashore.

57 Three of the four spans of Les Ponts Couverts cross the Canal du Moulins that circles old Strasbourg. The tall spires of the cathedral dominate the city with an exquisite tracery of warm sandstone reaching to the sky. The view from the panoramic Vauban Terrace overlooks one of the best preserved medieval sites in Europe.

83   A cruise on the River Vecht is filled with whimsied turnings, each with an image to delight the eye. The lovely little drawbridge at Breukelen with strong diagonal lifts and delicately hung roadway is a tidy and memorable tableau.

111   The double set of Holtenau locks is at the junction of the Kiel Canal and Kieler Fords. The Baltic Sea is to the left; the city of Kiel on the right. This 100-kilometer canal connecting the North Sea and the Baltic is the busiest canal in the world.

131   At Söderköping, near the eastern entrance to the Göta Canal, before an interested audience of lock watchers, each yacht puts a crew member ashore to handle lines and assist the lockkeeper. There is a guest harbor at Söderköping, one of the nine ports along the canal where both fuel and provisions are available.

161   The Danube flows through eight countries, eight cultures, past mountain, hill and plain, 2888 kilometers from the Black Forest to the Black Sea. On a hazy summer morning in Budapest, seen through the round arches of the Fisherman's Bastion, the river glides quietly past the Parliament Building.

197   The Swan Inn at Streatley alongside Goring Lock is nestled under a hillside. The steep hills on both sides of Goring Gorge, a vestige of glacial scouring, are unusual along the Thames. There are 179 meters of dock space under the willows and an excellent English inn beckoning from ashore.

223   A narrow boat rally at King's Norton offers a ride on a whistle-blowing, paddle-wheeled, narrow steamboat as a special treat for the children.

249   On the shore of the Moselle River at Cochem is a small riverside yacht basin. It has an opening downstream, protection from the wake of river traffic, and a ramp for launching trailer boats. For local color there is a castle on the hill, a picturesque town on the riverbank, surrounding vineyards and a barge heading downstream toward the Rhine.

251   On the Moselle River the excursion boats *Mosel* and *Traben Trarbach,* with bright reflections dancing in the water, leave the automated lock at Frankel below a hillside covered with vineyards.

259   Below the aqueduct at Håverud, Dalsland Canal, a lock cuts deep into the rock. The rush of water when the sluice gate opens calls for careful line tending and fending off at the upper end of the lock. In the quieter water at the far end, a sailor can tend, fend, and casually engage the canal watchers in easy conversation.

265   *Sirene,* on the River Vecht, is a graceful old yacht in a modern charter service. The carefully maintained, clipper-bowed 17-meter craft was built in 1893, a proper vessel to cruise the old world.

273   The fully fendered, smartly crewed, wooden motor yacht *Doutelle* heads up the Thames just past the Henley Sailing Club. The masts on open deck mounts can be easily dropped to pass under low bridges.

283   Five German yachts cruising together through the Göta Canal demonstrate organized passage-making as they enter the lock at Norrkvarn. Three of the yachts have starboard fenders and two have fenders rigged to port. A crew member of the last craft to enter leaps ashore with docklines ready, while others are on the gate at the far end to open the sluices when the near gates are closed.

Index

*Order this
classic print
by photographer
Stanley Rosenfeld
to hang in your
home or office*

For those who love waterway travel, the authors are offering, at their cost, a beautiful 21″ × 28″ art print of one of Stanley Rosenfeld's most handsome and serene photographs, "Reading the Ripples."

In this picture the late afternoon mist is rising from the Canal du Midi in Southern France as the lockkeeper ends his day. You can see this lovely scene reproduced in full color on page 28.

For readers of this book this art print, usually sold for $15.00, is being made available at $3.50, including postage and handling. Offer good only when entered on coupon below, and sorry—only one print per order. (Offer expires Dec. 31, 1981.)

Name _____

Street _____

City/State _____ Zip _____

Please send me "Reading the Ripples" by Stanley Rosenfeld. I enclose $3.50.

(Please add applicable sales tax.)

DETACH COUPON AND MAIL TO:

Floating Through Europe, Inc.
501 Madison Ave.
New York, N.Y. 10022